TRUMP THE PRESS

TRUMP THE PRESS

DON SURBER'S TAKE ON HOW
THE PUNDITS BLEW THE
2016 REPUBLICAN RACE.

———

Don Surber

ISBN-13: 9781533360199
ISBN-10: 1533360197
Library of Congress Control Number: 2016908396
CreateSpace Independent Publishing Platform
North Charleston, South Carolina

Trump has a better chance of cameoing in another Home Alone movie with Macaulay Culkin—or playing in the NBA Finals—than winning the Republican nomination.

—Harry Enten, *FiveThirtyEight* Politics, June 16, 2015

TABLE OF CONTENTS.

CHAPTER 1

AN ARMY OF GOLIATHS.

UNIVERSITY OF TENNESSEE LAW PROFESSOR Glenn Harlan Reynolds published his treatise *An Army of Davids* in March 2006 on the impact of the Internet on commerce, politics, and society. Reynolds was an early adopter of the new technology. He became the godfather of the blogosphere after he launched his *Instapundit* blog two weeks before 9/11. A decade after the book's publication, its prophecies came true.

The Internet helped people be more self-reliant and independent. Life was better, thanks to this new technology. For example, Jeff Bezos and his Amazon.com company could compete with the local shopping mall by providing goods quickly through the services of an overnight delivery service. Traditional retailers followed suit. People in Poca, West Virginia, had access to Fifth Avenue stores without a catalogue or a visit to New York City. Moreover, these changes applied to journalism.

"Where before journalists and pundits could bloviate at leisure, offering illogical analysis or citing 'facts' that were in fact false, now the Sunday morning op-eds have already been dissected on Saturday night, within hours of their appearing on newspapers' websites," Reynolds wrote.

In the Bible, David used a slingshot and slew Goliath, the giant who protected Philistines. Our modern media Goliaths protected the federal government.

However, some members of the army of Goliaths learned to use the slingshot quite well. The conservative commentariat's vanguard —*National*

Review and the *Weekly Standard*—plunged into the Internet pool and expanded their influence. But they were still Goliaths. They still talked among themselves. They still rarely left Washington. From their offices near the Potomac, they immediately dismissed Donald Trump as a celebrity, not a person.

This book points out their folly. Who am I to judge? I am a veteran journalist (literally, as I was a reporter for the European edition of *Stars & Stripes* in my Army days) who retired after more than thirty years in newspapers.

I began 2015 by accepting the conventional wisdom about the deep bench of Republican governors in the race. But I liked Trump's message. No one else was willing to say what he said: Build the wall. Challenge political correctness. Make America great again. My first choice, Scott Walker, faded, while Donald Trump blossomed. The napalm-like vitriol used on Trump by conservative commentators intrigued me. The hotter their hate, the more I realized his prospects were rising.

The incessant attacks on Trump, often over minor matters, helped solidify his base because he refused to back down. The more the pundits loathed him, the more his supporters admired him. He was honest, confident, intelligent, and right. Trump took on the enforcers of political correctness—the press. Good choice. In America, the only people less liked than the media work for the government.

Many pundits knew not what was going on outside their small circle of friends. They reminded me of what *New Yorker* movie critic Pauline Kael told the Modern Language Association on December 28, 1972. "I live in a rather special world. I only know one person who voted for Nixon. Where they are I don't know. They're outside my ken. But sometimes when I'm in a theater, I can feel them," Kael said.

However, Trump supporters were in the ken of John Nolte, a feisty editor-at-large at *Breitbart News*. "If our Media Elite are wondering from their velvet bubbles why Donald Trump has captured the imagination of Republican voters, that can be summed up in a single word: fight. The Donald is fearless, and he fights like a Leftist, not a milquetoast

Republican henpecked by the media into a soft-bellied Walter Mitty who dreams of but will never be president," Nolte wrote on June 25.

Of all the political paragraphs written in 2015, that was the one I most wish were mine.

Another media person who saw Trump rise to become the Republican elephant in the room was Scott Adams, the creator of the *Dilbert* comic strip. He cheated. He read Trump's book *The Art of The Deal* and measured Trump accordingly. I liked Adams's commentary so much that I named him Pundit of the Year on my blog—http://donsurber.blogspot. com.

While every presidential election is historic, few have included anything as entertaining as Trump's nomination. The press committed mediacide by blowing its last shred of credibility trying to stop Trump. Making a billionaire the underdog was nearly impossible, but the Washington press corps was up to the task.

Congratulations.

CHAPTER 2

A CAUSE WITHOUT A REBEL.

———————

WE LIKE TO THINK OF our heroes as cowboys, Roy Rogers riding tall
in the saddle on Trigger, the smartest horse in the world. The cowboy
fights the bad guys, saves the ranch, and wins the girl. He has a code that
includes humility, sacrifice, and self-reliance.

However, our heroes are seldom altruistic. Rick Blaine in the movie
Casablanca ran an upscale nightclub and gambling den. He was a slump-
shouldered chain smoker. Cynical, self-centered, and bitter, Blaine still
nursed a broken heart from an affair that ended badly in Paris. He
acquired letters of transit by chance. They were magical slips of paper
that allowed the bearer to escape the Nazis and leave Casablanca via a
plane bound for Portugal.

As time went by, this burnt-out expatriate American did the right
thing by putting others ahead of himself. He let a wanted man escape
the Nazis with those letters of transit. The corrupt police captain Louis
Renault looked the other way. When Renault said that he would round-
up the usual suspects, he signaled he would use his power of corruption
for good. Their heroism was not in shooting down Nazis but in sabo-
tage. A gin-joint owner and a crooked cop were the last, best hope for
Casablanca and the world.

But it was only a movie.

Nearly seventy-five years later, a real-life garish casino owner rode
into the presidential sweepstakes on an elevator down from his opulent
and ostentatious penthouse.

The pundits laughed. But that was OK. As union leader Nicholas Klein said at his union's convention in Baltimore on May 14, 1918, "First they ignore you. Then they ridicule you. And then they attack you and want to burn you. And then they build monuments to you. And that is what is going to happen to the Amalgamated Clothing Workers of America."

Over time, people misattributed to Gandhi a more polished version. "First they ignore you, then they ridicule you, then they fight you, and then you win."

There was no ignoring Donald Trump. He was a flawed vessel. Boastful, tacky, and vain, Trump led the lifestyle of the rich and famous, long after that television show expired. In a column in *Slate*, Reihan Salam, executive editor of the *National Review*, recalled growing up in Brooklyn in the 1980s and 1990s. "Trump was the living embodiment of gaudy success—a kind of mash-up of Santa Claus, Scrooge McDuck, and Vito Corleone. When I was a kid, it was not at all uncommon to hear friends and classmates declare that they wanted to be Donald Trump when they grew up. They didn't want to be real estate developers or casino magnates. They literally wanted to *be* Trump, which seems doubly strange in hindsight, as so few of the kids I have in mind were white," Salam wrote on February 11, 2016.

Trump could be rude and nasty. His comments turned off many people, particularly women. His campaign brought out the nastiness in others. He came off as a bully.

And his business acumen also came into question. Graduates of Trump University (and later the New York State attorney general) filed lawsuits against the school, claiming it was a charade. Four times his businesses sought Chapter 11 protection from creditors in federal bankruptcy court, which many pundits sloppily called filing for bankruptcy; the filings were to avoid bankruptcy by reorganizing and renegotiating his outstanding loans.

Trump's litigation over the years provided a mother lode for opposition research. For example, he tried in 1993 to use the state's power of eminent domain to force Vera Coking to sell her house at 127 South Columbia Place in Atlantic City. She and her husband had paid $20,000 for the property in 1961. Her husband later died. In the 1970s, she turned down a million-dollar offer from Bob Guccione, publisher of *Penthouse.* Coking fought Trump in court and won.

In 2010, she moved into a retirement home. Her family put the house up for sale seeking $5 million, but there were no takers. Carl Icahn bought it at auction for $583,000 on July 31, 2014, and demolished it on November 19, 2014.

Trump's politics were ever evolving. He had been a Republican, an independent, and a Democrat before becoming a Republican again. Previously, he supported abortion, universal health care, and amnesty for illegal aliens. On top of that, he led the push to demand Obama show his birth certificate, believed the Bush administration knew of 9/11 before the attack, and bought into the long-discredited link of vaccines to autism.

Pundits spent most of the nomination process believing Republicans had better messengers.

"I truly, honestly, and with all my heart and mind think Donald Trump's most ardent supporters are making a yuge mistake. I think they are being conned and played. I feel like a guy whose brother is being taken advantage of by a grifter. I'm watching helplessly as the con artist congratulates him for taking out a third mortgage," Jonah Goldberg of the *National Review* wrote on July 11.

But the people burned by politicians were not looking for a better messenger; they wanted a better message. The only one delivering it was a loud braggart with an odd duck hairstyle in gold with streaks of silver.

His message was clear: make America great again.

Many Americans did not feel great. Between immigration—which had tripled since the 1970s—and unbridled free trade, Americans had half the opportunities for manufacturing jobs than the previous generation enjoyed. Closed factories littered the landscape. In 1978, my mother, her two sons-in-law, and her son all worked in factories. In 2015, only two of her fifteen grandchildren did. Some joined the professional class, true, but most found jobs in retail and other areas that paid far less than manufacturing. Adjusted for inflation, wages fell too.

Oh, the US Chamber of Commerce said free trade created jobs. However, the economy would have created jobs in transportation and retail regardless. The United States had a net gain of only 6.5 million jobs between 2000 and 2014, while the population grew by 36.7 million. And 43 percent of those new jobs went to immigrants, both legal and illegal, the US Bureau of Labor Statistics reported.

We needed to rein in free trade and illegal immigration.

Official Washington could not care less. No one in Washington ever faced the prospect of the factory in that company town—government— closing its doors for good, much less the loss of even one department.

Salena Zito of the *Pittsburgh Tribune-Review* understood Trump's supporters. "At first the media dismissed Trump, which only made angry voters support him more. That led to a ratings bonanza for national media outlets; they decided to legitimize—and to exploit—his run. In short, they still don't get Main Street's anger and frustration, but they are more than willing to cash in on it with Trump. Everyone—Trump and the media elite—is riding the populist wave to the bank. Everyone except Trump's supporters," Zito wrote on August 22.

She was not enamored of him.

"Trump often promotes nastiness in pursuit of legitimate policy concerns. Yet his populism also taps into real frustration with two things: first, today's political correctness and the one-size-fits-all progressive moralism of America's cultural leaders; second, the paternalistic GOP establishment, which patronizes the nation's populists for their votes while holding them at arm's length as if they were rabble," Zito wrote.

Working people had a cause without a rebel.

"But it goes well beyond economic issues. What drives this quest for authentic candidates is also cultural. I would ask my readers to consider: How many people who staunchly oppose gay marriage do you know? How many people who are pure creationists—who believe that God created the world largely as is—are in your circle of friends? I would guess that for a large number of readers, the answer is quite close to none," Sean Trende of *RealClear Politics* wrote on March 11, 2016.

Michael Goodwin of the *New York Post* was blunt. "My gut tells me much of the contempt for Trump reflects contempt for his working-class white support. It is one prejudice gentry liberals and gentry conservatives share," Goodwin wrote on March 20, 2016.

"It is perhaps the last acceptable bigotry, and you can see it expressed on any primetime TV program. The insults don't all seem good-natured to me. I grew up in central Pennsylvania, surrounded by the kind of people supporting Trump, and I sympathize with their worsening plight."

Trump did not live in the working-class neighborhood, but he understood the plight of those who did. He championed their cause when no one else would. On the eve of Operation Iraqi Freedom, Donald Rumsfeld said, "You go to war with the army you have, not the army you might want or wish you had at a later time."

This was true of presidential candidates. Trump was not Roy Rogers or even Rick Blaine. But he was not the tail end of Trigger either. Trump rallied a people whom the political class had ignored, which, my friends, is presidential leadership.

CHAPTER 3

TRUMP WON'T RUN.

———— • ————

"NOBODY'S GOING TO MISTAKE DONALD Trump for a presidential candidate, I don't think, other than Donald Trump," Chuck Todd said on his *Meet the Press* show on NBC on January 25, 2015.

John Fund of the *National Review* agreed after watching Trump's speech at the Iowa Freedom Summit. "His classic, brassy style won over some people in the audience, but it's hard to believe that The Donald is really running for president. He created the impression, instead, that he might simply be afflicted with adult ADD. Some in the audience bristled when he declared that President Obama should be in jail for a shady housing deal he had concluded as a senator, and when he declared that half the immigrants who enter the US illegally are really criminals," Fund wrote on January 25.

Stephen Hayes of the *Weekly Standard* handicapped the race four months before Trump entered.

"So in reverse order—from least likely to most likely—here's a look at the prospective GOP nominees. Trump seems convinced that there is a groundswell of support for a Trump White House. And he seems confident, well, about pretty much everything. 'Over the years I've participated in many battles and have really almost come out very, very victorious every single time,' he once said. 'I've beaten many people and companies, and I've won many wars. I have fairly but intelligently earned many billions of dollars, which in a sense was both a scorecard and acknowledgment of my abilities.' Clown show," Hayes wrote on February 23.

Others dismissed entirely the idea that Trump would run. He had considered running for president in 2000, 2004, 2008, and 2012. As he filed paperwork at last to explore a presidential run in the 2016 contest, political experts said he would not run.

"Voters never saw his name on a real ballot, and they likely never will. That's because while making a mockery of oneself and the democratic process might help drag a few eyeballs to Trump's TV show and help hawk a few ties to Tea Party daydreamers, actually running for president is something the walking haircut just won't do. Politics, a game of smoke and mirrors, fudged facts, and shady dealings, remains too legitimate a venture for Trump," Kia Makarechi of *Vanity Fair* wrote on January 20.

Michael Scherer of *Time* magazine agreed. "Sarah Palin and Donald Trump are not running for president. Despite what you might have heard, there is a big difference between a presidential campaign and a reality show," Scherer wrote on January 26.

His proof?

"There is no evidence that either is any more serious about an actual campaign this time—no fundraising, no staff hires, no grassroots organizing in early states. But both have the same incentives to make the nation, and the political press corps, think differently. And the political press corps, struggling at the moment to interest a nation exhausted with politics in another 20-month campaign, has an incentive to write about Palin and Trump, who truth be told are simply more fun than actual presidential candidates," he wrote.

The next day, Stephen Collinson of CNN agreed. "Just when you thought it was safe to go back on the Republican campaign trail, Sarah Palin and Donald Trump are back. All it took to set Twitter abuzz at the first big GOP campaign bash at the weekend was for The Donald and the 2008 vice presidential nominee to clear their throats and muse, yet again, about presidential campaigns," Collinson wrote.

He saw an ulterior motive. "Trump, who thrives on attention, and Palin, who needs to maintain a brand on the fringes of conservative media, for whom the oxygen of publicity as a new campaign grinds into gear seems too enticing to ignore," he wrote.

On February 26, Chris Cillizza of the *Washington Post* asked, "The real question is not whether Trump will run or not. The real question is why any of us even care."

That was not the dumbest thing Cillizza wrote in 2015.

Meanwhile, on Fox News on April 17, George Will bet an imaginary hundred dollars on who would win the Republican nomination, dividing it among several contenders. He concluded by saying, "One dollar on Donald Trump in the hope that he will be tempted to run, be predictably shellacked, and we will be spared evermore this quadrennial charade of his."

Be careful what you wish for.

The contempt in Washington for Trump was intense. "Donald Trump has a long record of clownishly pretending he's going to run for president, and people take him seriously—including a lot of people at this network, which drives me crazy. I think Donald Trump is a bane of humanity," Jonah Goldberg of the *National Review* said on Fox News on April 20.

Columnists for the New York City tabloids also swore he would not run.

"Stop pretending—Donald Trump is not running for president," Kyle Smith of the *New York Post* wrote on May 30.

"If Trump did get into the race, and practiced his usual habit of being a giant publicity vortex, he would merely deprive more serious candidates of opportunities to get their messages out before Trump's inevitable exit from the race," Smith wrote in that column.

Bernie Goldberg, a former CBS reporter who became a media critic, reviewed Trump's appearance on Fox News in May 2015. "Sure, it easy to say anything about anything when you're just talking on television. Sitting behind the desk in the Oval Office is a little harder. But despite his money, Trump connects with the other 99 percent. He's not PC and he knows how to talk to people fed up with politics as usual. No, progressives wouldn't vote for him. But Republicans would and so might a lot of low-information types who don't know much about politics but know they like Trump. He could also pick up some moderates who are tired of the Clintons and their shenanigans," Goldberg wrote on May 14.

"So, I could think of a lot worse things than Donald Trump running for president. But he won't. And here in the United States of Entertainment, the long, long run to the White House won't be nearly as interesting without him."

While these experts in Washington and New York were writing Trump off, Byron York of the *Washington Examiner* was in Iowa talking to Chuck Laudner, who ran Rick Santorum's upset win in the 2012 caucuses. Trump had hired Laudner to run his campaign months before Trump entered the race.

"He addressed a crowd of over 500 at Simpson College in Indianola, and last week, he had a crowd of over 800 at Wartburg College in Waverly. In addition to college stops, Trump has been headlining fundraising events for Republican candidates and organizations. Trump has done events for the Polk County Republican Party, state Senator Jack Whitver, Secretary of State Paul Pate, and the Scott County GOP. In each instance, Trump has helped each draw impressive crowds," Laudner told York.

After Trump formally entered the race, pundits clung to the belief that he was not running for president. Leading the charge against Trump was Fox News contributor Karl Rove, who was Bush 43's campaign manager. Rove cited as evidence that Trump had not immediately filed a declaration of candidacy form with the Federal Election Commission.

Ah ha! Got you.

"He will delay filing that piece of paper. He got into the race on Tuesday, and by Friday, he still couldn't file a one-page piece of paper that required his name and his address and his signature on it," Rove said on Fox News on June 22.

In the inner sanctum of Washington, people considered this document crucial.

"Remember, we found out about Hillary's paid speeches and Rubio's liquidated IRA from their financial disclosures. They didn't submit a one- or two-page summary. So if Trump is only submitting this summary, it actually is proof he isn't that serious about this—it's about trying to get into the debates but keeping up appearances in time for him to start a new season of *The Apprentice* in January. That said, he is one helluva promoter, and he will get plenty of folks to bite as we will see over the next 48 hours," Taegan Goddard, publisher of *Political Wire*, wrote on June 16.

Yes, and Clinton's paid speeches and Rubio's liquidated IRA embarrassed them so much that they immediately ceased campaigning. Not!

The next day, Trump did file the form, and reporters found...nothing. Not a thing. Still, the pundits declared he was not serious about running. As usual, the experts were right. Donald Trump did not seek the presidency, and this book does not exist.

Oh wait, he did run. Read on.

CHAPTER 4

HOW DARE HE RUN!

———————

THE POLITICAL EXPERTS IN WASHINGTON said the Republicans had a deep bench of capable, battle-tested, former and current governors, headed by Scott Walker of Wisconsin, who had slain the public-union dragon. But others of similar executive ability also entered the tournament of candidates: Chris Christie of New Jersey, Rick Perry of Texas, John Kasich of Ohio, Bobby Jindal of Louisiana, Mike Huckabee of Arkansas, George Pataki of New York, Jim Gilmore of Virginia, and Jeb Bush of Florida. Surely, one of these men would prove himself the worthiest of the nomination.

Also entering the arena were three rookie senators—Ted Cruz, Marco Rubio, and Rand Paul—policy wonks better suited for the vice presidency. There were other candidates as well.

Best of all, Democrats were stuck with Hillary Clinton, a divisive first lady, mediocre senator, and disastrous secretary of state. She believed the nation owed her the presidency because she had endured the public humiliation of her husband's decades of sexual impropriety. Americans wanted new. She represented the old.

Socialist senator Bernie Sanders, former Maryland governor Martin O'Malley, and former senators Jim Webb and Lincoln Chaffee joined her in the race, but few experts gave them any chance.

Then, on June 16, 2015, Trump entered the Republican race uninvited. The party apparatchiks welcomed Trump with crossed arms and clenched fists. Many in the press made no secret of their contempt for

Trump. Conservatives in Washington went out of their way to distance themselves from this intruder. Liberals made fun of his hair.

"While Trump is a ludicrous figure with no chance to win, there are lots of other candidates who have an equally low chance (zero) to make it to the nomination. Still, it is worse having Trump there, since he obviously is using this opportunity purely as self-promotion and to air his obnoxious attitudes," Jennifer Rubin of the *Washington Post* wrote on June 16.

Radio talker Erick Erickson lumped Trump with Dr. Ben Carson, a retired brain surgeon who gained a following as a black conservative who stood up to President Obama.

"Trump and Carson are not future nominees. Their campaigns, objectively, do not have those things it takes to run a campaign across 50 states. They do not have the experienced consultants, they do not have the pundits who can help them generate free media attention, and they do not have the understanding of what it really takes to run a political campaign because they are not politicians and are not surrounded by people who can offset their lack of understanding," Erickson wrote on June 19.

Somehow, with no help from pundits, Trump found a way to get on television.

Trump became Al Czervik, a character portrayed by Rodney Dangerfield in the movie *Caddyshack*. In that movie, the nouveau-riche Czervik leads the charge of the hoi polloi to take over Bushwood Country Club, run by the stuffy Judge Elihu Smails, played by Ted Knight. The caddies and groundskeepers whom Trump led to the Bushwood Republican Party were working-class independents, disillusioned Democrats, and those not registered to vote. In fact, Trump's social-media director was his former caddy, Dan Scavino.

None of the other candidates led anyone to the party.

Over four decades, Trump learned to play the press like Pablo Casals played cello. His first wife, Ivana, christened him "The Donald." In the media center of the world—New York City—Trump became a top celebrity who could dominate news cycles. He both feuded with and courted the press, winning headlines and making his name a brand. Some New Yorkers saw him as the man they loved to hate. The now-defunct *Spy* magazine spoofed him as a "short-fingered vulgarian," which infuriated him. Trump told the editors in a note accompanying a picture of his hands, "If you hit me, I will hit you back 100 times harder."

Trump was a competitor who strove to win any contest he entered. His presidential campaign was no different. Experts in Washington did not understand that. Stuart Rothenberg, a political forecaster widely respected in Washington and largely unheard of outside the capital, gave Trump no chance. "To be taken seriously, you need political credentials," Rothenberg wrote.

Others agreed.

"His candidacy has been a joke from the start. He makes for great copy, but so did Jack the Ripper," Democratic strategist Peter Fenn of *US News and World Report* wrote on July 20.

The experts scorned Trump's call to make America great again because the press aped academia in dismissing patriotism as martial music played by a Pied Piper. The press also saw his riches as a liability. But his supporters liked that he was wealthy. He could not be bought. A media that regularly decried billionaires who buy politicians missed Trump's point.

"I've watched the politicians. I've dealt with them all my life. If you can't make a good deal with a politician, then there's something wrong with you. There's something certainly not very good, and that's what we have representing us. They will never make America great again. They don't even have a chance. They are controlled fully by the lobbyists, by the donors, and by the special interests," Trump said in declaring his candidacy.

I cannot remember a candidate admitting that he used lobbyists to get what he wanted. Washington was corrupt. Grifters had taken over the capital. As porn star Mercedes Carrera tweeted on January 11, 2016, when asked if she would run for vice president, "I'm not sure I'm a big enough whore to be a politician."

Trump supporters wanted Washington cleaned up. However, the pundits were too busy counting words to appreciate what those words said.

"In his announcement speech, he said 'I' 195 times, and also declared 'I'm really rich.' Sure, he's just looking for some media coverage in between tapings of his horrible TV show, but his message of common sense—and his disgust for politics as usual—is resonating with some. Still, he'll be out of the race in no time and back to his golf courses," Joseph Curl of the *Washington Times* wrote on June 16, 2015.

Conservatives complained that Trump would draw attention away from better candidates. This begged the question: If they were better candidates, why did they not figure out how to get the same free air time that Trump got? Earned media is just that. But as Democrats wanted to redistribute Trump's fortune, so conservatives wanted to redistribute his fame.

"Donald Trump is a great entertainer and developer, but his ideas of what to do as president won't grow the economy. The Club for Growth has issued very substantive and detailed white papers on the records of the major announced Republican candidates for president. There is no need to do a white paper on Donald Trump. He is not a serious Republican candidate, and many of his positions make him better suited to take on Hillary Clinton in the Democratic primary. It would also be unfortunate if he takes away a spot at even one Republican debate," Club for Growth president David McIntosh said. "The 2016 Republican presidential field is already the most pro-growth in recent history, with great ideas for cutting taxes, repealing Obamacare and replacing it with patient-centered, free market reforms, and moving the country forward with free trade."

McIntosh did have a point. Trump was once liberal. Trump had supported Clinton, former House Speaker Nancy Pelosi, and other targets of the right.

However, the ice-cold reception to new ideas was stunning. Reagan's party of the big tent had collapsed into a pup tent, just big enough for the sixteen candidates who wanted to recycle the platform from the 2012 campaign, which they had recycled from 2008. This time it would work. And if not this time, there was always 2020, 2024, 2028, and so forth. Running on the same theme every four years worked so well for President William Jennings Bryan.

Oh wait, he was never elected, despite three nominations. Never mind. You know what I mean.

Republican strategist Rick Wilson, whose advice was so valuable that none of the seventeen Republicans running for president hired him, predicted gloom and doom. (Remember when Reagan called the Democrats the party of gloom and doom?)

"You could sense the orifices of the RNC leadership and the GOP presidential campaigns tightening the longer Trump's discursive announcement ran, and the more the media giggled and simpered, happy to have chosen the clown prince of the 2016 cycle. Well, he's here now, and he's filing, so it's time for the GOP to get real about dealing with him. Obviously, the debates are the inflection point, so here's some counsel on using them to contain the damage," Wilson wrote.

But Wilson had some good news; The Donald wouldn't last.

"Don't overestimate him. Trump is probably ultimately self-limiting. He likely won't invest enough of his own qwan [money] in the race to truly change the game, and it remains to be seen if he will adhere to those election rules like financial disclosure, filing deadlines, expenditure reports, and other irritants the little people face," Wilson wrote.

Comedian Larry Wilmore was among the liberals welcoming Trump. "How did you know, comedy gods? I've got a show, and Trump's running for president. Good news for me, horrible news for our writers because all of our jokes are officially writing themselves," Wilmore said.

But at least one liberal saw Trump as destroying the nation by daring to run for president as an outsider.

"In all, the ability of Donald Trump, a man conspicuously unqualified to be president, to take captive the run-up to the 2016 presidential campaign, is reducing the entire political scene to a joke. The phenomenon is detrimental not only to the Republican Party but also to the single most important civic event in our society every four years," Jules Witcover of the *Baltimore Sun* wrote on July 15.

Only someone as entrenched in the federal government (as Witcover became after decades of covering Washington) would dismiss Trump's forty years as a chief executive officer as making him "conspicuously unqualified" to be president, especially while a community organizer with less than a term in the Senate sat at the Resolute desk in the Oval Office.

"The arrogance is stunning, is truly stunning here. He is what you see on television. He is consistently that guy. And that guy is funny, and that guy is smart, but that guy is not the guy I want running the presidency of the United States. Now, I don't think Donald Trump is Barack Obama by any stretch of the imagination. But Donald Trump is a progressive. He's not a conservative," radio talker Glenn Beck said

Beck was correct. Trump was no liberal or conservative. He was a pragmatist. That appealed to the public because after a decade and a half of ideological battles in Washington, many Americans yearned for results.

Columnist Charles Krauthammer warned America that Trump's announcement speech disqualified Trump.

"It was stream of consciousness. I think his single most important statement was 'I am very rich.' That's the basis for the campaign. But you know, look, you say, can you take him seriously? Can you really take seriously a candidate who says Mexico is not our friend. It is sending us immigrants who are criminals, drug dealers, and rapists...It will damage the party because, like say an Al Sharpton or even a Ross Perot, having those kind of people on stage who aren't really serious candidates diminishes the stature of the others who are," Krauthammer said on Fox News.

Yes, how dare a candidate not speak only from a script that has been field-tested on a focus group. No teleprompter, then no presidency for you.

"But his thesis is this, and I do think it has some resonance. All of our troubles are caused by Mexicans, Chinese, Japanese, Saudis, and others. I am going to extract tribute from all of them. He said, Entitlements? I won't have to cut entitlements. The Chinese will fund our entitlements. How? I'm right. I'm the author of *Art of The Deal*. Trust me. I'll make the deal. I'll make the Mexicans pay for the wall. I'll make the Saudis empty their treasury to support our infrastructure. Look, this is a campaign that's run on know-nothing xenophobia," Krauthammer said.

It seemed as if all the political experts in Washington agreed that Trump had no business running for president because he would lose the nomination.

"We trust Trump will not be the Republican nominee. But Trump could win significant support from Perot-type voters in primaries who will then be up for grabs in the general election," Bill Kristol, editor of the *Weekly Standard*, wrote on June 24.

But experts are not always right.

"Science alone of all the subjects contains within itself the lesson of the danger of belief in the infallibility of the greatest teachers of the preceding generation…As a matter of fact I can also define science another way: Science is the belief in the ignorance of experts," Nobel physicist Richard Feynman said.

Meanwhile in Florida, radio talker Rush Limbaugh watched the Trump announcement on television and told his listeners the next day, "So I'm watching. I've got the sound up, which is very rare, and the phone started ringing, and nobody in the rest of the office here picked it up, and I just yelled, 'Answer the [blank, blank] phone,' because I wanted to hear what Trump was saying. And I stopped myself. Wait a minute. Look what just happened here. There hasn't been a single other person give a political speech in years that if the phone rang and interrupted them, I'd have been mad."

CHAPTER 5

TRUMP CANNOT WIN.

———✦———

THE DAY AFTER TRUMP ENTERED the race, Chris Cillizza of the *Washington Post* declared Trump's candidacy dead in a piece headlined, "Why no one should take Donald Trump seriously, in one very simple chart."

The chart he showed said more Republicans disliked Trump than liked him. "Among Republicans—you know, the people who decide the identity of their party's presidential nominee—Trump has a *net negative 42 rating*. As in 23 percent of Republicans had a favorable view of Trump while 65 percent(!) had an unfavorable one. Want even more? Compare the number of Republicans who feel strongly favorable to Trump (11 percent) to those who feel strongly unfavorable (43 percent). No one in the field is anywhere close to those numbers; New Jersey Gov. Chris Christie is the only candidate other than Trump to have higher unfavorable than favorable ratings among his own party," Cillizza wrote.

"And it's not even (or only) his brutal image problems that doom Trump. Just one in ten Republicans (11 percent) have no opinion of him. So, Trump is both extremely well-known and extremely disliked by the members of the party he is running to represent.

"You cannot and do not win anything when your numbers look like Trump's. I can't say it any more clearly than that. There's nothing you can say or do—not that Trump would ever even consider going on an image rehabilitation tour—to change how people feel about you. Republicans know Trump. And they really, really don't like him."

Yes, in Washington people think that one poll taken months before anyone votes means the campaign is over. Perhaps we should worry. Washington has the people who have our nuclear codes.

"Trump, of course, knows this. His goal is attention, not winning. And in truth, even that would be fine if Trump had an issue (or issues) that he cared about and wanted to draw attention to via his presidential bid. He doesn't. He just says stuff. Lots and lots of stuff. And it's not clear that he's spent more than the five seconds before he speaks thinking about what he's going to say," Cillizza wrote.

Cillizza merely repeated a mistake made the day before by *FiveThirtyEight*, a numbers-crunching site run by economist Nate Silver.

"Taking into account name recognition, Trump's net favorability rating (favorable minus unfavorable) of –32 percentage points stands out for its pure terribleness at this point in the campaign. Like his unfavorable rating, it is by far the worst of the 106 presidential candidates since 1980 who are in our database," Harry Enten of *FiveThirtyEight* wrote.

Enten said only one conclusion was possible.

"For this reason alone, Trump has a better chance of cameoing in another *Home Alone* movie with Macaulay Culkin—or playing in the NBA Finals—than winning the Republican nomination," Enten wrote.

Guess Culkin better get cracking on that new *Home Alone* sequel, and the Cleveland Cavaliers should make room on their roster for The Donald.

But Enten's boss—Nate Silver—agreed. "At *FiveThirtyEight*, however, we're fairly agnostic about what will happen to Trump's polling in the near term. It's possible that he's already peaked—or that he'll hold his support all the way through Iowa and New Hampshire, possibly even winning one or two early states, as similar candidates like Pat Buchanan and Newt Gingrich have in the past. Our emphatic prediction is simply that Trump will not win the nomination. It's not even clear that he's trying to do so," Silver wrote on August 11.

But others believed Trump had a good chance of winning. John McLaughlin, eighty-eight, said so on his weekly panel show, *The McLaughlin Group*, on July 10.

"Do you realize this man's achievement? Do you realize the buildings that he's put up? They're enormous," McLaughlin said.

Howard Stern of Sirius XM was another believer. "You could actually be president. This is looking like a reality," Stern told Trump on the air on August 24, 2015.

But overwhelmingly, pundits said The Donald's campaign was DOA.

"Mr. Sanders and Mr. Trump won't win their party's nomination, but in trying, they could make the path to the White House that much rockier for whoever eventually does," Karl Rove wrote on July 8.

In 2012, Rove raised $350 million from Trump and others for an independent PAC called American Crossroads. Republicans lost in ten of the twelve Senate campaigns and five of the nine House races that Rove's group supported. The day after the election, Trump mocked Rove as the election's biggest loser.

But Rove had the pulse of Washington pundits. "Basically nobody who follows politics in any depth thinks either Donald Trump or Bernie Sanders could be elected our next president. And yet here we are, with the unelectables rising to the top of their parties' polls. Trump leads basically every GOP poll of the 2016 race, and Sanders—an independent socialist senator from Vermont—just crested Hillary Clinton in his very first poll in New Hampshire. So how is it possible that the chattering classes are still giving them almost no chance—not only to win the presidency, but even their parties' nominations? There's actually a very good reason: It's because people do care about electability. They just don't care about it yet," Aaron Blake of the *Washington Post* wrote on August 13.

That was the same day that Krauthammer offered his forecast in the same publication. Krauthammer called The Donald the clear front-runner but hedged.

"Nonetheless, his core support, somewhere around 20 percent (plus or minus a couple), remains as solid as that once commanded by Ron Paul and Ross Perot. Which means Trump will likely continue to lead until the field whittles down to a handful, at which point 20 percent is no longer a plurality. Teflon Don. Solid constituency, fixed ceiling. Chances of winning his party's nomination? About the same as Sanders winning his," Krauthammer wrote. He gave Sanders no chance.

Jonah Goldberg of the *National Review* feigned pity for Trump. "Poor Donald Trump. It wasn't supposed to be like this. For years, wherever The Donald went, he met people who told him he should run for president. His retinue of sycophants surely saw little to gain from explaining that birthers, celebrity worshippers, and devotees of *The Apprentice* are not a statistically meaningful sample of the electorate. Nor did it dawn on him that some people say 'you should run for president' the way you tell your long-winded uncle 'you should write a book.' History is full of failed men who mistook flattery for insight," Goldberg wrote on July 8.

James Fallows of the *Atlantic Monthly* agreed. "Donald Trump will not be the 45th president of the United States. Nor the 46th, nor any other number you might name. The chance of his winning nomination and election is exactly zero," Fallows wrote on July 13.

John Podhoretz, editor of *Commentary* magazine, was sure the collapse of Trump was near. "The thing is, as Nate Cohn of the *New York Times* reminded me yesterday on Twitter, Trump's mid-20s numbers are exactly at the level every one of the not-Romneys in 2011—Michele Bachmann, Herman Cain, and Newt Gingrich in particular—reached at one point or another in that storied year. At those moments when the not-Romneys were riding high, they had all kinds of negatives the way Trump does and yet seemed to have earned a passionate following that didn't care about any of it. And yet, they were all laid low eventually," Podhoretz wrote on August 4.

"The problem for the GOP is not that Trump might not crater; it's that when he does, he might decide to get Hillary Clinton elected in 2016 by running as a third-party candidate. How to manage Trump so he doesn't do that is on the minds of everyone in the theoretical GOP top tier, which is why they're treating him gently. But if they have to stop treating him gently—if, especially, the Jeb Bush SuperPAC with $103 million decides it has to stop treating Trump gently the way the Romney people decided they had to get rough with his rivals—they will do what they have to do and they will have an effect."

Bush went after Trump. Bush's poll numbers fell, and Trump's rose.

By now readers likely are thinking, gee, no one knew, so why pick on all those pundits who blew Trump off? Because not everyone followed the crowd and marched off the cliff. A week before Trump officially entered the race, Chris Matthews of MSNBC foretold the events to come. "Trump, if he goes in will not be going in to show off. He will be going in to win the nomination. And that means trouble for the other candidates. Can they take a punch? Can they? Can they stand there on that debate stage and laugh off a direct shot from Donald Trump? Can they act as if the man has not just attacked their character, their dignity, their rationale for being there in the first place?" Matthews said on June 9, 2015.

"So, all bets are off. Trump inside the ring means trouble for everyone else. The only question is whether he can take a showman's performance in the debates and convert it into victory in the caucuses and primaries. But those are months from now. What happens if the big name, the big noise coming out of debates this summer, which begin in August, by the way, is Donald Trump? Will there be any life in other Republican candidates once he's done his number on them?"

But the conservative commentariat in Washington missed Trump, just as their churlish commissar, Krauthammer, had written off another populist candidate two presidential elections earlier.

"When, just a week ago, Barack Obama showed a bit of ankle and declared the mere possibility of his running for the presidency, the chattering classes swooned. Now that every columnist in the country has given him advice, here's mine: He should run in '08. He will lose in '08. And the loss will put him irrevocably on a path to the presidency," Krauthammer wrote on October 27, 2006.

But this time it was different. We had reached peak Trump.

CHAPTER 6

PEAK TRUMP.

———◆———

OIL EMBARGOES IN THE 1970s by OPEC, a group of totalitarian govern-
ments that wanted to hold at their mercy the free nations of the world,
created fear in the West of running out of oil. President Carter stoked
those fears by dusting off the idea of peak oil, a time when the production of oil would begin to decline as reserves ran out.

In 1919, David White, chief geologist of the United States Geological
Survey, predicted the United States would reach peak oil in 1922.

In 1953, Eugene Ayers, a researcher for Gulf Oil, predicted peak oil
would reach the United States by 1960.

In 1956, M. King Hubbert, a geoscientist for Shell, predicted peak
oil would reach the United States by 1971.

In 1977, Carter predicted the world would reach peak oil in 2011.

Each prediction failed because experts overlooked the incentive for
capitalists to develop new fields and new technologies, which expanded
the world's reserves of oil. George Phydias Mitchell's company developed hydraulic fracking, which led to a glut of oil on the market by 2011.

Learning nothing from this, conservative pundits began talking
about peak Trump from the day he announced he was running for
president.

We reached peak Trump on June 16.

"On Tuesday, Donald Trump laid out the most entertaining campaign launch in presidential history. The stagecraft—descending his
elevator in his tower behind his sexy wife—was magnificent. The Donald

knew that the crowd expected The Donald, and thus he gave them Peak The Donald," Ben Shapiro wrote in *Breitbart News*.

We reached peak Trump on July 9.

"On Wednesday, we reached peak Donald Trump, with two national TV interviews, including one by NBC News' Katy Tur. We also learned on Wednesday that RNC Chair Reince Priebus called Trump and asked him to tone down his rhetoric on immigration—yet another acknowledgement of how the New York real-estate mogul is hurting the party. But here's a fairly safe prediction: Trump's poll position in the GOP race is going to go down. It might not happen tomorrow, or next month before the first debate, or the month after that. But it's going to happen. And it won't be due to immigration, but instead past statements on a slew of important issues to the GOP base," Chuck Todd of NBC wrote.

We reached peak Trump on July 21.

"Trump reached peak Trumpness during his speech today," the *Week* reported.

We reached peak Trump on July 22.

"Memo to Donald Trump: We are past PEAK TRUMP! Sell-by date approaching. Plan EXIT STRATEGY before Iowa! ADIOS amigo! #ArtOfTheWithdrawal," Bill Kristol wrote.

We reached peak Trump on August 19.

"Though Donald Trump is maintaining a healthy lead in polls for the Republican presidential nomination, there is mounting evidence that he has already peaked," Philip Klein of the *Washington Examiner* wrote.

We reached peak Trump on August 20.

"Donald Trump's 'Time' Magazine Cover Lets Us Know We've Reached Peak Donald Trump," Alicia Lu of the *Bustle* headlined her article.

We reached peak Trump on August 20, for a second reason.

"Trumpmentum has been losing steam ever since the debate. I hopped over to RealClear Politics this morning to take a look at their latest poll averages, and it shows something interesting: Donald Trump may have hit his ceiling. On August 5, he hit a peak at 24.3 percent. He then plateaued for a few days and has been falling ever since. He now stands at 22.0 percent," Kevin Drum of *Mother Jones* wrote.

We reached peak Trump on September 16.

In an article titled, "The Five Reasons That 'The Donald' is Done by December," Jeff Wald of the *Huffington Post* wrote, "On Wednesday September 16, 2015 at 4:23 p.m. EST, I tweeted that we had just reached 'Peak Trump.' I believe that was the moment 'The Donald' reached his maximum appeal to the American public. I could have added something along the lines of, 'and our long national nightmare shall soon be over'; although you only get 140 characters."

We reached peak Trump on September 24.

"Trump may have passed his peak, polls indicate," wrote David Lauter of the *Los Angeles Times*.

We reached peak Trump on September 30.

"As a card-carrying member of the media, it has certainly felt to me, starting around the second debate, that the limits of Trump's candidacy have come clearer: He's out of his depth on policy, his campaign is progressively less inventive and unusual, and fear of Trump is leading to consolidation around his most politically talented challengers—namely Rubio and Fiorina. But Trump still leads in the polls, and the level of media coverage he's getting now is about the same as before he peaked in the polls," Ezra Klein of *Vox* wrote.

We reached peak Trump on October 23.

"I said before that we'd reached Peak Trump, and the polling since has borne that out. Improbably, Ben Carson is on the way up. But the race is getting nuanced, and technicalities might play a big part in the early race momentum next year," Neil Stevens of *Red State* wrote.

We reached peak Trump on October 27.

"There's buzz this morning about a new CBS/New York Times national poll that shows Ben Carson leading Donald Trump by 4 percentage points. It's the first time since mid-July that a pollster that puts out results regularly has shown anyone but Trump leading the

Republican primary nationally. 'Peak Trump' has been declared, erroneously, almost as many times as 'peak oil.' Is there reason to believe it's real this time?" Kyle Wingfield of the *Atlanta Journal-Constitution* wrote.

We reached peak Trump on January 14, 2016.

"Trump's Rant about the 'Son of a Bitch' Who Installed His Microphone Last Night Was Peak Trump," ran the headline to a Jack Holmes's piece in *Esquire*.

We reached peak Trump on March 5.

"I think we may have passed peak Trump, as it will be known. I don't think Mr. Romney was under any illusions that he was going to talk Trump's supporters out of supporting him. I think he knows the axiom that you cannot reason people out of a position they have not been reasoned into," George Will said on Fox News.

Trump had more peaks than the Himalayas. But the peak Trump cliché did inspire Jonah Goldberg of the *National Review* to write one of his best paragraphs in the campaign on August 11, 2015.

"While Rasmussen and other allegedly reputable polls suggest that we may have hit peak Trump already, I'm not buying it. Every time reason and logic suggest Trump's moment should start winding down, he surges ahead. Well, I'm not taking the bait this time. I'm only going to predict success for Trump from now on, on the theory that reality will prove me wrong. So Trump will win the Republican primaries. Even his opponents will vote for him. Even his opponents' mothers and children will vote for him. Humans shall rise from the grave to pull the lever for him. He is unstoppable. He shall be president for life. You can take that to the bank," Goldberg wrote.

But four days later, he took off the curse and wrote, "It's obviously too soon to tell for sure, but I think we've reached Peak Trump."

The conservative commentariat would rather be in agreement than be right.

CHAPTER 7

DOUBLE-AGENT MAN.

———————

As Trump fed the cable news networks new material in news cycle after news cycle, the conservative commentariat double downed on its belief that he was not serious about running for president. Never mind that he was throwing away a popular TV show, which NBC canceled due to his presidential run, and that he was investing millions of his own money on his campaign, these cerebral conservatives could not comprehend his commitment to his cause.

"The US has become a dumping ground for everybody else's problems," Trump said in his announcement speech on June 16, 2015.

The crowd applauded.

"Thank you. It's true, and these are not the best and the finest. When Mexico sends its people, they're not sending their best. They're not sending you. They're not sending you. They're sending people who have lots of problems, and they're bringing those problems with us. They're bringing drugs. They're bringing crime. They're rapists. And some, I assume, are good people," Trump said.

Conservatives in the capital took umbrage that anyone would connect illegal immigration to violent crime because that offends liberal sensibilities, and conservatives in Washington would rather die than offend a liberal.

"That plays well with many far-right Republican primary voters desperately clinging to an America that no longer exists. But such rhetoric is the death knell for the GOP—and the party knows it," Jonathan Capehart of the *Washington Post* wrote.

John Fund of the *National Review* gave his explanation. "But just maybe Trump is a double agent for the Left. He is nearly a cartoon version of what a comedian such as Stephen Colbert considers a conservative—the kind of conservative Colbert played on Comedy Central until this year. He reinforces all the Left's negative stereotypes of conservatives as ignorant blowhards," Fund wrote on June 21.

Thus began one of the loopier claims in American history, that Trump was a secret agent working for the Democrats. Well, he did live a lifestyle that James Bond would envy, filled with gorgeous models as his wives, a 757 jet, beautiful homes, including a stunning Manhattan apartment, and of course, weekends at the Mar-a-Lago resort in Palm Beach, Florida.

To be sure, conspirators had some evidence. "Former president Bill Clinton had a private telephone conversation in late spring with Donald Trump at the same time that the billionaire investor and reality-television star was nearing a decision to run for the White House, according to associates of both men," the *Washington Post* reported on August 5.

"Four Trump allies and one Clinton associate familiar with the exchange said that Clinton encouraged Trump's efforts to play a larger role in the Republican Party and offered his own views of the political landscape.

"Clinton's personal office in New York confirmed that the call occurred in late May, but an aide to Clinton said the 2016 race was never specifically discussed and that it was only a casual chat."

But Trump socialized with many politicians. Trump said that as a businessman, he had to donate to both parties because the size of government dictated that corporations pay tribute to those who run it. Pay to play.

In the first Republican debate in Cleveland, the moderators asked Trump about his donations to the Clintons.

"Well, I'll tell you what, with Hillary Clinton, I said be at my wedding and she came to my wedding. You know why? She didn't have a choice because I gave. I gave to a foundation that, frankly, that foundation is supposed to do good. I didn't know her money would be used on private jets going all over the world. It was," Trump said.

Months later, Tucker Carlson, editor in chief at the *Daily Caller*, called that Trump's finest moment in the first debate. "Even then, I'll confess, I didn't get it. (Why would you pay someone to come to your wedding?) But the audience did. Trump is the ideal candidate to fight Washington corruption not simply because he opposes it, but because he has personally participated in it. He's not just a reformer; like most effective populists, he's a whistleblower, a traitor to his class," Carlson wrote on January 28, 2016.

But the belief that Trump wanted to elect Clinton by undermining Republicans was tenacious because it reflected a Washington-based belief that only the political class could govern the country. And by govern, they meant rule. Since he was not a politician, Trump could not win, Rove said on Fox News on June 22, 2015.

"Ignore him. He is completely off the base. I mean, you know, 'I'm gonna negotiate with ISIS. I have a secret plan to deal with ISIS, but I can't tell you about it because of my enemies. As president I have the unilateral authority to levy a 35 percent tax on any company that opens plants abroad.' I mean this guy is not a serious candidate," Rove said.

However, Trump was serious. His campaign was not some lark financed by others. He put his money where his mouth was. He also paid what economists call an opportunity cost to make money by delaying production of his television show. That came four months before his formal announcement.

"Everybody feels I'm doing this just to have fun or because it's good for the brand. Well, it's not fun. I'm not doing this for enjoyment. I'm doing this because the country is in serious trouble," Trump told the *Washington Post* on February 25, 2015.

But Trump ran anyway. He had studied presidential politics and learned how to campaign. He did not advance in business by ignoring his homework. His mastery of the New York media was not serendipity. He spent decades learning how to play the media game. He learned the political game.

"The one thing I've always found to be true with Trump is, I think he learns faster than any other political figure I've known except Bill Clinton," former Speaker of the House Newt Gingrich said on CBS on September 6.

But everyone else in politics knew The Donald was a gift to the Democrats. While conservative pundits bemoaned Trump's entry into their race, many a liberal rejoiced.

"Democrats are jumping with glee over news that Donald Trump is officially exploring a run for president," *Huffington Post* reported on March 18.

The day he entered the race, Lisa Feldmann of the *Christian Science Monitor*, reported, "The Democratic National Committee couldn't be happier."

Feldmann concluded, "We know, it's not fair to count anybody out at this very early stage. But Trump's candidacy is as quixotic as they come. A March poll by NBC News and the *Wall Street Journal* reports that fully 74 percent of Republican voters say they could not see themselves supporting Trump. No Republican contender scored worse."

Democratic National Committee press secretary Holly Shulman issued a press release mocking him. "Today, Donald Trump became the second major Republican candidate to announce for president in two days," Shulman said. "He adds some much-needed seriousness that has previously been lacking from the GOP field, and we look forward to hearing more about his ideas for the nation."

The joy continued all summer long.

"I am a person of faith—and The Donald's entry into this race can only be attributed to the fact that the good Lord is a Democrat with a sense of humor," Democratic consultant Paul Begala told the *Washington Post* on July 1, 2015.

Others agreed.

"And while it is said that voters have a very short memory and have not yet really focused on the 2016 decision, the memory of Trump's attacks will be enduring for at least the next two years. It is quite unlikely that this will escape Hispanic voters' minds," Bill Humphrey and Stephan Richter wrote in *The Globalist* on July 8.

Pointing out that NBC canceled his shows, they concluded, "Getting ever madder due to the loss of very profitable television deals might induce him to stay in the race as an independent and split the conservative base. And that is precisely what Ross Perot did in the 1992 race, with known results and benefits for the other Clinton."

Academia weighed in.

"As a political scientist, I am reluctant to make predictions about elections, especially about the behavior of a single individual. But I'm willing to make an exception this year, because the presidential campaign is turning out to be such an exceptionally crucial (and entertaining) one. Here is what I see as the step-by-step best case scenario for putting a Democrat in the White House next year, with a little help from Donald Trump," Professor Peter Dreier of Occidental College (Obama's alma mater) wrote on July 22, in *Talking Points Memo.*

Dreier made seventeen points outlining how Trump would help Democrats. ("2. Trump refuses to apologize or abandon his campaign for the GOP nomination. Throughout 2015, he continues to attract large crowds and major media coverage as he travels around the country appealing to the Tea Party and Hair Club for Men crowds.")

But as summer became autumn and autumn became winter, Democrats discovered their gift was a Trojan horse.

"About 20 percent of likely Democratic voters say they would buck the party and vote for Republican presidential candidate Donald Trump in a general election, according to a new poll. The willingness of some Democrats to change sides could be a major problem for Democratic front-runner Hillary Clinton this fall," the *Hill* reported on January 9, 2016.

Apparently internal polls at Camp Clinton showed the same thing.

"If Donald Trump takes the Republican nomination, our party will lose more than the presidency. Years of progress will be ripped away. Obamacare will be repealed. Marriage equality will be rolled back. Get excited to visit the wall on the Mexico border—and get ready to pay for it if President Trump can't magically get Mexico to cough up the cash for it," Clinton's campaign manager Robby Mook wrote supporters on January 28.

Maybe Trump was an incompetent double agent.

CHAPTER 8

GEORGE WALLACE OR DER FÜHRER?

———◆———

PUNDITS SAW TRUMP AS CHUM in the summer of 2015. Even the *Wall Street Journal* wrote off Trump in an editorial on July 9.

"But in any case he's a political fad who will fade as voters learn that he's no conservative. He donates money to Democrats because he says 'you're gonna need things from everybody,' which is not the best tea party appeal. He loves corporate welfare, especially government seizure of property so he can build his properties. He gives no evidence of knowing anything about public policy, other than he'd stand up to China and the menace of Mexico—though he concedes that 'some' Mexicans 'are good people.'"

Larry Sabato also crossed Trump off the list from the get-go. A professor and director of the University of Virginia Center for Politics, he published *Sabato's Crystal Ball*. It might has well been a bowling ball that summer, for in June 2015, Sabato and company produced for *Politico*, "The Myths of 2016: What everyone gets wrong about the election."

The first myth he attacked was "the giant Republican field is unpredictable, almost anybody's game." Sabato got that right, but he predicted the wrong people emerging.

"Republicans are hungry to reoccupy the White House, and the realistic among them understand the party won't win without pitching a bigger tent. There may be no single GOP frontrunner, but there are just a few politicians who have the resources, positioning and potential to expand the base. They are former Florida Gov. Jeb Bush, Florida Sen.

Marco Rubio and Wisconsin Gov. Scott Walker, not necessarily in that order," the *Sabato's Crystal Ball* team wrote.

Three months later, Walker ran out of money and quit the race. In February 2016, Bush lost South Carolina and quit. The next month, Rubio lost his home state of Florida and quit.

However, getting the story wrong was rampant in DC that summer. The lefty *Huffington Post* dismissed Trump as irrelevant.

"After watching and listening to Donald Trump since he announced his candidacy for president, we have decided we won't report on Trump's campaign as part of The Huffington Post's political coverage. Instead, we will cover his campaign as part of our Entertainment section. Our reason is simple: Trump's campaign is a sideshow. We won't take the bait. If you are interested in what The Donald has to say, you'll find it next to our stories on the Kardashians and *The Bachelorette*," the *Post* posted on June 17.

Michael Ramirez, one of the few conservative cartoonists to win a Pulitzer, drew a cartoon of a deep space probe and captioned it, "Scientists photograph the most remote object in our solar system."

The punchline? "It's Donald Trump's chances of being elected president."

Not every journalist in Washington was blind to Trump's potential. On May 10, a month before Trump formally entered the race, Byron York of the *Washington Examiner* wrote, "The bottom line is, by the various measurements journalists use to evaluate campaigns—crowds, staff, money, candidate time on the ground—if the Trump campaign were being conducted by anyone else, journalists would take it quite seriously."

However, all most political pundits knew about The Donald was that he was rich and tacky and that he had a TV show and odd hair. They knew nothing about how he helped revive luxury hotels in New York City or how he helped save Atlantic City. They did not care to learn. The press decided to mock him incessantly until he would go away, like they had Palin in 2008.

"He'll be out before Iowa. You read it here first," Joe Nocera of the *New York Times* wrote on September 29. The newspaper moved him to sports six weeks later.

The experts never asked themselves why a businessman would tear himself from a multi-billion-dollar enterprise he had built and campaign for such a high office if he were not confident of winning.

"His miserable comments about Mexican immigrants have already cost him business. NBC, which came under heavy pressure from a Hispanic media-watchdog group and many viewers, severed ties with him, as has Macy's, which carried his clothing line. Trump's political and ideological forays have generally been promotional brand extensions, lasting only as long as they were, in his view, good for business; the whole con might end well before the first snows in Sioux City and Manchester," David Remnick, editor of the *New Yorker*, wrote on July 8.

Of more importance, they never sought to find out why people followed him. Bret Stephens of the *Wall Street Journal* in fact hated them all. "If by now you don't find Donald Trump appalling, you're appalling," Stephens wrote on August 31.

But York stood up for them. "Here's the important thing to remember about Trump, or any other political candidate, for that matter: Maybe you think he's a clown. But some voters, perhaps a significant number of voters, take him seriously. They're not dumb. So the question is, what concern of those voters, what need, is being addressed by Donald Trump?" York wrote on May 10.

The answer from the pundits was simple: racism. Former Nixon speechwriter Ben Stein called Trump the second coming of George Wallace. "But without George Wallace's charm," Stein said on NewsMax TV on July 14.

Rimshot.

Stein joined the chorus in calling Trump a danger to the party. "I can't see him doing anything but damage to the Republican Party," he said.

Given the record-low confidence level Americans had in a Congress run by Republicans, there was not much left to damage. But two days earlier, Chuck Todd, on his *Meet the Press* show, denounced Trump along those same lines.

"We've seen versions of Donald Trump over the years. And I just don't mean versions of this Donald Trump, but I mean, you know, a George Wallace and things like this. This does happen. And they do strike a chord," Todd said.

On the same show, historian Doris Kearns Goodwin said that instead of reporting his words and letting viewers and readers decide, the press should shun him. "We, as journalists, have a responsibility to figure out which candidates are likely to be our leaders. I remember talking with Tim Russert about this. Rather than who's got the most money, who's saying the most outrageous thing, who has the highest polls, who is likely to be a leader? They've shown qualities already. This guy has shown qualities I cannot imagine him as a presidential leader," Goodwin said.

However, Trump did show leadership, which was what bothered her most. He led people with ideas that did not have her approval. Those ideas were open to anyone who had the gumption to stand up to the liberals. Mickey Kaus, one of the first journalists to blog, pointed this out a decade earlier.

"Much is being made, in the press, the blogs, and the email I'm getting, of the split in the Republican party on immigration: there are pro-crackdown conservatives on the one hand, and rich Republican business backers who need immigrant labor on the other. I'm not sure this internal struggle is such a close thing, though, at least this year. Republicans facing the loss of Congress need to mobilize their base, not their lobbyists. They need voters, not money. That points in only one direction, no? Sometime before November, that should become obvious," Kaus wrote on March 27, 2006.

As Trump rose in the polls, the *Huffington Post* ate its words and moved him back from entertainment to its politics section. On January 28, 2016, the *Huffington Post* editors made it mandatory for all writers to end any story on Trump with the following disclaimer: "Note to readers:

Donald Trump is a serial liar, rampant xenophobe, racist, misogynist, birther and bully who has repeatedly pledged to ban all Muslims—1.6 billion members of an entire religion—from entering the US."

So what did George Wallace think of Donald Trump? Not much. Black comedian George Wallace joked about the September debate on CNN. "Donald Trump is adamant about building this wall, is he not? He's gonna stop the Mexicans, the Mexicans are building tunnels. If he's gonna build a wall, they're building tunnels."

He had a point about tunnels, but a wall would make border crossing more difficult. At any rate, his was a far better analysis of the situation than what pundits offered.

But calling a presidential candidate George Wallace was a politically correct way of calling him Hitler. Sadly, a few people were willing to go there.

"I've often objected in my column to invoking Hitler as popular analogue because it trivializes the suffering and slaughter of the Jews. Now I'm not so sure. Remember that before there could be a Holocaust, there was the identification of the Jewish race as the enemy. Trump's apparent identification of Muslims as 'a problem,' with his threat of a Muslim registry and a religious test at the border, sounds terribly familiar," *Washington Post* columnist Kathleen Parker wrote on December 8.

She had violated Godwin's Law, named for attorney Mike Godwin, an early adopter of computer technology, joining Internet chats when the people online were mainly academics.

"As an online discussion grows longer, the probability of a comparison involving Nazis or Hitler approaches," Godwin posted sometime in the early 1990s.

His observation caught on, as his words became an admonition not to call people Nazis because that mocked the slaughter of two-thirds of European Jewry by the Germans under Hitler. Through usage, the law came to mean conceding the argument. When you called someone Hitler or a Nazi in an online argument, you lost.

A quarter of a century after Godwin's warning, Parker went there, as did others. Jeffrey Tucker of *Newsweek* may have been the first, when he filed a column on July 17, after hearing Trump speak for an hour.

"You would have to be hopelessly ignorant of modern history not to see the outlines and where they end up. I want to laugh about what he said, like reading a comic-book version of Franco, Mussolini or Hitler. And truly I did laugh as he denounced the existence of tech support in India that serves American companies ('how can it be cheaper to call people there than here?'—as if he still thinks that long-distance charges apply). But in politics, history shows that laughter can turn too quickly to tears," Tucker wrote.

The stretches to make The Donald into der Führer were strained.

"There are three qualities to Trump's presidential campaign that invoke parallels to Nazism. The first is his intense cult of personality, which, for Trump supporters, is particularly driven by his reputation as a successful businessman who can fix things, and by his willingness to brazenly defy the taboos of political correctness," Matthew Rosza wrote for MSNBC on November 15.

But Obama had developed a cult of personality eight years earlier, and he promised to fix things, even stealing the cartoon character Bob the Builder's catch-phrase: "Yes, we can."

Trump's call to build a wall to keep illegal aliens out, and his later call to better scrutinize people entering from Islamic nations were a light year from taking real citizens, seizing their property, putting them in concentration camps, working them as slaves, and then killing them in mass murders.

Pundits portrayed him as anti-immigrant, but Trump hired immigrants at his resorts and even married immigrants. His mother was an immigrant. What he opposed was illegal immigration. Most law-abiding Americans did, which was why he was winning.

As he approached the point where his nomination appeared inevitable, the *Washington Post* threw the kitchen sink at Trump on March 2, 2016.

"Some readers ask how Donald Trump can be a threat to democracy if he is putting himself forward as a candidate. If he ends up attracting a majority of American voters, what could be more democratic?" the editorial said.

"First, you don't have to go back to history's most famous example, Adolf Hitler, to understand that authoritarian rulers can achieve power through the ballot box. In the world today, it has become almost commonplace for elected leaders to lock the door behind them once they achieve power. Vladimir Putin in Russia, Hugo Chávez in Venezuela, Yoweri Museveni in Uganda, Recep Tayyip Erdogan in Turkey—all found ways once in power to restrict opposition, muzzle the media, and erode checks and balances."

The Washington Post's logic, if one could call it that, was that since Hitler won an election, all elections result in the election of a Hitler.

Roger Simon, chief political columnist of *Politico*, (not to be confused with Roger L. Simon of *PJ Media*) went off the deep end in a November 25, 2015, column.

"Trump is no fool. He is a man with a plan. Armed with his celebrity status, his vast wealth and his adoption of the big lie as his favorite campaign tactic, he sees the White House within reach," Simon wrote.

"He is ready for Hillary. He tipped his hand just the other day. 'I don't think she has the stamina to be president' he said. 'I don't think she has the strength or the stamina to be president.'

"Donald Trump has the stamina. Donald Trump has the strength. Donald Trump has the will.

"America has been stabbed in the back for the last time. 'We're tired of being run by stupid people!' he shouts. 'The American dream is dead. But we're going to make it bigger and better and stronger than ever before!'

"Bigger. Better. Stronger. One dream! One nation! One leader! Der Donald! Hail!"

Trump supporter Ann Coulter mocked the Hitler histrionics in a column on March 9, by listing the similarities between Hitler and Trump. They included the following:

* Adolf Hitler was a teetotaler. Donald Trump is a teetotaler.
* Adolf Hitler was a vegetarian; Donald Trump has never smoked.
* Adolf Hitler's favorite food was liver dumplings, a dish very similar to meatloaf. (*Ed.: They're not remotely similar.* No one knows that.) Donald Trump's favorite food is meatloaf.

Conservatives in Washington should have called out people on their side who called him Hitler and trivialized the Holocaust. But just like the Bushwood Country Club, the conservative commentariat protected its own first.

CHAPTER 9

POPULISTS NEVER WIN.

———◆———

PUNDITS LUMPED SANDERS AND TRUMP together as doomed candidates who could not win because they were populists, and populists never win.

"Trump's presidential campaign is a racist clownshow. And no, polls from July 2015 don't say very much about who will be president in January 2017. But there's more to Trump's burgeoning popularity than immigrant-bashing alone. He's running as a full-blown plutocrat populist, and populism is, well, popular—especially after a grinding recession. That should be concerning to his 2016 opponents, since the platform Trump has outlined on the trail has a long and successful history in American politics," Zach Carter of the *Huffington Post* wrote on July 22.

Like many pundits throughout the campaign, Carter called Trump a clown. They were half right. He was a clown punching bag. Every time they knocked him down, he bounced up and hit them back.

On July 28, writing in *US News and World Report*, Nicole Hemmer, a researcher at the University of Sydney, predicted Trump's bubble would burst because other bubbles had burst before:

"Lacking any sufficiently pure candidate, the populist right settles instead for shock value. This explains why voters in search of an ultra-conservative candidate have ended up backing people like Trump (whose policy positions are nebulous), or a latter-day Newt Gingrich, who prior to his 2012 rise had accused House conservatives of right-wing social engineering and partnered with then-House Speaker Nancy Pelosi, a Democrat, to combat climate change.

"The same thing that makes a primary bubble—anti-establishment populism—also explains why these bubbles burst. For former Texas Gov. Rick Perry, the first beneficiary of populist support in 2012, the crash came when he voiced support for the DREAM Act, calling fellow candidates heartless if they opposed legislation to fund education for children of undocumented workers. This was the real oops moment of Perry's campaign—he never led the polls again after making that remark. The populist right believed that the comment revealed Perry as just another stooge for the pro-amnesty establishment."

On August 11, Walter Russell Mead of Bard College declared Trump's appeal "nihilistic populism," not to be taken seriously.

> In part, also, Trump's popularity is the result of harmless good fun; our two-year presidential electoral cycle is a ridiculous spectacle and the reporters and pundits who discuss the horse race in such diligent detail are chasing will o' the wisps and wasting time. Many of the people who answer the polls that get analyzed to death in long, thumb sucker pieces aren't thinking seriously about how they will vote more than a year from now. You can also tell a pollster that you plan to vote for Trump simply, as George Wallace used to put it back in 1968, to "send them a message." Trump offers average Americans the chance to pull the Establishment's chain, and then watch the wonks and the pundits jerk and squeal. This is a lot of fun for the tens of millions of people out there who think the whole political class consists of high-minded incompetents and unprincipled parasites. Nihilistic populism, that is, can also be a powerful phenomenon.

Salena Zito of the *Pittsburgh Tribune-Review* saw some good in Trump's populism, as a sacrificial lamb. "Populism's impact on political parties is complicated: Johnson won in a landslide, yet Goldwater's populist candidacy became a catalyst for the conservative movement. Goldwater's loss gave liberals the moment to overreach—and they did.

Within three-and-a-half years, Johnson dropped his re-election bid, and Republican Richard Nixon won the presidency twice," Zito wrote on August 22.

On September 3, Larry Sabato of the University of Virginia told everyone to take a chill pill. Trump's lead in the polls would not last.

"Most mainstream analysts think Trump fever will break once the winnowing process reduces the number of Republican candidates so that other contenders—augmented by a large majority of GOP leaders who abhor Trump—can define him as insufficiently conservative. The identity of the actual Republican presidential nominee, though, remains obscured," Sabato wrote.

He used the last two Republican presidential nomination processes as his guide. "In the meantime, just keep two facts in mind. First, polls taken in 2015 about the 2016 presidential contest are as solid as a sand castle built on the sea shore—and it's hurricane season. Second, voters (especially in Iowa and New Hampshire) are just test-driving candidates like cars. They find features of several contenders to be appealing, but they realize no final purchase is needed until February," Sabato wrote.

On September 14, Charles Wheelan, a fellow at the Rockefeller Center at Dartmouth College, wrote that the world (i.e., the United States and Britain) were in a populist revival.

"In the eyes of policy wonks (like me) and the political establishment (like Hillary Clinton and Jeb Bush), these are not serious people. They have little chance of getting elected, and could not get their wacky ideas passed even if they did," Wheelan wrote.

However, former Speaker of the House Newt Gingrich, who once was a history professor, had a far different take on the subject of populism.

"Donald Trump is not unique. He is, in fact, part of a clear populist pattern in American history. The first great populist rebellion was Thomas Jefferson and James Madison against the Federalist elites. By the end of their insurgency, they had invented the Democratic-Republican Party and the Federalist Party disappeared. This was a bitter struggle in which the Federalists tried to put their opponents in jail through the Alien and Sedition Acts," Gingrich and his colleague Craig Shirley wrote for *NewsMax* on August 27.

Andrew Jackson followed in 1824 (a losing effort, but he won in 1828). Gingrich left out other populist presidential candidates, including Ronald Reagan in 1980 and Barack Obama in 2008. Both brought new voters to their party, although Obama's victory was far smaller than Reagan's.

"It's dangerous, however, to focus simply on the personal characteristics of populist insurgents. They have to be colorful to attract the popular support and they have to be vivid to ignite the energy—but there is also something far deeper going on," Gingrich and Shirley wrote. "Millions of Americans supported Jefferson because they were fed up with a Federalist elite that people believed would sell them out. Millions supported Andrew Jackson because they deeply distrusted the Bank of the United States and other instruments of elite power over the average citizen. Similarly, Trump is gaining ground because Americans are deeply unhappy with their current elites."

Pundits paid no attention to Gingrich. What did he know about populism?

I mean, besides leading the Gingrich Revolution in 1994, which gave Republicans control of the House of Representatives for the first time in forty years.

CHAPTER 10

HE FIGHTS.

———◆———

WHILE TRUMP'S RIVALS SPENT THE summer working on their campaign strategy and raising money from millionaires and billionaires, he campaigned. He had worked out his strategy before entering the race and had already raised all the money he would need. He raised that money over the course of four decades by building a multi-billion-dollar resort and casino conglomerate that included the Miss USA and Miss Universe pageants and other television productions.

His plan was simple: use the summer lull in news to dominate the cable news networks, and make the race a referendum on him.

Trump copied the marketing plan that Aaron Spelling and Fox broadcasting used to make *Beverly Hills 90210* a hit series. The series finished in eighty-eighth place after its first season. But that summer, when the other networks showed reruns, Fox offered fresh episodes of *90210*, which drew viewers and developed a following. The show moved up to forty-eighth place in its second season.

Providing fresh material to the cable news networks in the summer boosted Trump's ratings as well. He knew television better than its talking heads did. By the end of July, he took the lead in the public opinion polls and never looked back.

The Washington press was awful. Most members knew little about him and showed even less curiosity about finding out who he was. They could not even get his hair right. Many in the press just assumed he wore a toupee because somebody somewhere said it once. Luke Russert of MSNBC said on the air on July 20, "John McCain's arms were so badly broken, he can barely comb his hair. Donald Trump can't comb his hair 'cause it's fake."

The press loved to mock this nonexistent toupee until Trump decided it had gone on long enough. At a rally in Greenville, South Carolina, on August 27, Trump invited Mary Margaret Bannister—a stranger—up on stage to pull his hair and prove it was not a toupee. The showman had one-upped his critics. He usually did.

Drawing on four decades of experience with the New York media, Trump used the carrot-and-stick approach to the media, praising those who went along and smacking those who did not. He knew his audience hated the press as much as it hated Congress and both political parties. His criticisms of the press endeared him to the public. Battling the press made him a fighter, which was part of his attraction to the ignored rank-and-file Republicans: he fights.

And Trump criticized reporters to their faces. He confronted Anderson Cooper in an interview on July 23.

> TRUMP: You started off the interview with a poll that I didn't even know existed.
>
> COOPER: I started off
>
> TRUMP: I think it's very unfair. You talk to me a poll I never even saw. All I know is, I have a very big group of support, and I think one of the reasons is.
>
> COOPER: At the moment with Republicans, you're way out in front.
>
> TRUMP: Let me tell you, the people don't trust you, and the people don't trust the media.

That day, Trump also took on a Telemundo reporter at a rally in Laredo, Texas. "Many feel that what you said, when you said that people that cross the border are rapists and murderers," the reporter began.

Trump cut him off. "No, no, we're talking about illegal immigration, and everybody understands it. And you know what? That's a typical case of the press with misinterpretation. They take half a sentence, then they take a quarter of a sentence. They put it all together. It's a typical thing," Trump said.

At a press conference in Iowa on August 25, Trump ejected Univision commentator and anchorman Jorge Ramos who spoke out of turn.

"Go back to Univision," Trump told Ramos.

But minutes later, Trump let Ramos back in, and the two had it out.

Trump had sued Univision after it dropped his beauty pageants over his plans to build a wall between Mexico and the United States. Months later, the two quietly settled the matter out of court.

Beating the press worked for Trump for the same reason George H. W. Bush's confrontation with Dan Rather on CBS on January 25, 1988, worked. Confronting the press showed people the candidate was willing to fight. Over the years, too many Republicans kowtowed to the press. Not Trump.

"George Will is a disaster. The guy is a disaster. Another one, Karl Rove. No, he's terrible. Terrible. He's terrible. Karl Rove still thinks Mitt Romney won the election. Karl Rove ought to be on Wall Street. He raises money pretty well. He raised last cycle, the last presidential election, he raised $434 million and didn't win one race. Can you believe that?" Trump told a rally in Dallas on September 14.

He fought.

"The *Des Moines Register* is a terrible paper as far as I'm concerned. Very liberal paper by the way," Trump told a town-hall meeting in New Hampshire on October 26.

And fought.

"I've become immune to it. Honestly, I've seen things that are so bad with the press," Trump told a rally in Sparks, Nevada, on October 29.

In the nineteenth century, it was a bad idea to argue with a man who bought ink by the barrel, but in the twenty-first century, Trump engaged people who had every hour of the day on cable news to mock him because his supporters wanted him to fight.

And fighting back brought free publicity. The cable news critics would run his clips in order to bash him, but that backfired because people agreed with what they saw in the clips. Trump beat the media at its own game. The media as a whole was unaware, but Rush Limbaugh spotted it early.

"You know, these people are gonna have to learn—and I doubt that they will—that they can't deal with Trump the way they deal with every standard, ordinary, everyday politician, because he's not one. He's a businessman, and if they don't start looking at him that way—and a winning businessman, a competitive business—if they look at him, and they continue to try to react to Trump and shape coverage of Trump based on politics, they're gonna miss this," Limbaugh said on July 23, 2015.

Far from being out of control, Trump calculated the news he generated. He spoke to his audience of disenchanted voters using language the politicians had banished. This scored with voters. When he was politically incorrect, the cable news networks repeated his message in the hope of bringing him down. Instead, they were spreading his word.

For example, he broke a taboo by daring to point out that illegal aliens committed crimes. Before he said this, he knew three things: it was true, his audience knew it was true, and the media pretended it was not true. Pundits foolishly seized on this issue believing they could discredit him.

"With his outrageous remarks about immigrants from Mexico carrying drugs and raping and murdering people, Trump has thrown a monkey wrench into the race for the Republican presidential nomination. That polls show him second in New Hampshire is troubling to say the least. Trump will never be president, but he might ensure Hillary Clinton is," Cal Thomas wrote in his column on July 3.

To the delight of the conservative commentariat, Univision and Macy's dropped their partnerships with Trump in light of his remarks.

"Donald Trump has spent the past decade toying with adding the final career move necessary for him to achieve the Platonic ideal of pompous American windbaggery: becoming a politician. Now that he has actually jumped into the ring, he is finding out very quickly that the things you say while running for president as an immigrant-bashing faux populist can get you in serious trouble," Ben Domenech, publisher of *The Federalist*, wrote in the *New York Daily News* on July 2.

Writing in the *National Review* on July 6, Linda Chavez, president of the Becoming American Institute, blurred the lines between illegal aliens and legal immigrants. "If we conservatives hope ever to expand our ranks and actually elect a conservative to the White House, we need to begin mending fences with Mexican Americans and other Hispanics, not defending the likes of Donald Trump."

Mending fences? What fences? That was the problem. There were no fences. And innocent people paid the price for the refusal of Washington to fence the border. Five days before Chavez's column appeared, on July 1, an illegal alien shot and killed Katie Steinle, thirty-two, on Pier 14 in the Embarcadero district in San Francisco, which is a sanctuary city. He was a career criminal, whom officials had deported five times, before he jumped the border a sixth time.

The murder of Katie Steinle did draw indignation from some in the conservative commentariat.

"If laws are not enforced, what is the point of having them?" Thomas wrote in his column on July 13.

"If politicians are so afraid of losing the Hispanic vote that they do nothing in response to the murder of Kathryn Steinle, they should be removed from office. The notion that Hispanics won't vote for a party that stands for justice is racist."

That was ten days after Thomas castigated Trump for pointing out the rapes and murders by illegal aliens.

CHAPTER 11

MEET THE TRUMPKINS.

———•———

A FEW PUNDITS IN WASHINGTON supported Trump's ideas, if not his presidential ambitions. They shared his opposition to political correctness and amnesty for illegal aliens. Trump's detractors took to calling his supporters *Trumpkins*. But who doesn't like pumpkins? They make good jack-o'-lanterns for Halloween and pie filling for Thanksgiving. They are native to America. Only someone out of his gourd would not like pumpkins.

Fox News anchor Sean Hannity was among those delighted when Trump announced his candidacy.

"We've got a problem in this country if he can make that statement and CNN refers to it as 'racially tinged.' Floor-to-ceiling drugs confiscated by people crossing our southern border. You want to talk about crime? Well, who's coming from Latin America and Mexico? Are they rich, successful Mexicans, Nicaraguans, El Salvador residents? No! Why would they leave if they're so successful? It's people who have not had opportunity in Mexico and so they will raise all this money and give it to these human traffickers. Human traffickers take full advantage of them, take every penny they've got, and then maybe get them across the border in a perilous journey," Hannity said on June 29, 2015.

Another Fox News pundit, Monica Crowley, agreed. "Voters want a straight talker. And is he brash? Is he outspoken? Absolutely. But he's also giving voice to what a lot of voters are believing about the state of the country right now. And he's fearlessly doing it. I mean the question about whether or not he's good for the Republican Party I think is immaterial," she wrote on July 2. "Because he's performing two great services for the rest of the candidates if they're smart enough to follow his lead: Number one, he is not caving in to the leftist intimidation tactics, right?" In fact, he egged the left on. "And number two, by being this brash and outspoken. Could he say things in a more graceful way? Maybe. But guess what? He's doing a lot of political blocking for the other candidates. Because he is saying things that need to be said, and if the other candidates are smart, they might wrap it up in more diplomatic language. But he is actually going out there, kind of as the lead rabbit running around on the field."

The rabbit was winning the race because big donors had gelded many of the gilded greyhounds. The only donor Trump had to worry about was himself.

Patrick Buchanan, himself a former presidential candidate, liked the cut of Trump's jib. "Politically incorrect? You betcha. Yet, is Trump not raising a valid issue? Is there not truth in what he said? Is not illegal immigration, and criminals crossing our Southern border, an issue of national import, indeed, of national security?" Buchanan wrote on July 2. "Women and girls crossing Mexico on trains are raped by gangs. The coyotes leading people illegally across the US border include robbers, rapists, and killers, who often leave these people to die in the desert."

Buchanan ended his column with the best summary of the 2016 campaign: "Americans are fed up with words; they want action. Trump is moving in the polls because, whatever else he may be, he is a man of action."

Radio talker Mark Steyn praised Trump for not apologizing for the silly gotcha gaffes called by the media. It was, he said, "a lesson for other candidates, too. You know, the strangulated, constipated artificiality in which the candidates talk about things, where they say something mildly infelicitous, and then some spokesperson comes out and regrets that they misspoke. Trump basically does nothing but misspeak, and he never apologizes for it. Even the Hispanics don't seem to mind him saying that Mexicans are just a bunch of rapists," Steyn told Fox News on July 31.

Ann Coulter, the bombastic columnist and author, praised Trump for being in touch with working people, as she told *Breitbart News* on July 6, 2015.

But I really think he is magnificent. I'm almost stunned at how good he's being especially considering the world he lives in. He's a fancy Manhattanite—and I'm sure—who vacations in the Hamptons. All of his friends disagree with him. You very rarely see this in any place—in any group of people—and he really is just standing up for the American working class like I've never seen. The American working class really likes him, and always has, and I think his next move should be that he should point out that he's the only one who cares about black jobs. I mean have you seen the black unemployment rate? How dare liberals accuse him of racism? They don't even have an argument. He's the one trying to defend American jobs and particularly with the black youth unemployment rate. How about letting Americans take those jobs instead of the foreign-born poor?

Jeffrey Lord of the *Conservative Review* described the anti-Trump movement on June 18, 2015. "A serious chunk of the conservative base of the Republican Party looks at the Washington GOP Establishment—defined as everyone from Speaker John Boehner and Senate Majority Leader Mitch McConnell to the Republican National Committee, the US Chamber of Commerce, and some quarters of the conservative commentariat—and they see not conservatives but Insiders. People who have long ago abandoned the field to join—if I may borrow a phrase thrown at Trump—a clown car of Insider-dom. People who spend their time talking to one another in Washington or New York or both and are utterly clueless of what's going on in everyday America," Lord wrote.

Proponents of open borders lectured Republicans about the need to court the Hispanic voters to expand the party. But Trump was bringing in voters by saying we should wall off the border; elitists resented that because he was bringing the wrong people to the party: caddies and groundskeepers.

In the movie *Blazing Saddles*, the Waco Kid consoled Sheriff Bart after the townspeople shunned him. "What did you expect? 'Welcome, sonny'? 'Make yourself at home'? 'Marry my daughter'? You've got to remember that these are just simple farmers. These are people of the land. The common clay of the new West," the Waco Kid said. "You know: morons."

That is exactly how most pundits viewed Trump supporters. Every poll showed he did better among people without college degrees than people with degrees. Everyone in the DC elite had at least one degree. They thought Trump's support came from the common clay of the country.

You know: morons.

"To date, earned media coverage has largely dictated this race and while Trump has been masterful in manipulating the media to low information voters, the real campaign is only just beginning. And when it comes to negative ads Trump's opponents have a lot of material to work with. As much as voters claim to dislike negative ads the reality is that they are very effective and voters will be introduced to the real Donald Trump in the weeks ahead," Republican strategist Brian Walsh wrote in *US News and World Report* on September 15.

However, Trump's numbers grew despite the barrage of attacks from ads and pundits, or maybe because of the attacks. The home-audience conservatives noticed the difference between their lives and those of the in-studio conservatives on cable news.

"If you live in an affluent ZIP code, it's hard to see a downside to mass low-wage immigration. Your kids don't go to public school. You don't take the bus or use the emergency room for health care. No immigrant is competing for your job. (The day Hondurans start getting hired as green energy lobbyists is the day my neighbors become nativists.) Plus, you get cheap servants, and get to feel welcoming and virtuous while paying them less per hour than your kids make at a summer job on Nantucket. It's all good," Tucker Carlson, editor of the *Daily Caller*, wrote in *Politico* on January 28, 2016.

As his name suggested, Carlson had an upper-class upbringing. His father was once the ambassador to the Seychelles and later president of the Corporation for Public Broadcasting, and he married a Swanson Foods heiress. By 2016, Carlson had lived in Washington about twenty years. However, as Trump showed, well-to-do people can understand the working class, if they care to. Carlson cared to.

But for many pundits, Trump's supporters were just demographic statistics on a spreadsheet to people in the nation's capital, who generated numbers to predict the future. Their method was less messy than using the entrails of goats, as the Greek oracles did, and almost as reliable.

Nevertheless, Civis Analytics, a Democratic numbers-crunching outfit, gave a report to the *New York Times* on who supported Trump.

"He is strongest among Republicans who are less affluent, less educated and less likely to turn out to vote. His very best voters are self-identified Republicans who nonetheless are registered as Democrats. It's a coalition that's concentrated in the South, Appalachia and the industrial North," Nate Cohn of the *New York Times* reported on December 31, 2015.

Two months later, Trump swept the primary in Massachusetts, home of MIT and Harvard—the state with the most-educated populace in the nation.

"Trump appears to hold his greatest strength among people like these—registered Democrats who identify as Republican leaners—with 43 percent of their support, according to the Civis data. Similarly, many of Mr. Trump's best states are those with a long tradition of Democrats who vote Republican in presidential elections, like West Virginia," Cohn wrote.

All that was good news. Such a candidate could expand the base permanently, just as George W. Bush had done in West Virginia in 2000.

Until he took the state, Democrats had won the state fourteen times in the seventeen previous presidential races. Electing and reelecting Bush led to a change in the state's politics. Fourteen years after his election, the legislature flipped Republican for the first time in eighty-two years.

However, Trump also did well among Hispanics, scoring 24 percent in this analysis and 35 percent among other white people. That was a good number in a contest that included two Hispanic senators. Far from killing the Hispanic vote by promising to enforce immigration laws, Trump brought Hispanic Democrats and independents to the party.

"Trump's best state is West Virginia, followed by New York. Eight of Mr. Trump's ten best congressional districts are in New York, including several on Long Island. North Carolina, Alabama, Mississippi, Tennessee, Louisiana, and South Carolina follow," Cohn reported.

There could be only one answer: race. The analysis included "racially charged Internet searches" by congressional district. Once again, liberals tried to quantify the unquantifiable. No definition was given for "racially charged Internet searches," and there was no way of knowing if Trump supporters made all those "racially charged Internet searches." But people in journalism often stereotype poor white people as racist.

Attracting new voters is a plus, but Cohn concluded that attracting poor white people who had no college degree was a negative. He wrote, "Over the long run, the party will need to figure out a way to satisfy its newest converts while maintaining a message that's appealing to the rest of the country."

That was a weird take. He was adding people to the party, but they were the wrong kind of people. They were white, didn't graduate from college, and were poor. If they were illegal aliens from Mexico, the press would embrace them. But Trump's voters were people who live in places like West Virginia. The pundits sneered.

However, Trump's debate audiences drew three times the audiences that Obama drew in 2008. The system screwed many Americans over. They were not going to take it again. And pundits like Cohn missed the rebellion because they saw the American people as numbers on a spreadsheet.

Adrian Hanft, an apolitical interaction designer in Denver, asked a question that political pundits never asked. "If you aren't a supporter of Trump, there is a good chance you are baffled by his popularity and success. The trending explanation for his rise is the assertion that a third of the country is extremely angry and possibly racist. If that is true, I am deeply saddened. Could there be another explanation that doesn't require me to question the integrity, intelligence, or motives of a massive number of people?" Hanft wrote on his blog on March 19, 2016.

But to the political experts in America, the only acceptable answer to his query was a resounding no. Anyone who ever watched *Blazing Saddles* just knew that those white people out there in the hinterlands were all angry racists.

What America needed were fewer Waco Kids who dismissed the Trumpkins as morons, and more Tucker Carlsons who bothered to find out who the Trumpkins were—sprinkled with a few Adrian Hanfts who asked sensible questions.

The political press in Washington did not understand his supporters because they did not understand Trump. Not at all. They were as incurious about his true background as they had been about Obama's in 2008, but for opposite reasons. To find out who Trump was, my journey began with retired gossip columnist Liz Smith. She was there when Trump became The Donald.

CHAPTER 12

WHO IS DONALD TRUMP?

———————

MARY ANN MACLEOD TRUMP GAVE birth to Donald John Trump on June 14, 1946, in Queens, New York. Gossip columnist Liz Smith invented The Donald in Manhattan thirty-one years later. In her 2000 autobiography, *Natural Blonde*, Smith devoted an entire chapter to the Trumps.

Drawing on nearly forty years of experience with Donald and Ivana Trump and the rest of his extended family, Smith painted the portrait of a showboat who gave the tabloids fresh stories, gave the upper crust heartburn, and gave his family an empire worth billions.

> Everyone remembers exactly where he or she was when President Kennedy was shot. But I, typical gossip columnist that I am, remember exactly where I was when I first heard the word *Trump*. My friend and literacy ally Parker Ladd and I were in a car heading up Park Avenue. As we neared the statue of old Commodore Cornelius Vanderbilt that forces New York drivers to turn right and then left at what used to be the Pan Am Building and still is Grand Central Station, Parker said, "Have you ever met Ivana and Donald Trump?" I said I hadn't. He explained that Donald was a building tycoon and she a Czech ski champ, a blonde who talked a mile a minute with a deep accent. She had just bought some couture dresses from our mutual friend Arnold Scaasi.

The Vanderbilt statue is a fitting landmark for her story, for the commodore was born on May 27, 1794, on Staten Island, the son of a ferryboat operator. Like Trump, Vanderbilt followed his father's footsteps and then made his own path to become a billionaire.

"Mrs. Trump—Ivana—is really a very sweet, dear person. I think she's getting a bad rap," Ladd told Smith.

That sealed the deal. Someone in Gotham was unfairly maligned. This looked like a job for Super Gossip. "Before long, I met Mrs. Trump, and then I met her tall blond husband. I found them both refreshing, if a bit presumptuous and naïve socially, and I began to note their comings and goings. Little did I dream that their eventual 'going' would be something of my 'coming' to the fore in newsprint and other media. The Trumps were to have a profound effect on my career," Smith wrote.

"But before that, I became involved with the entire Trump family. I liked them—the daddy, Fred, who had slugged his way to the top in the Queens building business; his other mild-mannered son, Robert, and his adorable charity-minded wife, Blaine; Mary, the matriarch mother, a truly divine lady; the two sisters—Maryanne Barry, a New Jersey judge, and the other, Elizabeth Grau, a banker. I began going to many of the overachieving Trump family's anniversaries, weddings and birthdays."

The Donald lavished over-the-top praise on her and everyone else he liked. Ivana spoke a mile-a-minute in her thick Czech accent, which Smith couldn't decipher.

"The Trumps were always inviting me to go somewhere on their jet plane. I flew with them to San Diego; to a big party Barbara Walters and Merv Adelson were tossing just before that marriage came apart. I flew down to Palm Beach after the refurbishing of Mar-a-Lago and spent an all-girls weekend there with Ivana's mother, her girlfriends and ladies such as Helen Gurley Brown, Georgette Mosbacher, Shirley Lord, Barbara, et al," Smith wrote.

She was not the only fan of Trump in the carnivorous world of New York City journalism. Steve Cuozzo, restaurant critic and real-estate columnist for the *New York Post*, had a grudging respect for The Donald. Beneath the glamour and the headlines was a man who helped rebuild Manhattan.

"Whatever you think about his political views or crazy campaign, Trump doesn't get enough credit for being a transformative planner who is in love with the city. No matter how many times they watch *Taxi Driver*, younger New Yorkers and older ones who arrived recently have no idea of what the city was actually like in the mid-1970s through the mid-'90s. Notwithstanding Studio 54 and a short-lived Wall Street boom, the metropolis was reeling. Rampant street crime, AIDS, corporate flight and physical decay brought confidence to an all-time low," Cuozzo wrote on February 7, 2016.

His column was refreshing. Throughout the Republican nomination campaign, I marveled at the jaw-dropping vapidity of pundits who dismissed Trump because he was a billionaire, as if he had never accomplished anything. But Trump did more for New York than they realized.

"Trump waded into a landscape of empty Fifth Avenue storefronts, the dust-bowl mugging ground that was Central Park and a Wall Street area seemingly on its last legs as companies moved out. Except in Battery Park City, which was then as remote as an offshore island, few other developers built anything but plain-vanilla office and apartment buildings," Cuozzo wrote.

"Trump—almost by force of will—rode to the rescue. Expressing rare faith in the future, he was instrumental in kick-starting the regeneration of neighborhoods and landmarks almost given up for dead."

The first of Trump's landmarks became the Grand Hyatt Hotel at 109 East 42nd Street. Its original name honored Commodore Vanderbilt.

"An X-rated massage parlor stood in the lobby of the gloomy Commodore Hotel—symptomatic of East 42nd Street's decline. Trump, the hotel project's prime mover, replaced the brick facade with curtain-wall glass, designed a modern high-end hotel inside and made it attractive for tourism and business. It arrested the street's tailspin and set the stage for Grand Central Terminal's restoration in the 1990s," Cuozzo wrote.

That was leadership. That was vision. That was taking a risk. That was what America needed in a president. As the song said about New York, if you can make it there, you'll make it anywhere. And Trump did make it in the city that never sleeps. In April 1988, *New York* magazine included The Donald on its list of the hundred most important New Yorkers, "Because his buildings and his book and his ego are so much bigger than life."

The magazine ran a picture of Trump shaking hands with Brooke Astor as nouveau riche met the oldest money in the city. Smith wrote the piece on Trump.

"In my article, I spoke of Donald's rabid detractors and his love-hate relationship with the hoity-toity and the adoration of hoi polloi. I said if he smoked, he'd have his cigarettes monogrammed like so—$—with Ayn Rand's dollar sign. But I added that jealousy and spite played some part in making him the city's biggest target. Yes, he bragged and blew hard, but in my book he wasn't a real phony or a fake. I found him incapable of dissembling or doing the hypocritical things a lot of other rich New Yorkers do," Smith wrote.

Smith's profile of Trump did show that the personal attacks came from people who largely knew so little about the man. He may have been a braggart, but as Cuozzo's column showed, Trump had much to brag about: helping to rescue the greatest city in the world.

People who worked with Trump also knew him. They liked him. Donald Trump was a decent man. Political experts thought because he said, "You're fired!" on a television show that he was a mean old cuss. And they thought that because the public did not see him the way that they did, that Trump supporters were stupid. But did Trump's supporters misjudge him? Or did they merely see his television show as just that—a television show?

One of Trump's celebrity apprentices was a mechanic in Austin, Texas, named Jesse James, who parlayed his ability to rebuild motorcycles into an extensive business. He opened West Coast Choppers in his mom's garage at age twenty-three. He added T-shirts, beverages, and the like. Keanu Reeves and other celebrities were among his customers.

In 2000, the Discovery Channel launched the show *Motorcycle Mania*, which followed Jesse James around. He became wealthy. He married and divorced a porn star before marrying and divorcing Sandra Bullock and then marrying his fourth wife, Alexis DeJoria, a drag racer. Throughout his rise, James referred to himself as a "glorified welder."

On January 17, 2016, James wrote about being on Trump's *Celebrity Apprentice* series. While Trump did tell James on the show, "You're fired," James understood that it was nothing personal, just show business. James said no one wanted to see a nice guy on television. They wanted to see a guy who said, "You're fired."

But Trump was a nice guy, as James wrote in a Facebook post:

What I personally observed is a man that is perfect suited to run this country. He is respectful to the little guy (which shows he worked hard to get where he is) and he is also tough as nails when he needs to be. The people he will appoint to key top positions will be top shelf, and you can bank if they don't perform? They will get the boot. Lastly the best quality I observed about Donald Trump is being a dad. This is by far his strongest quality. Ivanka is an super smart, driven woman. She shakes your hand firm and looks you in the eye when she talks to you. Donald Jr. also has the same smarts and drive, but is also a pretty regular guy that has a "almost" restored '69 Camaro and loves to long range shoot (don't let anyone know I told you that). The poise in these two shows a lot in their parents. I think we are lucky to have his kids as part of the deal. So before you guys react to what I have written here. One thing you know about me is good or bad I will always tell it like it is. This guy is the Real Deal, and will Make America Great Again.

James was not the only associate of Trump who gave such a testimonial. Herschel Walker became a millionaire when Trump signed him to play for the New Jersey Generals in the old United States Football League.

"He was a guy that always did what he said he was going to do. And he invited me into his home. I've gotten to know that family well. I saw the way they were. They were a very good family," Walker said.

Trump took risks, which Dana White, head of the Ultimate Fighting Championship, appreciated. His sport was once the bane of state athletic commissioners across the country.

"When we first bought this business, it was banned in most states, it wasn't supported by the ACs, and no arenas wanted this thing. Donald Trump was the first one to have us come out at the Trump Taj Mahal. Not only did we host the events there, he actually showed up and supported the events. You will never hear me say a negative thing about Donald Trump," White said.

At a rally on April 28, 2016, in Evansville, Indiana, the legendary basketball coach of Indiana, Bobby Knight, vouched for Trump.

"I was very, very selective with players during the time I was here. And I'll tell you one thing, that man who was just up here a moment ago, I tell you that son bitch could play for me. This was a real neat thing for me because I have for some time leading up to where we are now felt that above anything else this country needed Donald Trump," Knight said.

Knight, seventy-five, had never voted in his life.

The hoi polloi also stood by him. On January 31, John Dickerson, host of *Face The Nation* asked The Donald why working-class voters liked him, given that "you don't ride three buses and have a second job and all that."

"No, no. I have the ultimate bus, right? It's called a 727. And now it is a 757, actually, when you think of it. But, somehow, I have always had great relationships with the workers. I work with them. I used to work during summer building houses in Brooklyn and Queens. I mean, I just work with them. These are incredible people. They have been hurt very badly. The middle-income people in our country have been hurt very badly. That's why I am doing a big tax cut for them," Trump said.

Perhaps no other man knew Trump better than Peter David Ticktin, his best friend at the New York Military Academy, which served as their high school. Ticktin went on to law school in Ontario. In his first year in practice, 1972, he successfully challenged and defeated the Uniform Summons. This caused the dismissal of every misdemeanor charge in the province that had used this form. In the 1980s, he relocated to

Florida, and went back to law school to pass the Florida Bar. In 1991, he began an eponymous law firm, which had fifteen other lawyers by 2016.

In short, Ticktin was a success in law as Trump was in real estate. Ticktin wrote about his experience in military school with Trump.

"In our senior year, together, Donald was my captain, and I was his 1st Platoon Sergeant. I sometimes joke that I ran his first company for him, Company A. People don't really change much from the ages of 17 and 18, and I know this guy. I know him to be a good decent guy. We lived and breathed an Honor Code in those years. It wasn't just a rule. It was our way of life. Neither Donald, nor any other cadet who graduated with us would ever lie, cheat, or steal from a fellow cadet. These values became irreversibly intertwined in the fabric of our personalities, of who we are," Ticktin wrote on Facebook on March 4.

Sir Arthur Conan wrote of the dog that did not bark, which solved the mystery of a stolen horse in one Sherlock Holmes adventure. Trump too had a dog that did not bark—or at least one that did not bad-mouth him.

"Of the 99 guys (no girls in those days) in our class, there is not one who I know who has a bad word to say about Donald Trump. Think of it. With all the jealousies which arise in high school and thereafter, with all the potential envy, not one of us has anything other than positive memories of this man. How could we? He was an A student, a top athlete, and as a leader, he was highly respected. We never feared him, yet we never wanted to disappoint him. He had our respect. He was never a bigot in any way, shape or form. He only hates those who hate. Of course he denounces the KKK," Ticktin wrote.

If Ticktin was the man who knew Trump best, the woman who knew him best might be his first wife, Ivana Trump. Theirs was an acrimonious divorce that dominated the news in New York City in 1991. But a quarter century later, she provided Dana Schuster of the *New York Post* with her insights into The Donald, which were published on April 3, 2016.

"He's no politician. He's a businessman. He knows how to talk. He can give an hour speech without notes. He's blunt," she said. As president, Trump would surround himself with "fantastic advisers, like Carl Icahn. Really brilliant minds. And he'd make a decision! Obama cannot make a decision if his life depends on it. It's ridiculous."

Trump collected no political endorsements until Christie announced his support on February 26. By that time, Rubio collected the backing of more than ninety politicians, some of whom he had actually met. Cruz collected another fifty. But Trump had testimonials from people who had worked with him over the years, who found he was an honorable man whose word was his bond.

CHAPTER 13

LEARNING HOW TO WIN.

———◆———

THE SUICIDE OF HER FATHER C. W. Post on May 9, 1914, made heiress Marjorie Merriweather Post the head of Post Cereal. She reigned for nearly a decade until handing the reins to her second husband, financier E. F. Hutton, who turned the company into General Foods, which became a conglomeration of food brands that continued to dominate the supermarket shelves nearly a century later. Easily the richest woman in America, she spent lavishly. In 1924, she began building a 110,000-square-foot palace in Palm Beach, Florida, which she named Mar-a-Lago (Spanish for sea to lake). She insisted on the finest.

"Gold is much easier to clean," she said.

She died on September 12, 1973. Donald Trump paid $5 million for the property in 1985 and began a restoration project that turned Mar-a-Lago into an exclusive resort, and his weekend home. One of the people he hired was Tony Senecal, who had worked for Mrs. Post, as he called her even decades after her death. In between times, he opened a tobacco shop in Martinsburg, West Virginia, and became the town's mayor. After Trump renovated and reopened the place, Senecal became his butler.

"When I first started, I wasn't the servant type. It was touch and go until Mr. Trump found out I was a former mayor. That made me a cut above," Senecal told Ronald Kessler of *NewsMax* on May 19, 2008.

Senecal did good work, and Trump wanted to promote him to concierge. He was serving Trump breakfast. Senecal recalled the conversation.

"So you're going to be the concierge. What do you think about that?" Trump asked.

"Well, I don't like it," Senecal said.

"Well, what do you want to be?" Trump asked.

"I thought as long as I was able, I would be your butler," Senecal said.

Trump rose and poked him in the arm. "And the butler's what you're going to be," Trump said.

OK, butlers are loyal. But Trump genuinely liked Senecal and told News Max, "He treats the members as equals. In fact, I think he might think he is above them. Every great place needs a Tony."

Senecal said Trump slept four hours a night. "He gets up and he reads five or six newspapers every day. I'm here by 5 o'clock with the newspapers, and there are many times when he opens the door and says, 'Let me have 'em.'"

Those papers were the *New York Times*, the *Wall Street Journal*, the *New York Post*, the *New York Daily News*, the *Palm Beach Post* and the *Palm Beach Daily News*. Eight years later, CNN's Carol Costello tracked down Senecal, then eighty-four.

"First of all, he's an incredibly generous person. He's generous to his employees. He's generous to strangers. Most of the time he's just a nice man. I mean, I lasted with him for twenty years. He had to be pretty good," Senecal said.

One family that knew of Trump's generosity were the widow and children of Lenard Dozier Hill III of Burke County, Georgia. While Trump bought and restored Mar-a-Lago in the 1980s, many farm families struggled. This had nothing to do with the developer, but as he read their stories in those six daily newspapers, Trump decided to take action.

Hill had committed suicide on February 4, 1986, in a foolish attempt to pay off his mortgage through life-insurance policies. Of course, those policies did not pay off for suicides. The bank foreclosed. Trump called Frank Argenbright, a wealthy Atlantan who had saved the farm of Oscar Lorick. Argenbright. At his expense, Trump flew Argenbright and the Hills to Trump Tower to work out a plan. Trump called the bank.

"I said to the guy, 'You listen to me. If you do foreclose, I'll bring a lawsuit for murder against you and your bank, on the grounds that you harassed Mrs. Hill's husband to his death.' All of a sudden, the banker sounded very nervous and said he'd get right back to me. Sometimes it pays to be a little wild," Trump later wrote in his best seller *The Art of the Deal*.

He raised the money and paid off the mortgage within ten months of Hill's death. Trump flew the family to New York City for a mortgage burning two days before Christmas 1986.

"I had just graduated from high school. He flew us to New York, and we went to Trump Tower and had breakfast with him. We saw a whole different side of him that was kindhearted, to reach out to us, to help us. Most people don't know and see that side. All they see is just the 'blurt' that people put on the TV. They don't see the other side of him, and that's what my family got to experience," Hill's daughter, Betsy Sharp, told the *Atlanta Journal-Constitution* twenty-nine years later.

Her brother, Leonard Dozier Hill IV, still lived on the farm in 2016. Sharp campaigned for Trump.

People may say, well that was just one farm saved, and he was rich. But what farm had Hillary Clinton saved? Bernie Sanders? Jeb Bush? Ted Cruz? For all Trump's bravado and billions, he was a man of the people.

Dilbert cartoonist Scott Adams posted on his blog a letter to Trump from Troy Morton, a black man, on March 2, 2016.

Now that it's clear you will be the Republican nominee, I want to share with you something so personal, painful, and uplifting, that I almost don't want to write it, but I will anyway…trolls be damned:

My whole life, up until yesterday, has been based on reaction to fear.

Growing up as a black man in Washington DC during the "crack '80s," when Marion Barry was mayor, I lived a lower middle class childhood in one of the most dangerous cities in America. Though I had many friends, I was also subject to the threats, intimidation, and bullying that happens when you're not like the people around you.

There was no father in my life to steel me against the world I lived in. My mother was strong, but it's not exactly the kind of strength I needed. I was a boy, and needed a Man.

Without strong male guidance, I learned to fear…but not how to face fear and win.

Morton was not the only person Trump inspired to win. Jim Herman tried for several years to make the PGA Tour and failed. He settled for a job as an assistant pro at Trump National in Bedminster, New Jersey. He recalled a chance conversation in 2006.

"I got into a nice conversation with Donald, Mr. Trump, one day. He's like, 'Why are you folding shirts and giving lessons? Why aren't you on the tour? I've played with tour players, you're good enough.' I don't know, maybe something like that gives you more confidence," Herman told Simon Evans of Reuters after winning the Shell Houston Open a decade later, at age thirty-eight, on April 3, 2016.

It was Herman's first win, but Trump was a winner—"a kind of mashup of Santa Claus, Scrooge McDuck, and Vito Corleone," as Reihan Salam had recalled from growing up in Brooklyn.

Troy Morton did Salam one better. "My life, in many important ways, mirrors the American experience. Potential to be great, but paralyzed by fear," Morton wrote.

This book is really a novel. The hero is imperfect, is discounted, is mocked, is opposed, is given up on, and is the winner in the end. The hero is the leader and the role model for his followers. Trump had inspired Morton and many others who were knocked down to get up again. No one was going to keep them down.

"Winning is always possible, but becomes probable if you never back down, never quit, and become your dominant self. Once the battle is won, treat the vanquished with kindness and respect. Be the bigger man. You taught me how to win," Morton wrote.

Trump had done what a successful presidential candidate does; he had made an emotional connection with his supporters. The billionaire who seemingly had everything understood the plight of others who did not. He embraced them and they hugged back. He had built that bridge with the public—the hoi polloi, as Liz Smith had put it—over a lifetime in business. The imperfect messenger had more strong points than he had flaws. And his message was perfect: "Make America Great Again."

Now let us see how he Trumped the press over the next year.

CHAPTER 14

THE McCAIN MUTINY.

———— ◆ ————

TRUMP GENERATED NEWS TO FEED CNN, Fox News, and MSNBC throughout the summer of 2015. To do so, he often reached into his utility belt and pulled the feud out. Feuds among celebrities were fun. Fans could chew popcorn and watch the sparks fly. The gossips of New York understood the entertainment value, but the political reporters did not. Ordinarily, Trump avoided starting a feud because that would make him the bully. However, he knew how to provoke one, which is why he held a rally on July 12, 2015, in Phoenix, which drew five thousand supporters. Trump praised Mexicans and denounced illegal aliens.

"During his speech, Trump turned the lectern over to Jamiel Shaw Sr., the father of a high-school student killed by an [illegal alien], who spoke about why he is supporting the candidate," CNN reported.

Trump went to the backyard of Senator John McCain for one reason. He wanted the 2008 Republican nominee to react. He did.

"It's very bad. This performance with our friend out in Phoenix is very hurtful to me, because what he did was he fired up the crazies," McCain told Ryan Lizza of the *New Yorker* the next day.

McCain also took a personal shot at Trump. "He was a big Democratic supporter. Some of this stuff is going to come out: he gave more money to Democrats than Republicans; he had Hillary Clinton at his wedding. You know, he's attacking Hillary Clinton after she was in the front row of his—I don't know which wedding it was," the twice-married McCain said of the thrice-married Trump.

That was what Trump wanted. His audience disliked McCain for the same reason the press liked him: McCain was a Republican in name only. McCain gifted Trump a news cycle, and The Donald made sure his rebuttal would be outrageous enough to stretch the feud through many news cycles.

First, Trump went on MSNBC's *Morning Joe* show on July 17. "I supported John McCain. He let us down because he lost but, you know, it was a hard one after what had happened with the economy. But I supported him, raised a lot of money for him. John McCain was very disloyal to me," Trump said, which was true. In the 2008 campaign, Trump was an official bundler for McCain, not only donating the maximum amount but getting others to contribute $88,250 to McCain's campaign.

The next day, Trump held a rally in Ames, Iowa, and attacked McCain. "He was a war hero because he was captured. I like people who weren't captured. Perhaps he is a war hero, but right now, he said some very bad things about a lot of people," Trump told the crowd on July 18.

On cue, critics reacted with indignity.

"When is Donald Trump going to stop embarrassing his friends, let alone the whole country?" Sir Rupert Murdoch tweeted hours later. Murdoch headed News Corporation, which owned Fox News.

Joseph Curl of the *Washington Times* saw this as the coming implosion of the Trump campaign. "Already becoming a laughingstock, Mr. Trump will continue to be outrageous and say incredibly stupid things. Americans will (rightly) conclude that the guy is an undisciplined egomaniac and dismiss him. But until then, it's going to be a blast to watch. Now, we get to wake up each day and say, 'I wonder what stupid thing Trump will do today?' And when he implodes, we'll all have to get serious," Curl wrote.

Curl seemed unaware that he did just what Trump wanted him to do. He thought about Trump from the moment Curl woke up.

Bill Kristol went on ABC News to denounce Trump. "He's dead to me."

The *National Review* also wasted no time in denouncing him. "The Arizona senator gets a lot of grief from people on the right, including around here, but even the conservatives who loathe and despise the man (I'm not one of them, by the way) almost never question McCain's service. I should note that decent people in general don't speak that way about McCain either. But Trump simply doesn't know where the lines are on the right because he's not a conservative and he can't help himself," Jonah Goldberg wrote on July 18.

Four days later, Goldberg took another bite of that apple. "Of course Trump wouldn't hesitate to attack John McCain's war-hero status. Trump's bottomless insecurity cannot countenance the idea that his critics have any legitimacy. Of course Trump won't apologize—because his dog-and-pony show is predicated on the idea that he 'tells it like it is' and 'fights.' He's the omniscient master of *The Apprentice*. He can't behave like the Biggest Loser," Goldberg wrote on July 22.

He ended the column, "Donald Trump stakes much of his fortune on the alleged value of the Trump brand. Hillary Clinton's candidacy rests on a similar assumption about the Clinton name. Both fail to take into account the fact that personality trumps brand."

Frank Luntz, whose focus groups giving reactions to events were in vogue at Fox News, said the exchange hurt Trump.

"This is a big deal because it demonstrates character. It demonstrates judgment. Up until this point, that exchange was because I was asking him questions about the words that he was using and whether they were proper for a presidential candidate. But that exchange suggested that he really doesn't appreciate the significance of being a POW and what that means in American society," Luntz said on July 19, 2015.

However, Trump's support grew because McCain was part of the problem in Washington, where he was in his fifth term as a senator and seeking a sixth. While people certainly respected his service as a POW, they had had it with his service as a senator. But pundits liked McCain because he was the one Republican who was willing to fight.

Republicans.

CHAPTER 15

BLOOD IN THE WATER.

REINCE PRIEBUS, HEAD OF THE Republican National Committee, brought order to the debates for 2016, limiting their number and choosing the media outlets. He wisely excluded MSNBC and the *Des Moines Register.* But that did not stop the newspaper from trying to cause trouble.

Trump passed Bush on July 20, to take the lead in the *RealClear Politics* poll average, which averaged the latest national polls. The next day, the liberal *Des Moines Register* ran an editorial: "Trump should pull the plug on his bloviating sideshow."

Timing is everything in politics and comedy.

"In just five weeks, he has polluted the political waters to such an extent that serious candidates who actually have the credentials to serve as president can't get their message across to voters. In fact, some of them can't even win a spot in one of the upcoming debates, since those slots are reserved for candidates leading in the polls," the editorial said.

The newspaper also called him "a feckless bloward."

Typically, politicians indulge the press these temper tantrums, for fear of hurting news coverage. Trump was not a politician. He hit back twice as hard.

"I am not at all surprised by the *Des Moines Register*'s sophomoric editorial. It was issued immediately after the release of the ABC News/ *Washington Post* poll showing me with 24 percent and an eleven-point lead over my nearest rival. As one of the most liberal newspapers in the United States, the poll results were just too much for them to bear.

The *Des Moines Register* has lost much circulation, advertising, and power over the last number of years. They will do anything for a headline, and this poorly written non-endorsement got them some desperately needed ink," Trump said in response.

This burnished his reputation as a tough fighter. But this delighted the *Des Moines Register* editorial board, which found a substitute for Iowa's quadrennial first-in-the-nation caucus to generate publicity. Oh, not for the paper, which Gannett owned, but for themselves. A good showing in the Iowa caucuses could impress the brass at Gannett, headquartered in suburban Washington.

In the 2008 campaign, then-editor Carolyn Washburn used her role as moderator of a Republican caucus debate as her ticket out of Iowa by ridiculing the candidates.

> WASHBURN: I want to take on a new issue. I would like to see a show of hands. How many of you believe global climate change is a serious threat and caused by human activity?
> FRED THOMPSON: Well, do you want to give me a minute to answer that?
> WASHBURN: No, I don't.
> THOMPSON: Well, then I'm not going to answer it.

That exchange helped win her Gannett's Editor of the Year award in 2008 and a promotion to editor of the *Cincinnati Enquirer.*

However, without the debate, the newspaper trashed Trump. The gimmick drew national attention. All went well until Trump decided to milk another news cycle from the nontroversy by banning the paper from covering his events.

This stunned Amalie Nash, the *Register*'s editor. How dare a politician retaliate.

"As we previously said, the editorial has no bearing on our news coverage. We work hard to provide Iowans with coverage of all the candidates when they spend time in Iowa, and this is obviously impeding our ability to do so. We hope Mr. Trump's campaign will revisit its decision instead of making punitive decisions because we wrote something critical of him," Nash said on July 25.

The wall between reporting and editorials is imaginary. The plum jobs of covering the Iowa caucuses did not go to people who bucked the editorial position of the newspaper.

After the nontroversy died down, on September 17, the newspaper tried to revive the feud with an editorial: "Trump's overt sexism is too much."

But where the earlier editorial was just silly name-calling, this editorial was a rather graphic and sexist stereotyping of Trump as a lounge lizard. "Every woman has met a Donald Trump. He's the jerk at the bar, family reunion, or sporting event who disrespects women. He laughs the loudest at his own jokes and thinks the world revolves around him. He puffs up his chest and stares at yours. If you tell him to back off, he asks if you're menstruating," the newspaper wrote.

The newspaper's staff had divulged a little too much personal information. However, the newspaper merely continued a story line from the first debate hosted by Fox News on August 6, Bret Baier, Chris Wallace, and Megyn Kelly were the moderators. Kelly came loaded for bear. She did not ask boring policy questions. She went for the throat. This was a television show, after all.

> KELLY: Mr. Trump, one of the things people love about you is you speak your mind, and you don't use a politician's filter. However, that is not without its downsides, in particular, when it comes to women. You've called women you don't like fat pigs, dogs, slobs, and disgusting animals.
>
> (LAUGHTER)
>
> TRUMP: Only Rosie O'Donnell.
>
> (LAUGHTER)
>
> KELLY: Your Twitter account has several disparaging comments about women's looks. You once told a contestant

on *Celebrity Apprentice* it would be a pretty picture to see her on her knees. Does that sound to you like the temperament of a man we should elect as president, and how will you answer the charge from Hillary Clinton, who was likely to be the Democratic nominee, that you are part of the war on women?

TRUMP: I think the big problem this country has is being politically correct.

(APPLAUSE)

TRUMP: I've been challenged by so many people, and I don't frankly have time for total political correctness. And to be honest with you, this country doesn't have time either. This country is in big trouble. We don't win anymore. We lose to China. We lose to Mexico both in trade and at the border. We lose to everybody. And frankly, what I say, and oftentimes it's fun, it's kidding. We have a good time. What I say is what I say. And honestly, Megyn, if you don't like it, I'm sorry. I've been very nice to you, although I could probably maybe not be, based on the way you have treated me. But I wouldn't do that. But you know what? We—we need strength, we need energy, we need quickness, and we need brain in this country to turn it around. That, I can tell you right now.

Trump had won the evening on that exchange. A national audience of twenty-four million people—three times the viewership of any previous primary debate—had seen an angry woman attack Trump, only to have him brush her aside.

But Trump decided to wring a few more news cycles out of the story. Days later, on CNN, Trump told host Don Lemon, "You could see there was blood coming out of her eyes. Blood coming out of her wherever."

This led to a nontroversy over whether he meant she was on her period, something he vehemently denied. He said that by "whatever," he meant her nose.

"Only a deviant would think anything else," Trump replied.

Nevertheless, the exchange helped boost both. Trump showed he can take the heat, and Kelly showed she can deliver it. Radio talker Erick Erickson pulled Trump's invitation to a confab Erickson hosted and invited Kelly to replace him. Liberals call such protests faux outrage. They may have a point.

Joshua Green of *Bloomberg News* said Trump triumphed. "When it became clear last week that Trump was the Republican front-runner, everyone assumed that the big battle shaping up in Republican politics was going to be between Trump and former Florida Governor Jeb Bush. But judging by Thursday's raucous, electric debate, Trump may have sensed his true opponent before anyone else had a clue: It's Fox News. Throughout the evening, Trump and his inquisitors battled back and forth like gladiators. Both parties emerged as huge winners. Though nearly devoid of substance, it was the most entertaining debate I've ever seen," Green wrote.

However, there also was substance because presidential temperament is consequential. Trump bested her.

Out in Hollywood, *Variety*'s media critic, Brian Lowry, declared both Trump and Kelly the winners.

What does seem clear is that Trump's sniping has prompted other media figures to defend Kelly—journalists tend to circle the wagons in such cases—which buttresses her claim to be an independent voice. Fox has even retaliated by suggesting that Trump is afraid of Kelly. At the same time, Trump has shifted the focus, at least partially, from how well he fares against his debate rivals to the nature of his exchanges with the moderators.

Granted, this Trump-Kelly sparring match has dragged on long enough as to have grown a trifle tiresome. But for the candidate and Fox News, the net effect feels like a win-win in terms of how it plays to different key constituencies. And if that leaves behind some hurt feelings or a bloody nose in the short term, from an image perspective, it couldn't work out better for both sides if the whole thing were as choreographed as a "Rocky" movie.

But viewers saw something the experts missed.

"During that first debate, I turned to my wife and remarked that if Hillary happened to be viewing, she must be having some very uncomfortable thoughts about facing such an unconstrained political pit bull on a debate stage with the whole world watching. My wife's broad grin confirmed my thought that there must be millions of watching Americans who were seeing and feeling the same thing," Russ Vaughn of the *American Thinker* blog wrote on April 21, 2016.

As for this business of Trump demanding a woman get on her knees and beg The Donald for another chance, it was a joke, according to the target, Brande Roderick, a stunning blonde and *Playboy* pinup.

"Like him, I didn't even remember him saying that. I've always had a positive experience around Donald. He's always been encouraging. He's never been disrespectful to me. I don't condone men being derogatory, but I think he's just on television. He's trying to be funny. He didn't mean anything horrible by it," Roderick later told MSNBC.

An NBC poll after the debate showed Trump was the clear winner among the candidates on the stage—23 percent said Trump had won, 13 percent said Cruz, 11 percent said Carson, 8 percent said Carly Fiorina (who wasn't in the debate), 8 percent said Rubio, 7 percent said Bush, and 7 percent said Walker.

Of course, the pundits got it wrong as usual.

CHAPTER 16

AN ARMY OF VINCENT CANBYS.

———•———

ON NOVEMBER 22, 1976, FILM critic Vincent Canby of the *New York Times* reviewed *Rocky*. He panned the film that launched Sylvester Stallone's career.

"The problem, I think, comes back to Mr. Stallone. Throughout the movie we are asked to believe that his Rocky is compassionate, interesting, even heroic, though the character we see is simply an unconvincing actor imitating a lug," Canby wrote.

The reviews of Trump's first debate were even more off-base.

"The moderators of the GOP debate Thursday night at the Quicken Loans arena gave Donald Trump plenty of rope—and sure enough he hanged himself. Right out of the box, the candidates were asked to pledge their support to whomever ultimately wins the GOP nomination; the only hold-out was Trump, who refused to make that commitment and who elicited boos from the audience," Liz Peek of the *Fiscal Times* wrote for Fox News online.

"Later, in response to a sharp question from Megyn Kelly about his history of calling women 'fat pigs' and 'slobs,' Trump argued that the big problem with the country was political correctness. He concluded, 'If you don't like it Megyn, too bad; you haven't been very nice to me.' Bad decision, Donald."

Peek's chopped quoting of him is an old journalism trick, but the problem for her was the audience heard the full quote and put his remarks in context. Botching a review of a film is easier because no one has seen is easier than reviewing a debate for people who saw it too.

Krauthammer got in his digs as well.

Look, you had on that stage very strong candidates. And if you were to take away the glitz, and the buzz, and all of the smoke, you would have seen the strongest field of candidates that the Republicans have had in thirty years. And I think one of the reasons, that at the end of the debate, Donald Trump decided that he would make this into a war on the moderators, and the war's on Fox, is because I think, he thinks he lost. If you win a debate, you don't start a war attacking the moderators, and he has succeeded. He's a brilliant showman. He has succeeded in doing—taking all the attention from what actually happened in the debate. And I think the GOP'll rue the day because this is a great opportunity to show off the field.

I'm worried about the GOP and changing the White House a year and a half from now. And it won't happen if these good candidates are completely obscured.

Throughout the campaign, commentators kept referring to all these brilliant candidates who were in the shadow of Trump, who was in command of the stage. Pardon me, but shouldn't a president take charge and be in command? Americans were looking for a commander-in-chief, not the Shadow. Trump had developed leadership skills in business, which clearly outshone those who had carefully climbed the political ladder to the middle.

The morning-after reviews were largely against Trump.

"Trump lost, beginning from the third-party question right at the start. He had any number of moments that were the worst moments he has had in the campaign. When he stuck with his shtick it was jarring on that stage, and when he tried to sound like a politician—talking of how he evoked on issues and in his closing statement, for instance—he sounded less assured and deft than the real politicians," Rich Lowry, editor of the *National Review*, wrote.

His colleague, Jonah Goldberg, also said Trump lost.

"Trump's refusal to say he wouldn't run as a third-party candidate wasn't shocking, but it was good to get on the record. And when he 'explained' why he raised his hand in favor of a potential third-party run, the words spilled out like someone flipped over a homeless man's shopping cart. His exchange with Megyn Kelly made it seem, if but for a moment, that King Joffrey had survived to become a real estate mogul from New York. I don't think this is the 'end of Trump.' But one can hear the distinct hiss of air escaping from the hot air balloon," Goldberg wrote.

Radio talker Michael Medved agreed. "The losers? Trump and Paul both fared poorly in the opening of the debate, but recovered somewhat as time went on. The Christie-Paul spat helped neither of them. The questions to Trump were appropriately tough; he's the frontrunner, after all. But the hostile tone of the challenges from the moderators may help him with his preferred presentation of himself as the victim of an establishment cabal. His defenses on issues of corporate bankruptcies and buying political favors won't play well, nor will his grimaces and over-broad gestures, or the overall impression of blustery, vulnerable pomposity," Medved wrote.

Rick Wilson, a Republican strategist who spent most of the campaign tweeting R-rated comments about Trump, also said Trump lost.

"Trump had a terrible night, though his fan boys will never admit it. Rank and file GOP voters (I was in a room full of them) were horrified by the third-party blackmail from Trump. His interactions were testy, thin-skinned and narcissistic; in short, Peak Trump. His devotees will stick, but he didn't win new parts of the GOP coalition to his cause. Every time he opens his mouth, Hillary's ad makers get another script concept. He didn't like the format, and though Fox gave him the lion's share of the time tonight, he showed he's not ready for political prime time. He showed that edge between 'not pc' and 'not a gentleman' is a narrow one," Wilson wrote.

Republican strategist Alex Castellanos said this was the end.

"They thought he might be Reaganish, that he might grow to be a president. That's dead now. That's what the Megyn Kelly moment did. It killed his opportunity for growth. The fire that is Donald Trump is now contained. It's not going anywhere. He is not growing. He was just going to hang on to that white hot core, his numbers may dip or rise a tinny bit. He is no longer a huge threat to dominate and control the Republican Party. And that one moment that you noticed, that you thought was the most important, that's what did it," Castellanos told CNN on August 7.

Republican strategist Sara Fagen agreed. "But this just feels like that summer fling in high school that your parents tell you not to do but you can't help yourself. But by the time we get back to school, I think Donald is going to be fading well into—into the background of this race," Fagen said on ABC on August 9.

Larry Sabato, director of the University of Virginia Center for Politics, made a similar call. "The key moment of this debate—the minute that will be most remembered—is the one at the beginning. Headline: 'Trump refuses to pledge party loyalty, won't rule out running as an independent.' That answer went over like a lead balloon in the arena, and I suspect it was no more popular at home with strong Republicans," Sabato wrote.

Of course, the one surefire way to keep Trump from running as a third-party candidate was to nominate him. Pardon me for being logical.

While the writers on the opinion pages of the nation's newspapers were generally useless, one of the scribblers in the funny pages understood fully what was going on. The postdebate assessment by Scott Adams, creator of the *Dilbert* comic strip, was spot on. Adams realized Trump used his mastery of salesmanship and negotiation to win the election. Adams shared his observations on his blog on August 13, "Allow me to describe some of the hypnosis and persuasion methods Mr.

Trump has employed on you. (Most of you know I am a trained hypnotist and this topic is a hobby of mine.)"

Adams wrote, "For starters, Trump literally wrote the book on negotiating, called *The Art of the Deal*. So we know he is familiar with the finer points of persuasion. For our purposes today, persuasion, hypnosis, and negotiating all share a common set of tools, so I will conflate them. Would Trump use his negotiation and persuasion skills in the campaign? Of course he would. And we expect him to do just that."

Adams was analyzing Trump not as a partisan, but as a salesman, which is what a politician is. Policy statements and position papers are props; the politicians are all Willy Lomans, "out there in the blue, riding on a smile and a shoeshine," as Arthur Miller wrote in his play *Death of A Salesman*.

Trump's speeches planted an anchor in the mind of the voter to make his sale, Adams said. Trump used that approach to frame the debate.

"And what did you think of Trump's famous 'Rosie O'Donnell' quip at the first debate when asked about his comments on women? The interviewer's questions were intended to paint Trump forever as a sexist pig. But Trump quickly and cleverly set the 'anchor' as Rosie O'Donnell, a name he could be sure was not popular with his core Republican crowd. And then he casually admitted, without hesitation, that he was sure he had said other bad things about other people as well," Adams wrote.

The pundits focused on Kelly, whom the pundits loved, while the audience focused on O'Donnell, whom conservatives scorned.

"When Trump raised his hand at the debate as the only person who would not pledge to back the eventual Republican candidate, he sent a message to the party that the only way they can win is by nominating him. And people like to win. It is in their nature. And they sure don't want to see a Clinton presidency," Adams wrote.

I do not wish to steal the entire post by Adams, but he pointed out how Trump repeatedly said things that went over the heads of the pundits and into the hearts of the home audience. The Trump approach was the only way to beat political correctness because political correctness was all about suppressing opinion. Liberals lose when the issue is abortion but win when it is choice. In eschewing political correctness, Trump forced liberals to speak English again.

Not only did Trump win the debate, but Adams said he owned Fox News by challenging its most popular female presenter. Not only was Trump challenging the liberal mainstream media, but the conservative media as well.

Adams then made a stunning prediction eleven months ahead of the nominating convention in Cleveland:

"As far as I can tell, Trump's 'crazy talk' is always in the correct direction for a skilled persuader. When Trump sets an 'anchor' in your mind, it is never random. And it seems to work every time. Now that Trump owns Fox News, and I see how well his anchor trick works with the public, I'm going to predict he will be our next president. I think he will move to the center on social issues (already happening) and win against Clinton in a tight election."

Drawing a cartoon is difficult. Drawing a conclusion is easy. Adams did both well, while many pundits in the conservative commentariat lacked the talent to do either. The political world was changing. On Fox News, George Will misread the change, thinking it would blow over.

"Henry Wallace tapped into something, with the far left of American Politics in the late '40s; the John Birch society tapped into something; George Wallace tapped into something; and it was up to the grown-ups in the labor movement in the late 1940s, and the grown-ups in the conservative movement in the 1960s to read those elements the riot act, and say: Come back in, but come back in on our terms because we are not going down the road you want to go," Will said.

Meanwhile, Roger L. Simon, screenwriter and head of *PJ Media*, pointed out what should have been obvious by August.

"We're still over five months from the Iowa caucuses and—astoundingly—it's increasingly looking like the 2016 presidential election, not just the nomination, is Donald Trump's to lose," Simon wrote on August 19.

"It's not only the polls, which are swinging his way. He has changed the nature of our electoral politics into a reality show with himself as star. Read his interview in Wednesday's *Hollywood Reporter* if you're looking for confirmation. Everybody else in both parties looks boring by comparison. We pretend to be interested in the others but The Donald is all we really care about, even bourgeois liberal critics when they try to dismiss him. (The *WaPo*'s David Ignatius is now likening Trump to Putin, as if The Donald were about to invade the Crimea. Well, he might put a hotel there.)"

Simon nailed it. Trump had taken command of the presidential race. Trump's supporters did not care what the pundits said any more than they cared what Vincent Canby said about the movies.

Besides panning *Rocky*, over the years *Times* film critic Canby also panned *Deliverance, One Flew Over the Cuckoo's Nest, Blazing Saddles, The Exorcist, A Christmas Story, Witness, Mask, The Natural,* and *Rain Man.* When Canby was seventy, management at the *New York Times* at last figured out he was not very competent at reviewing movies.

The *Times* made him the newspaper's chief theater critic instead.

Too bad Washington's theater district was too small to justify reassigning Krauthammer and his cohorts to review plays instead of debates.

CHAPTER 17

SEND IN THE CLOWNS.

———

DONE RIGHT, GATHERING A GROUP of people from a target audience was a good way for a marketer or a politician to test a message. Done wrong, and you have how Frank Luntz did it. A longtime political consultant, he had a cottage industry of setting up focus groups for Fox News to help its coverage of planned news events. He also appeared on CBS News the next day to share his thoughts.

The first debate was the "destruction of a candidacy," according to Luntz's next day comment—Trump's.

"Trump was the number one person walking into that debate. Almost all of his supporters (of the focus group) abandoned him because of what he said," Luntz said on CBS the next day.

Luntz pointed to Trump's exchange with Fox News star Megyn Kelly. "When you're talking about a Republican presidential nomination, when these people want to defeat Hillary Clinton, that's not the language, that's not the strategy, that's just not what they want to hear," Luntz said.

Well, forget the nomination then.

"Make no mistakes, his popularity may even go up slightly, but the negativity around him—because in the end you still have to be liked by the majority of Republicans to get the nomination," Luntz said.

Trump had blasted Luntz on Twitter shortly after the debate.

"I won every poll of the debate tonight by massive margins by the *Drudge Report* and *Time* magazine so where did you find that dumb panel," Trump tweeted.

"Frank Luntz is a low-class slob who came to my office looking for consulting work and I had zero interest. Now he picks anti-Trump panels!" Trump wrote.

"Your so-called focus groups are a total joke. Don't come to my office looking for business again. You are a clown!" Trump tweeted.

On CBS, Luntz did not deny having sought business from Trump. Indeed, months later, *Breitbart News* reported Luntz's company did $340,000 worth of work for Rubio over the years.

"I've been called a lot of things in my life but I've never been called a clown and those focus groups are accurate," Luntz said.

However, his focus group results were at odds with postdebate polls. As for clown, the Beltway boys and girls, as well as the editors of the *New York Daily News*, repeatedly dismissed Trump as a clown. On July 28, Kevin Williamson of the *National Review* wrote a piece headlined "Fifteen Elephants and a Clown," eviscerating Trump for daring to seek the presidency.

"One would think that a life spent in public might inspire at least a smidgen of concern about the wide world. He might have had any sort of life he chose, and Trump chose a clown's life. There is no shortage of opportunities for engagement, but there is only one thing that matters to Trump, and his presidential campaign, like everything else he has done in his seven decades, serves only that end," Williamson wrote.

He launched personal attacks on Trump's late father and Trump's latest wife, which undercut the argument that Trump was uncouth.

"But who could witness that scene—the self-made man who started with nothing but a modest portfolio of 27,000 New York City properties acquired by his millionaire slumlord father, barely out of his latest bankruptcy and possibly headed for another one as the casino/jiggle-joint bearing his name sinks into the filthy mire of the one US city that makes Las Vegas look respectable, a reality-television grotesque with his plastic-surgery-disaster wife, grunting like a baboon about our country's 'brand' and his own vast wealth—and not see the peerless sign of our times?" Williamson wrote.

He also called Trump "a ridiculous buffoon with the worst taste since Caligula." And Trump was the vulgar one?

In response, Rush Limbaugh said, "I like Kevin Williamson. I wish Kevin would write something like this about Hillary. I wish some in our conservative media would let go with some of this stuff for Democrats."

But the conservative commentariat always liked to sacrifice Republicans to gain the favor of Democrats. Consider satirist P. J. O'Rourke.

"Also typical of modern Americans is Trump's bad taste. True, he doesn't dress the way the rest of us do—like a nine-year-old in twee T-shirt, bulbous shorts, boob shoes, and league-skunked sports team cap. And Trump doesn't weigh 300 pounds or have multiple piercings or visible ink. He puts his own individual stamp on gaucherie. And we like it. We're a country that cherishes being individuals as much as we cherish being gauche," O'Rourke wrote on June 16.

David Harsanyi of the *Federalist* had written Trump off in an earlier column on April 25, 2015: "Friendly Reminder: Donald Trump Is a Clown Who Shouldn't Be Taken Seriously."

The *Daily News* story on June 17, on Trump's entry in the race read, "The carload of Republicans running for president now has a clown."

Chris Matthews of MSNBC wrote on July 14, "It's Tuesday, and that means it's time to rev up the right-wing clown car. This week, Donald Trump takes the lead in the Republican presidential field."

However, in his defense, Matthews was fair—he called them all clowns.

Heritage Action leader Michael Needham said on Fox News on July 19, "Donald Trump's a clown."

Stephen Hayes of Fox News said of the first debate, "Early impressions? Rubio and Christie did very well. Walker, Kasich were solid. Jeb Bush seemed nervous, halting. Trump was a clown show."

Mary Elizabeth Williams of *Salon* magazine agreed with Hayes. "Donald Trump, clown prince of slime: Why are we still pretending this sexist joker is a serious candidate?" she asked.

Ross Douthat of the *New York Times* needed 113 words to call Trump a clown in his article on August 7, 2015, after the debate:

"I doubt that Trump's numbers are going to come back to earth just because he rambled incoherently about Scotland and single-payer; that mistakes the essence of his appeal. But in the two hours last night it did feel like you could see the outline of a primary campaign in which the clown-car antics go on, but the depth of the field prevents them from simply overwhelming the debate, and rather than just the tedious establishment-versus-populist emptiness of 2012 we get a certain amount of demagoguery but also a series of overlapping substantive debates— over immigration, Common Core, entitlements, foreign policy—between not just one or two but several plausible would-be nominees."

Jim Geraghty of the *National Review* avoided calling Trump a clown and made the same point. Geraghty wrote on September 11, "If Trump wants to be judged as an entertainer…maybe he should *run for the job of entertainer*, not President of the United States."

Readers get the point. They called him a clown, and he in turn called some of them clowns. So what is the big deal? A lot, because when you call someone a clown, you can hardly be taken seriously yourself. That applied to Trump as well as his many critics.

CHAPTER 18

DOWN GOES DONALD.

———•———

THE CONSERVATIVE MEDIA—MAINLY FOX NEWS and subsidized publications such as the *Weekly Standard* and *National Review*—was a closed club. Andrew McCarthy of the *National Review* took Trump to task for his feud with Megyn Kelly after that first debate.

"Trump should apologize because a gentleman does not speak the way he spoke; it was uncivil and unmanly," McCarthy wrote on August 8.

His call for civility echoed the sensibilities of the erudite founder of the magazine, William F. Buckley Jr., who debated liberal Gore Vidal live on ABC television on August 27, 1968.

"Now listen, you queer—stop calling me a crypto-Nazi, or I'll sock you in your goddamn face, and you'll stay plastered!" Buckley said in front of a shocked home audience of ten million people.

Over the years, writers at his magazine often traded insults with The Donald, and the magazine even tried to use Trump's comments to raise funds. Early in the campaign, Trump responded to one of the many, many insults by star writer Jonah Goldberg over the years.

"I'm worth a fortune. I went out, I made a fortune, a big fortune, a tremendous fortune, bigger than people even understand. Then I get called [a failure] by a guy that can't buy a pair of pants. I get called names?" Trump said.

Goldberg responded in a column on July 11: "Trump Fans, It's Time For An Intervention."

"What I find so gaudy about Trump is his constant reference to the fact that he made a lot of money, and his expectation that it somehow makes him immune to criticism or means that he's a better person than his GOP competitors, never mind yours truly. Moreover, I find it horribly disappointing that his fans like this about him. If you met someone in real life who talked this way, you would think he's a jerk. But somehow he's awesome when he does it on TV?" Goldberg wrote.

Finally, someone admitted to what really galled many in the conservative commentariat the most about Trump: He succeeded. He made money. He wore nice clothes. He married models. And people admired him for this. His name was on the top of a luxury hotel, while they struggled for bylines.

The magazine tried a lighthearted exploitation of the feud by using it as a money-raising promotion.

"So we think Donald Trump is wrong, but can't be entirely sure. That's why we hope NR readers will turn The Donald's unique you-can't-buy-pants-Goldberg insult into an opportunity for Jonah's many fans to express some small-but-symbolic financial solidarity with NR. And to help keep Jonah in pants. Our goal: to raise $5,000 by Sunday at midnight," the magazine said on July 10.

This was not a joke. The magazine survived mainly through sugar-daddy donations and not its advertising and subscriptions. In its first fifty years, it lost $25 million, but Buckley's family was well off.

Trump once again had entered a feud with a man who bought ink by the barrel, or at least whose boss did. But Trump's campaign lived by the news cycle, and this rhubarb was worth a few mentions on cable news. He framed the debate as whether or not the critic who called him a failure could afford a pair of pants. Brilliant.

Just as Vidal had trolled Buckley, Trump hit a nerve in Goldberg, who struck back in a column, "Rudeness is Not a Conservative Principle," on August 8, tying it to Trump's feud with Megyn Kelly.

"So now The Donald is in hot water for making a crude menstrual insult. This is as good a time as any to make a simple point, one I make to young conservative activists all the time. Just because being rude or crude is un-PC that is not, in itself, a defense of being rude or crude. You would think social conservatives in particular wouldn't lose sight of this. But many have, at least going by my email and twitter feed," Goldberg wrote.

He ended his call for civility with an appeal to pragmatism.

"And, even if you think Trump's comments are funny or entertaining or not that big a deal or just a gaffe, at least ponder for a second about whether you think they will help Republicans win the presidential election. Everyone loves Reagan. Everyone says we need a great communicator. Well, the point of being a great communicator is to communicate. That is to say, it is to persuade people. If you think that Trump is the right guy for that project, you're the one who just doesn't get it," Goldberg wrote.

Whether Goldberg's message got through to the Trumpkins is unknown, but unlikely considering his lengthy string of rants against Trump. Certainly the message did not get through to editor Rich Lowry when he appeared on Kelly's show on September 23, to discuss the second debate.

> KELLY: Let's start with that. People say it's sexist to say her business career was a disaster. Has anybody said that?
>
> LOWRY: No, no one disputes that. Trump obviously attacks everyone, but she's become a much bigger target, and I think part of what's going on here is that last debate. Let's be honest. Carly cut his balls off with the precision of a surgeon.
>
> KELLY: What did you just say?
>
> LOWRY: He knows it.
>
> KELLY: You can't say that.
>
> LOWRY: He knows he insulted and bullied his way to the top of the polls. No one was able to best him ever, except for this tough lady on that stage. And it must kill him. He must be simmering about it to this night.

Buckley years later regretted threatening on national TV to punch Vidal, but at least he did not threaten to castrate his rival because, as McCarthy wrote, "a gentleman does not speak the way he spoke; it was uncivil and unmanly."

However, Trump deserved denunciation because he mocked Fiorina's looks in a profile of Trump in *Rolling Stone*. Writer Paul Solotaroff began the article began with a tour of The Donald's Boeing 757 jet.

"I follow him into the stateroom of the 757, past three rows of sleeper seats wrapped in eggshell calfskin, with seat-belt buckles of plated gold and the family crest stitched in every headrest; past the conference center, with its mahogany table and a dozen executive high-backs snugged around it; past the in-plane theater, with its oyster-shape couches and the 57-inch flatscreen tuned to Fox; past the bumped-out bulkhead and the first of two bedrooms, this one fitted with mohair couches that convert to a full-size bed; and then the master bedroom, with its silk-spun walls and bathroom fixtures finished in rosy gold," Solotaroff wrote in the story published on September 9.

Air Force One seems like a step down from that luxury. But another paragraph in the article created a controversy.

"With his blue tie loosened and slung over his shoulder, Trump sits back to digest his meal and provide a running byplay to the news. Onscreen, they've cut away to a spot with Scott Walker, the creaky-robot governor of Wisconsin. Praised by the anchor for his 'slow but steady' style, Walker is about to respond when Trump chimes in, 'Yeah, he's slow, all right! That's what we got already: slowwww.' His staffers at the conference table howl and hoot; their man, though, is just getting warm. When the anchor throws to Carly Fiorina for her reaction to Trump's momentum, Trump's expression sours in schoolboy disgust as the camera bores in on Fiorina. 'Look at that face!' he cries. 'Would anyone vote for that? Can you imagine that, the face of our next president?!' The laughter grows halting and faint behind him. 'I mean, she's a woman, and I'm not s'posedta say bad things, but really, folks, come on. Are we serious?'"

Trump's critics leaped on his attack. Jim Geraghty used humor.

"Donald Trump thinks Carly Fiorina isn't physically attractive enough to hold the office of Lyndon Johnson, Richard Nixon, William H. Taft, Grover Cleveland, and Rutherford B. Hayes," Geraghty wrote in the *National Review* on September 10, 2015.

The controversy was real but beneficial to many people. It boosted sales of *Rolling Stone*, which had discredited itself a year earlier with a false report of a gang rape at the University of Virginia. The Fiorina controversy gave pundits a new source of outrage. The controversy also raised the profile of Fiorina and gave her the high moral ground and sympathy. This time, Trump paid dearly for the news cycles that he coveted.

At the Republican debate the next week, on September 16, CNN and the Republican National Committee bent their rules to put Fiorina on the stage. CNN wanted her because it was good television. Republicans wanted her on stage because she could slow Trump. Their donors wanted cheap labor and opposed Trump's plan to build a wall.

As expected, the debate panelists asked her about his crude remark.

"I think women all over this country heard very clearly what Mr. Trump said," Fiorina said to applause.

Trump's response was "I think she's got a beautiful face, and I think she's a beautiful woman."

Every pundit in Washington jumped on this exchange. They declared Fiorina the winner and champion of the debate. To paraphrase Howard Cosell's phrase when George Foreman knocked out Joe Frazier on January 22, 1973: Down goes Donald. Down goes Donald. Down goes Donald.

"What really happened, we had one instance where Donald Trump was challenged, and Carly did it. She did it in a very concise and cutting way. And for the first time, Trump had no answer. And that was an electric moment," Krauthammer said on Megyn Kelly's show.

Down goes Donald. Down goes Donald. Down goes Donald.

"Republican frontrunner Donald Trump lost Wednesday's Republican presidential debate, and one person deserves more credit for his defeat than anyone else: Carly Fiorina. The former Hewlett-Packard CEO and failed 2010 Senate candidate outshined the entire impressive GOP field. She also proved particularly deft at skewering Trump," columnist John McCormack wrote in the *Weekly Standard.*

Down goes Donald. Down goes Donald. Down goes Donald.

"The winner of the night was a scrappy Fiorina who earned an A+ grade. Her ferocity made Trump crawl under a rock, and from there he called her beautiful after he had gone out of his way to basically call her ugly and that no one wanted a president with her face," Raoul Lowery Contreras, a contributor to the *Hill*, wrote.

Down goes Donald. Down goes Donald. Down goes Donald.

"The good news is that this was a debate that wasn't Trump-centric, where it wasn't all about The Donald. As a result, he seemed to lose interest in the proceedings in the second half. The fact checkers will have a field day with his claims about his own business record, or his stupid charge that Bush said he wants to cut women's health services. With Fiorina offering a much stronger outsider option, it's hard to imagine that The Donald will hold his prohibitive lead when the full impact of the debate sinks in," radio talker Michael Medved said.

Down goes Donald. Down goes Donald. Down goes Donald.

"Fiorina showed she can bloody Trump, and her back-and-forth with him may soon be seen as a tipping point. She succeeded at making him uncomfortable," James Hohmann and Elise Viebeck of the *Washington Post* wrote.

Down goes Donald. Down goes Donald. Down goes Donald.

"So the question after the second Republican debate is this: Will it take a week for Carly Fiorina to sit atop the GOP polls, or will it take two weeks? Because after Wednesday night's debate, it's going to happen," John Podhoretz wrote in the *New York Post.*

Down goes Donald. Down goes Donald. Down goes Donald.

"Carly Fiorina nailed it in the second Republican debate. That's the assessment of GOP insiders in a special edition of the POLITICO Caucus, our weekly survey of the top operatives, activists, and strategists in Iowa and New Hampshire. They offered their reactions immediately after watching Wednesday's 8 p.m. prime-time debate in Simi Valley, California," *Politico* reported.

Down goes Donald. Down goes Donald. Down goes Donald.

"Fiorina performed like an all-star and showed substance and style that will move her up in the game," Ed Rollins, Republican political consultant, told *Politico*.

Down goes Donald. Down goes Donald. Down goes Donald.

"Trump's breathtaking criticism of her appearance created the most predictable question, and she knocked it out of the park with an answer that managed to make Trump look small and mendacious, while also reinforcing a Trump criticism of Jeb Bush for dissing women's health care services," Ed Kilgore, managing editor at the *Democratic Strategist*, said.

Down goes Donald. Down goes Donald. Down goes Donald.

"One is loath to say this since predictions of Trump's political demise have repeatedly been wrong, but there is a very good chance we've seen Peak Trump," Jamie Weinstein of the *Daily Caller* wrote.

Down goes Donald. Down goes Donald. Down goes Donald.

And of course, we had the cutting comment by Lowry.

But the controversy did not matter because Fiorina failed to generate enough support to include her on the prime-time stage in the next debate. Her campaign later ended before the second primary.

Meanwhile, Trump continued to lead the polls by a wide margin. Why did it not matter to Trump supporters? In that *Rolling Stone* article, Solotaroff provided an insight that none of the pundits who leaped on the that-face comment cited:

"In all the hysteria, however, what's often missed are the qualities that brought Trump here. You don't do a fraction of what he's done in life—dominate New York real estate for decades, build the next grand Xanadus for the super-rich on the far shores of Dubai and Istanbul, run the prime-time ratings table for more than 10 years and earn a third (or sixth) fortune at it—without being immensely cunning and deft, a top-of-the-food-chain killer. Over the course of 10 days and several close-in encounters, I got to peer behind the scrim of his bluster and self-mythos and get a very good look at the man. What I saw was enough to make me take him dead serious. If you're waiting for Trump to blow himself up in a Hindenburg of gaffes or hate speech, you're in for a long, cold fall and winter. Donald Trump is here for the duration—and gaining strength and traction by the hour."

But the pundits said Trump had jumped the shark.

CHAPTER 19

JUMPING THE SHARK.

———◆———

As *HAPPY DAYS* BEGAN ITS fifth season on September 20, 1977, the gang visited Los Angeles. Arthur Fonzarelli—the Fonz—played by Henry Winkler, answered a challenge and water-skied over a shark. Thirty years later, comedian Jon Hein popularized the phrase "jumping the shark" to connote that moment when a television series had passed its peak. Pundits appropriated the term to mark a moment when the candidacy turned and headed for death.

In the case of The Donald, they said he jumped the shark before he jumped into the race. Trump jumped the shark on February 26, 2015.

"Donald Trump says he's serious about 2016 bid. Shark, jumped? What better way for the host of this success to call attention to himself—and perhaps negotiate a few more bucks out of NBC—then to threaten to chuck the whole thing in an effort to run for the post of what used be called the leader of the free world?" Peter Grier of the *Christian Science Monitor* wrote.

Trump jumped the shark on July 9, 2015.

"But by Thursday afternoon Trump appeared to have jumped the shark of his own self-indulgence, thanks to his inflammatory comments about Mexican immigrants. And now the fallout might not hurt him only politically: Trump's big plans for an over-the-top Washington hotel are also crumbling before his famously squinty eyes, along with the gilded name brand he has spent so many years polishing. Abandoned by two celebrity chefs, José Andrés and Geoffrey Zakarian, who were supposed to be developing restaurants at his $200 million, Pennsylvania Avenue property, which is slated to open next year, Trump is now fighting with both for abruptly departing the Trump Organization ship, along with more than a dozen corporate sponsors and business partners," political gossip Kate Bennett wrote in *Politico*.

Trump jumped the shark on July 13, 2015.

"Donald Trump jumps the stupid shark by promising to kick an escaped drug lord's ass," Sarah Jones, managing editor of *Politics USA* wrote.

Trump jumped the shark on July 20, 2015.

"He was a controversial character who said some useful things, I think, and brought some people into the Republican tent. But he jumped the shark yesterday," Kristol said on ABC News, referring to Trump's disparaging remarks about McCain's war service.

Trump jumped the shark on July 21, 2015.

"The reality TV star jumped the shark with another outlandish statement designed to attract media attention—an attack on Sen. John McCain's war heroism," Shawn Steel wrote in the *Washington Times*.

Trump jumped the shark on August 8, 2015.

"But Donald Trump might have finally jumped the shark with his recent comments about Fox News's Megyn Kelly," Matt Lewis wrote in the *Telegraph*.

Trump jumped the shark on August 24, 2015.

"OK, this is now officially out of control. Donald Trump's dominance of media coverage of the Republican presidential primary has jumped all of those sharks that have shown up off the North Carolina coast. All of them," Rem Rieder of *USA Today* wrote.

Trump jumped the shark on September 18, 2015.

"Donald Trump has jumped the shark…It is not that Trump's poll numbers are immediately going to crater. He is still leading all the polls. But when we look back at the 2016 presidential election, the second Republican candidate debate might well emerge as a crucial turning point for Trump," Bill Schneider of Reuters wrote.

Trump jumped the shark on November 13, 2015.

"John Fund asks if Trump jumped the shark last night. It feels like we've heard about Donald Trump's imminent collapse many times in this cycle, and he's only slid a little. But last night's Trump rant against Carson in Iowa, punctuated by his question, 'How stupid are the people of Iowa? How stupid are the people of the country to believe this crap?' feels like a turning point," Jim Geraghty of the *National Review* wrote.

Trump jumped the shark on December 7, 2015.

"Donald Trump Jumps the Greatest Shark Ever!" was the headline. "On Monday, Republican presidential candidate Donald Trump set media heads spinning with his proposal to ban all Muslims—including tourists—from entering the United States 'until our country's representatives can figure out what is going on,'" wrote Joel Pollak, senior editor-at-large for *Breitbart News*.

Trump jumped the shark on January 6, 2016.

"I tweeted out a response to Donald Trump's raising questions about my natural-born citizenship. It was a link to Fonzie jumping the shark, and I think I'm going to let my response stick with that tweet... One of the things that media loves to do is gaze at their navels for hours on end by a tweet from Donald Trump or me or from anyone else. Who cares? Let's focus on the issues. Let's focus on the issues that matter," Cruz said.

Trump jumped the shark on January 26, 2015.

"With Fox News Debate Boycott, Has Trump Finally Jumped the Shark?" ran the headline to a Walter Hudson piece on *PJ Media*.

Trump jumped the shark on February 28, 2016.

"I'm not OK with Donald Trump's refusal to denounce David Duke and the KKK. Of course he's heard of David Duke. Trump has jumped the shark," Bush 43's first spokesman Ari Fleischer tweeted.

If elected, Trump will be a healthy president, given the oceans of sharks he jumped just to get to the White House.

By the way, *Happy Days* continued for another seven years after the Fonz jumped that shark.

CHAPTER 20

THE COMIC-BOOK DEBATE.

———

THE TALK ABOUT SHARK JUMPING was an admission that Trump was the Fonz while the other candidates fought over who was Potsie or Ralph Malph. The Fonz and company headed for a showdown with the media at the third debate on CNBC on October 29, 2015. The event became the only time all the Republican candidates came together to battle a common foe.

CNBC billed the third debate as "Your Money, Your Vote," but the lead moderator, John Harwood, quickly dashed any hope of having a civil discussion of financial issues with his first question for Trump.

> HARWOOD: Let's be honest. Is this a comic book version of a presidential campaign?
> TRUMP: It's not a comic book, and it's not a very nicely asked question, the way you say that.

One could almost hear the giggles in the room when CNBC staffers came up with that question in the pregame meeting. However, their mirth and merriment ended quickly. Ted Cruz took his next opportunity—a question by Carl Quintanilla about a government shutdown—to level Harwood and CNBC.

> CRUZ: You know, let me say something at the outset. The questions that have been asked so far in this debate illustrate why the American people don't trust the media.
> (APPLAUSE)

CRUZ: This is not a cage match. And if you look at the questions: Donald Trump, are you a comic book villain? Ben Carson, can you do math? John Kasich, will you insult two people over here? Marco Rubio, why don't you resign? Jeb Bush, why have your numbers fallen? How about talking about the substantive issues?

(APPLAUSE)

CRUZ: And, Carl, I'm not finished yet. The contrast with the Democratic debate, where every fawning question from the media was, Which of you is more handsome and why? And let me be clear—

QUINTANILLA: You have 30 seconds left to answer, should you choose to do so.

CRUZ: Let me be clear. The men and women on this stage have more ideas, more experience, more common sense than every participant in the Democratic debate. That debate reflected a debate between the Bolsheviks and the Mensheviks. And nobody watching at home believes that any of the moderators have any intention of voting in a Republican primary. The questions that are being asked shouldn't be trying to get people to tear into each other. It should be what are your substantive—

QUINTANILLA: I want the record to reflect, I asked you about the debt limit and got no answer.

HARWOOD: We're moving on.

A week shy of his sixtieth birthday, Harwood was the graying-at-the-temples stereotype of an anchorman. His résumé included a Nieman fellowship at Harvard. Dad was a newspaperman. Mom was an activist who had worked for Bobby Kennedy's presidential campaign in 1968. Two days before the debate, Mollie Hemingway of the *Federalist* wrote a column detailing why Harwood should not run the debate. She cited his defense of Clinton in her e-mail scandal, his mocking of Republicans, and his history of softball questions for liberals.

"The problem isn't that Harwood is biased or not particularly worth reading or watching. That's between him and his employers. But why is he moderating a GOP debate? And why doesn't this debate have a conservative partner?" Hemingway wrote.

She proved prophetic. After the debate, Reince Priebus wrote a letter to NBC (owner of CNBC) threatening to give to another network a debate scheduled with NBC in February.

The reviews were scathing.

"I had to watch it again. I had to make sure I witnessed what I just witnessed. And upon absorbing the whole thing and double checking my notes from watching last night and again this morning before sunrise, they were practically identical. Conclusion: CNBC, a solid niche network with solid talent, just performed the worst moderation of any debate—and we're including all presidential, vice presidential, fictional...the one from *Old School* (Will Ferrell's Frank the Tank vs. James Carville, moderated by Jeremy Piven's Dean Pritcher), the one from *Clueless* (Alicia Silverstone vs. Amber on the plight of Haitian refugees)—in American history," Joe Concha of *Media-ite* wrote.

Brian Stetler, media critic for CNN, talked to his buddies at the rival network. "For the CNBC employees who boarded a charter plane right after Wednesday's bruising GOP debate, the redeye flight was physically smooth but emotionally turbulent. People were exhausted, but also rattled and worried," Stetler reported.

"'We were shell-shocked,' one source said. The poor reviews were piling up—declaring CNBC the biggest loser of the night—and the moderators Carl Quintanilla and Becky Quick knew more would be published by the time the flight landed in New York."

The network had a big night as fourteen million people tuned in, well beyond the record viewership for CNBC. Advertisers paid $250,000 for each thirty-second spot, according to Stetler. But Harwood had ruined the evening by being a jerk, as had the other moderators.

CNBC issued a one-sentence statement—"Journalists who ask presidential candidates substantive, challenging questions on interest rates,

Social Security, the debt limit, student loans, and taxes to name a few, should be applauded."—and then ordered its on-air staff not to talk about the biggest night in the network's history. It was a comic-book debate in which CNBC tried to push around the Republicans, except this time they shoved back. Hard. And they drew blood. The Republican Party canceled a debate scheduled with NBC, costing the network prestige and millions in revenues.

CHAPTER 21

TRUMP'S CANDIDACY MUST DIE.

———

IN 1970, STEVE WINWOOD AND his group Traffic dusted off the traditional British ballad "John Barleycorn Must Die" and made it the title track for their new album. The song was a wry tale of three men who vowed that John Barleycorn must die. But actually, they were distilling adult beverages. They buried him, but he rose. They cut him down. They skinned him to the bone. They ground him. But instead of killing him, they made him stronger—about seventy proof.

> Well there's beer all in the barrel
> And brandy in the glass,
> But little old sir John with his nut-brown bowl
> Proved the strongest man at last.
> Now the huntsman, he can't hunt the fox,
> Nor loudly blow his horn,
> And the tinker he can't mend his pots
> Without John Barleycorn.

In 2015, George Will had become one of the men who had determined that Donald Trump's candidacy must die. From Will's perch in Washington, he had gazed at the Trump Tower in Manhattan and decided he did not like Trump. Not one bit.

The *Wall Street Journal* called Will "perhaps the most powerful journalist in America." That was in 1986. Nearly thirty years, he was still influential, having joined the roster of dozens of pundits at Fox News, after ABC dumped him in favor of a man forty years younger. Roger Ailes hired pundits by the score after building Fox News into a $2 billion annual profit center.

Will's dislike of Trump was much like Brooke Astor's disdain for Trump—they both considered him a boor. She had scorned him as nouveau riche, while Will considered him his intellectual inferior. The feud was one-sided for many years. When Will took umbrage at Trump appearing beside Mitt Romney during the 2012 presidential run, Will's verbiage was polysyllabic but nevertheless impolite because he attacked the person not the idea. "I do not understand the cost benefit here. The costs are clear. The benefit? What voter is gonna vote for him (Romney) because he is seen with Donald Trump? The cost of appearing with this bloviating ignoramus is obvious it seems to me. Donald Trump is redundant evidence that if your net worth is high enough, your IQ can be very low and you can still intrude into American politics," Will said on ABC News on May 21, 2012.

Will's assumption that Trump was dumb reminded me of an on-air exchange between radio talker Don Imus and historian Michael Beschloss after the 2008 election.

BESCHLOSS: Yeah. Even aside from the fact of electing the first African American president and whatever one's partisan views, this is a guy whose IQ is off the charts—I mean you cannot say that he is anything but a very serious and capable leader and—you know—you and I have talked about this for years.

IMUS: Well. What is his IQ?

BESCHLOSS: Our system doesn't allow those people to become president, those people meaning people that smart and that capable.

IMUS: What is his IQ?

BESCHLOSS: Pardon?

IMUS: What is his IQ?

BESCHLOSS: Uh. I would say it's probably—he's probably the smartest guy ever to become president.

IMUS: That's not what I asked you. I asked you what his IQ was.

BESCHLOSS: You know that I don't know and I'd have to find someone with more expertise.

IMUS: You don't know.

Will had no idea what Trump's intelligence quotient was, but why let an uncomfortable facts get in the way of a good opinion? As the son of a philosophy professor, Will likely equated academics with intelligence and business with its opposite. Thus the more successful Trump was, the dumber he was.

Trump fired back in kind on Twitter, calling Will "the dumbest (and most overrated) political commentator of all time" and "strictly third rate."

Alexandra Petri, one of Will's stablemates at the *Washington Post*, gave Trump the TKO—technical knockout. "George Will got his man all right. But Trump wins this round. He always wins. Every time his name is mentioned, he grows in power," she wrote on May 30, 2012.

But Will was a slow learner. Three years later, Will launched a string of attacks on Trump. On July 5, 2015, Will discussed on Fox News the upcoming first Republican debate in Cleveland.

"Picture him on stage. He says something hideously inflammatory—which is all he knows how to say—and then what do the other nine people on stage do? Do they either become complicit in what he said by their silence, or do they all have to attack him? The debate gets hijacked. The process gets hijacked. At the end of the day he is a one-man Todd Akin. He's Todd Akin with ten different facets," Will said.

Akin was the Republican senatorial candidate in Missouri in 2012, who created a stir by saying raped women rarely get pregnant. The party demanded he apologize. He did. That was foolish because the party abandoned him anyway. The lesson to conservatives is never apologize. Republicans would rather look good in the eyes of Democrats than win.

Trump definitely was not that kind of Republican, which drove the conservative commentariat batty. Will was typical.

"In every town large enough to have two traffic lights there is a bar at the back of which sits the local Donald Trump, nursing his fifth beer and innumerable delusions. Because the actual Donald Trump is wealthy, he can turn himself into an unprecedentedly and incorrigibly vulgar presidential candidate. It is his right to use his riches as he pleases. His squalid performance and its coarsening of civic life are costs of freedom that an open society must be prepared to pay," Will began his column on August 12.

As if calling a man the town drunk was not a coarsening of civic life. Cognitive dissonance is a way of life in Washington. Perhaps it traces to the water system. Will's charge also was laughably inaccurate. Trump was a teetotaler.

The column continued to knock Trump and then Trump's supporters.

"Conservatives who flinch from forthrightly marginalizing Trump mistakenly fear alienating a substantial Republican cohort. But the assumption that today's Trumpites are Republicans is unsubstantiated and implausible. Many are no doubt lightly attached to the political process, preferring entertainment to affiliation. They relish their candidate's vituperation and share his aversion to facts. From what GOP faction might Trumpites come? The establishment? Social conservatives? Unlikely," Will wrote.

His column called for Republicans to bar Trump outright and, by implication, the supporters Trump brought to the party from outside Will's ken.

"A political party has a right to (in language Trump likes) secure its borders. Indeed, a party has a duty to exclude interlopers, including cynical opportunists deranged by egotism. This is why closed primaries, although not obligatory, are defensible: Let party members make the choices that define the party and dispense its most precious possession, a presidential nomination. So, the Republican National Committee should immediately stipulate that subsequent Republican debates will be open to any and all—but only—candidates who pledge to support the party's nominee," Will wrote.

The Republican Party wrote such a pledge, which Trump signed after wringing a few more news cycles of coverage out of the nontroversy.

Trump attributed Will's contempt for him to the fact that Will's wife worked for Scott Walker's ill-fated presidential campaign. When the governor dropped out, he took with him any dreams Will may have had of an ambassadorship to Vanuatu. However, Will soldiered on, bless his heart.

"Certainly conservatives consider it crucial to deny the Democratic Party a third consecutive term controlling the executive branch. Extending from eight to 12 years its use of unbridled executive power would further emancipate the administrative state from control by either a withering legislative branch or a supine judiciary. But first things first. Conservatives' highest priority now must be to prevent Trump from winning the Republican nomination in this, the GOP's third epochal intraparty struggle in 104 years," Will wrote on December 23.

He redefined conservatism as a Stop Trump movement. He became a reactionary who was willing to allow socialist Sanders become president to keep him and his friends in charge of the party.

"This is hardly the first time we have heard the United States singing lyrics like those of Trump's curdled populism. Alabama Democrat George Wallace four times ran for president with salvos against Washington's 'briefcase totin' bureaucrats' who 'can't even park their bicycles straight.' What is new is Trump promising, in the name of strength, to put the United States into a defensive crouch against 'cunning' Mexicans and others," Will wrote on August 26.

A month later, Will felt frisky about the odds of Trump folding.

"It is, however, unclear that Trumpkins will all migrate to one candidate when their hero departs, strutting while slouching. And although deferring delights can be virtuous, nothing is now more virtuous than scrubbing, as soon as possible, the Trump stain from public life," Will wrote on September 26.

However, the only thing scrubbed from public life were the names of Trump's opponents from the list on the blackboard of candidates. Little Sir Donald proved the strongest man at last, about seventy proof.

And George Will couldn't mend his pots without a little Trump hate.

CHAPTER 22

CEILINGS, NOTHING MORE THAN CEILINGS.

———

THE THIRD DEBATE LEFT THE press bleeding and Trump smiling. But anti-Republican press—which is to say, most of the Washington press—insisted he had limited appeal. In June, his ceiling was 11 percent.

"At the end of the day, it's quite possible that Donald Trump will get 11 percent in New Hampshire, but that might be his cap," Patrick Murray, the director of the Monmouth University Polling Institute, told *Politico* on June 25.

Yes, Trump had a ceiling. All the experts said so.

"Other people I spoke with in Las Vegas said that while Trump is a very entertaining speaker—'He's like watching a train wreck; you know you shouldn't look, but you do anyway'—he will probably hit a natural ceiling on his support," John Fund of *National Review* wrote on July 12.

And be thankful he had a ceiling.

"Trump clearly appeals to a certain base of GOP voters, who like the idea of a successful outsider and who are responding to his non-PC bravado. However based on these polls, it seems likely that Trump's support has a ceiling, and his poll numbers are rapidly approaching that ceiling. Trump doesn't have much room to grow, and we can only hope that he doesn't do any significant damage to the eventual nominee's general election chances before he inevitably peters out," Joshua Pinho of American Principles in Action wrote on July 8.

The ceiling was a little higher than first thought.

"However, the good news should be tempered by the fact that there is still probably a ceiling to Trump's support. It may just be a little higher than previously thought," Rob Garver of the *Fiscal Times* reported on July 14.

But he definitely was not the front-runner.

"Donald Trump is not the front-runner. Smarter polls would prove it...Senator Marco Rubio, Governor Scott Walker, and Ben Carson currently have the highest ceilings of support," Sam Wang of the *New Republic* wrote on July 20.

OK, his ceiling was a little over 22 percent. But that was it.

"The Morning Consult national survey of registered voters shows Trump with 22 percent support...Nonetheless, there are certainly signs suggesting he may be bumping up on his ceiling of support," Matthew Dickinson of *US News and World Report* reported on July 27.

Trump's was a low ceiling.

"Trump has a high floor and a low ceiling. He has a lot of enthusiasm going or some enthusiasm going, but he has got a ceiling," Karl Rove told Fox News on July 30.

OK, it was a 25 percent ceiling.

"Though there hasn't been any indication of a precipitous drop in Trump's numbers, his support seems to have met resistance at around the 25 percent mark after weeks of rising. Though that's still good enough to give him a double-digit lead in a crowded Republican field, it won't be as the field narrows. Past Republican candidates, such as Ron Paul in 2012 and Pat Buchanan in 1996, had a core base of dedicated followers, but had too low of a ceiling to capture the nomination. Trump seems to be in a similar position," Philip Klein of the *Washington Examiner* wrote on August 19, 2015.

Maybe it was a little higher than that.

"I think the question everyone is asking right now, as the race achieves some measure of stasis, is this: How much farther can Trump rise? Is 25 percent his ceiling, or his base?" Leon Wolf of *Red State* wrote on August 27.

Make that 30 percent.

"I think he's hit his ceiling of about 30 percent," Bill Kristol on ABC on September 6.

Retire, Donald.

"The famous Trump base has hit a ceiling. He should retire, and enjoy," Dan Henninger of the *Wall Street Journal* wrote on September 30.

Not enough people make him their second choice.

"There are signs that Trump is hitting the ceiling of his support. If you add in people who choose each candidate as their second option, Trump falls to an essential tie for second with Carly Fiorina. Carson leads," Philip Bump of the *Washington Post* wrote on September 30.

Readers get the picture. We know what happened. The pundits failed because they could not believe that an outsider waltzed into the sixteen-candidate race and swept into first place without their permission. If Trump were any other candidate, the talk would focus on his momentum and speculation about the bandwagon effect. Instead there were constant and insipid assurances that Trump had reached his ceiling.

"The first principle is that you must not fool yourself—and you are the easiest person to fool," Nobel physicist Richard Feynman said in his commencement speech at Caltech in 1974.

But the fools in the press kept insisting that Trump had a ceiling. They forgot the lesson of Paul Simon's song, "One Man's Ceiling Is Another Man's Floor."

For while Trump had not yet reached 40 percent in the polls, none of his opponents had reached 25 percent. By the end of November, Trump was in command of the race. And then came Islamic terrorism in San Bernardino, California, a moment that would raise and answer the question if who was most important figure in American politics, Trump or President Obama?

CHAPTER 23

Banning Muslims.

———◆———

A Muslim terrorist and his immigrant Muslim wife shot and killed fourteen colleagues and injured twenty-two other coworkers at an office Christmas party for the eighty or so employees of the county health department in San Bernardino, California, on December 2, 2015. This was the nation's deadliest terrorist attack since 9/11. Fortunately, police were able to find and kill the terrorists in a shootout a few hours later.

"You never let a serious crisis go to waste. And what I mean by that it's an opportunity to do things you think you could not do before," Obama's first chief of staff, Rahm Emanuel told the *Wall Street Journal* on November 19, 2008.

Obama leaped on this crisis to push for more gun control. "We should never that think this is something that just happens in the ordinary course of events because it doesn't happen with the same frequency in other countries," Obama told CBS News on December 2, 2015, the night of the massacre.

His attempt to exploit the tragedy was both foolish and ghoulish. Polling showed that. Four nights later, on Sunday, December 6, the president went on prime-time television to reassure the nation that this terrorist act was under investigation. The next afternoon, on December 7, 2015, Trump released a statement.

Donald J. Trump is calling for a total and complete shutdown of Muslims entering the United States until our country's representatives can figure out what is going on. According to Pew Research, among others, there is great hatred towards Americans by large segments of the Muslim population. Most recently, a poll from the Center for Security Policy released data showing "25 percent of those polled agreed that violence against Americans here in the United States is justified as a part of the global jihad" and 51 percent of those polled "agreed that Muslims in America should have the choice of being governed according to Shariah." Shariah authorizes such atrocities as murder against non-believers who won't convert, beheadings and more unthinkable acts that pose great harm to Americans, especially women.

This enraged pundits. Ben Shapiro wasted no time in trashing the plan. "Kiss Our Intelligence Apparatus Goodnight. We need to work with Muslims both foreign and domestic. It's one thing to label Islamic terrorism and radical Islam a problem. It's another to label all individual Muslims a problem. That's what this policy does. It's factually wrong and ethically incomprehensible," Shaprio wrote.

David French of the *National Review* also pounced, writing: "There is nothing wrong with closing our borders to select groups when confronted with actionable intelligence or to place some groups under greater scrutiny because of known threats. But to treat every single Muslim as a threat, regardless of whether they're from Raqqa, Erbil, Cairo, or Des Moines—and regardless of whether they've tweeted jihadist threats or bled on the battlefield alongside our troops—is to act mindlessly. I would also say Trump is acting maliciously, but I don't think Trump despises Muslims as much as he loves leading the news cycle. This is a political stunt and should be treated as such."

In a podcast on December 8, Stephen Hayes of the *Weekly Standard* called this the "greatest gift he could give Democrats."

"If Trump's proposal to ban all Muslims surprises you, you haven't been paying attention. If it pleases you, you're a bigot," Hayes also tweeted.

On December 8, Mika Brzezinski and Joe Scarborough reacted with horror on their MSNBC show.

"What scares me about this is that he is a pretty brilliant man and knows how to tap into how, what people are feeling and saying. And there is a vacuum, there is an opening for this created not just by the Obama administration but by the George W. Bush administration. The events of the past decade have really made this country ripe for these feelings and he's tapping into them," Brzezinski said.

"But George W. Bush as well as Dick Cheney and his statement we just showed, aggressively spoke out against this type of rhetoric," Scarborough said.

"That's great," Brzezinski said.

In his column on December 9, Mike Lupica of the *New York Daily News* bemoaned the 2016 presidential race in the wake of Trump's proposal.

"There has never been a lower point than this in modern presidential politics. If you think there has been, name it. We see how desperate they are to win at all cost. But at what cost to this country? We talk constantly about how unsafe everything has become in a terrorist world. You know what is less safe these days, and more vulnerable than ever? This country's good name," Lupica wrote.

On the same day, actor George Takei denounced Trump, citing internment camps set up in World War II to house Americans of Japanese origin. He was five when the government interred his family.

"It's ironic that he made that comment on December 7, Pearl Harbor Day—the very event that put us in those internment camps," Takei said on MSNBC.

However, Trump's plan did not cover citizens. He merely wanted to restrict noncitizen Muslims from entering the country. While Takei fell for one wrong spin, Democratic strategist Peter Fenn rolled out a different brand of nonsense in his column in *US News and World Report*.

"How many recruits will the Islamic State group gain from Trump's move toward fascism? How confused will young, angry, poor Muslims in the war-torn Middle East be, and how many Muslims will believe successful Donald Trump represents American thought and values and our approach to the world? How long will it take for us to undo this damage? How many years? What price will we pay? Those may be the scariest questions of all," Fenn wrote.

Hysteria had hit the Beltway. In his column on December 10, David Ignatius of the *Washington Post* psychoanalyzed Trump. "Trump's anti-Muslim rhetoric will live in infamy in US history. He obviously doesn't mind; his narcissistic personality is so extreme that every high-visibility outrage is for him a kind of validation," Ignatius wrote.

But on the same day, Krauthammer merely mocked the proposal in his column. "I decline to join the chorus denouncing the Trump proposal as offensive and un-American. That's too obvious. What I can't get over is its sheer absurdity. Here's a suggestion (borrowed from my Fox News colleague Chris Stirewalt) to shore it up. At every immigration station at every airport in America, we will demand that every potential entrant—immigrant, refugee, student or tourist—eat a bacon sandwich. You refuse? Back home you go!"

"True, the Stirewalt Solution casts the net a bit wide, snaring innocent vegetarians and Orthodox Jews. But hey, as Trump said Tuesday, 'We're at war—get it through your head.' Can't get squeamish about collateral damage."

Shane Goldmacher of *Politico* warned Trump's words hurt the Republican brand. "Muslim Republicans fear Donald Trump's escalating anti-Muslim rhetoric—capped this week by his call to block all Muslims' entry into the country—could turn Muslims away from the GOP for a generation, severing all ties with a constituency just as its population is bulging in three crucial presidential battleground states."

Matthew Continetti of the *National Review* echoed that sentiment. "The speed with which prominent Republican officials and conservative spokesmen condemned Donald Trump's proposal to ban Muslims from entering the United States revealed the true stakes in the 2016 election. The future of the GOP as we know it is in question—not the party's political future but its ideological one. Donald Trump's candidacy is already intensifying party divisions. Nominating him would alter the character of the Republican Party in a fundamental way," Continetti wrote on December 12.

Retired ABC News anchor Ted Koppel revived the counterintuitive argument that getting tough on terrorists somehow created more terrorists.

"They think they're being tough on ISIS and Trump thinks he's being tough on ISIS. [But in truth] Donald Trump is, in effect, the recruiter in chief for ISIS. ISIS wants nothing more right now than to have the world divided into Judeo-Christian on one side and the Islamic world on the other. It's exactly what Trump is doing for them," Koppel said on NBC.

Tom Friedman of the *New York Times* made the same argument: "Trump, by alienating the Muslim world with his call for a ban on Muslims entering the United States, is acting as the Islamic State's secret agent."

And it would not be a controversy without Bill Kristol declaring we had reached peak Trump again, which he did on December 10.

So what did Nation of Islam leader Louis Farrakhan, America's highest profile Muslim leader, think? No one in the mainstream media asked, but Paul Joseph Watson of the conspiratorial *Infowars* show did.

"Farrakhan drew attention to the Obama administration's disastrous policy of arming jihadists in Libya and Syria, noting that the blowback had, 'created a refugee crisis that is destabilizing the countries in Europe,'" Watson reported on January 11, 2016.

"'So when Mr. Trump said we can't allow these Muslim refugees into America, a lot of people were upset with him, but I know the hatred for America in the Muslim world is building," said Farrakhan, adding that US foreign policy had united Islamists against the West.

"'So in this way I think Mr. Trump is wise to vet anyone coming from that area into America because the hatred for America is in the streets now,' asserted Farrakhan, adding that if the US wasn't careful about the vetting process, it might be inviting its own destruction."

Also, not every journalist was ignorant of history.

"Almost every public figure appraising Republican presidential front-runner Donald Trump's proposed moratorium on Muslim immigration and travel to the US has reacted with horror, but the ban would not necessarily be unconstitutional, experts say. Recent US immigration history, in fact, is full of examples of discrimination against minority groups. Throughout the Cold War, non-citizen socialists were deported, and gays could be booted as 'sexual deviants' until 1990. An entry ban on HIV-positive people wasn't fully repealed until 2010," Steve Nelson of *US News and World Report* wrote on December 8.

However, lost amid all the vitriol pundits directed at Trump was any acknowledgement of the shift in leadership. Few pundits took notice of Obama's reaction and even less attention was given to Hillary Clinton's reaction. This was odd, considering the former was president, and the latter had been secretary of state. They should be the experts, not some reality-show celebrity, right?

CHAPTER 24

SCHLONGED.

———————

In the 1978 comedy *Animal House*, Dean Vernon Wormer thought he finally defeated Delta Tau Chi by revoking its charter and expelling its members. As the frat boys packed to leave Delta House, Bluto rallied them to their one last stand against the dean.

> D-DAY: War's over, man. Wormer dropped the big one.
> BLUTO: What? Over? Did you say over? Nothing is over until we decide it is! Was it over when the Germans bombed Pearl Harbor? Hell no!
> OTTER: Germans?
> BOONE: Forget it. He is rolling.

Throughout the campaign, supporters of Donald Trump often quoted Boone when their candidate said something indefensible. Telling it like it means never having to say you are sorry, to paraphrase another movie. At a rally in Grand Rapids, Michigan, on December 21, 2015, Trump discussed the 2008 Democratic presidential nomination race, when Barack Obama defeated the heavily favored Hillary Clinton.

"I may win, I may not win. But Hillary—that's not a president. Everything that's been involved in Hillary has been losses. Even her race to Obama, she was going to beat Obama. I don't know who'd be worse. I don't know. How does it get worse? She was favored to win, and she got schlonged," Trump said.

Schlonged?

He had thrown red tofu to his critics.

"What we're going to see—and what we got a taste of last night—was the misogynistic attacks on Hillary Clinton," David Brock, founder of a pro-Clinton super PAC, told MSNBC the next day.

Clinton's spokeswoman, Jennifer Palmieri, reacted angrily. "We are not responding to Trump but everyone who understands the humiliation this degrading language inflicts on all women should," Palmieri responded in a tweet.

Many interpreted schlonged as fornication.

"Who had 'Yiddish anatomical insult' in the Trump-offense ghoul pool?" Matt Taibbi of *Rolling Stone* tweeted.

Stuart Varney edited the schlonged clip when he showed it on his show on Fox Business News. "We bleeped it out—that was a reference to a male anatomy, OK? We bleeped it out," Varney told his audience.

But was "schlonged" really a synonym for fornication? NBC analyst Jeff Greenfield asked a few linguistic scholars and found that while the noun *schlong* is Yiddish for penis, the verb *schlonged* is not.

"On further review, Trump is right on this. 'I got schlonged' is a commonplace New York way of saying: 'I lost big time,' without the genital reference," Greenfield tweeted on December 22.

Several people found earlier uses of *schlonged* in previous elections, including Fritz Mondale's forty-nine-state loss to Reagan in 1984, when Geraldine Ferraro was his running mate.

So what was going on? *Dilbert* cartoonist Scott Adams gave a four-part explanation in a blog post on December 24. He said Trump knew what he was doing, and he schlonged the press.

"1. Schlonged has just enough deniability built into it (similar to saying someone sucks) that Trump could almost-sort-of-but-not-quite explain it away. That almost-but-not quite quality makes it news," he wrote.

His second point was the word sounded fun, like *osso buco*. His third point was people like schlongs. His was not a dry academic analysis.

"4. Schlongs also make you think of Bill Clinton and how hard Hillary must have tried to get a lock on his schlong. That doesn't help her," Adams wrote.

Bingo. Like Obama before him, Trump had schlonged the Clintons. Trump planned this. People mistook his extemporaneous speaking style for being undisciplined, but he had mastered speaking from an outline instead of a script.

Timing is everything in comedy and politics. This nontroversy was fun and light. People do like schlongs. And the story broke just in time for the Christmas break when politicians wisely took a time-out so their voters could relax for a few days. He dominated the news cycles without intruding on the public.

He did so by being newsworthy. When I was a young reporter, Tom Roser edited my work at the *Stars & Stripes*. One day, he pulled me aside and said there were a hundred thousand soldiers in Europe. Each one had a story. Most were boring. My job was to find the ones that weren't. Trump might have been a boor, but he was never boring. The media that fed off him resented this from the beginning.

"Trump is surging in the polls because the news media has consistently focused on him since he announced his candidacy on June 16," John Sides of the *Washington Post* reported on July 20.

He won the news cycles. They whined.

"The pity is this: this is the strongest field of Republican candidates in 35 years. You could pick a dozen of them at random and have the strongest Cabinet America has had in our lifetime, and instead, all of our time is spent discussing this rodeo clown," Krauthammer said on July 5.

A liberal editor agreed. "Here's a shocker, we are living in anti-establishment times. Who knew we would be sitting here September 6 looking at this landscape. This is a time you don't want to make predictions. It is a fluid rewrite the rules time. Now, this has been summer of Trump, but I think the media has done a great disservice to this country: wall to wall coverage of a bully. And has virtually ignored Bernie Sanders who is today -- but why, it's wall-to-wall coverage, wall-to-wall. It is free air time. It is obsessive. And I think in that it is a disservice. And gatekeepers are defining what is viable," Katrina vanden Heuvel, editor and publisher of the *Nation*, said on ABC on September 6, 2015.

Matthew Dickinson, a professor of political science at Middlebury College, earlier called on the media to get tough on Trump.

"Journalists should take his candidacy seriously by pressing him on the details of his policy pronouncements, and helping the public understand the differences between the public and private sector. The sooner the media begins evaluating The Donald on the details of his policies and his governing expertise, rather than on his deliberately provocative comments designed to mobilize a disaffected public, the sooner The Donald's political bubble is likely to burst," Dickinson wrote on July 19.

The idea of an army of Goliaths in the media ganging up on a candidate was decidedly unjournalistic, but not unprecedented because they took down Sarah Palin in 2008. But in Trump's case, the Goliaths of Washington were over their heads. He had wrestled to a draw the King Kongs of media in New York.

Critics began counting how much air time Trump received. The Media Research Center found that from August 7 to August 20, 2015, Trump received nearly seventy minutes of time on the nightly newscasts of ABC, CBS and NBC. The other sixteen Republican candidates split less than twenty-eight minutes among them.

Well, they just were not very interesting. Trump was. If you cannot command attention, how can you lead the free world?

Media Matters For America, a liberal group funded tax-free by billionaire George Soros, attacked only Fox News for giving him free air time.

"Fox News gave GOP presidential frontrunner Donald Trump at least $29.7 million in free airtime from May 2015 through the end of the year," the center reported on January 16, 2016.

But the site did not calculate the value of his air time on ABC, CBS, CNN, MSNBC, NBC, and other news networks. And Trump did all the networks, almost any time of day. While most Republicans disliked MSNBC, Trump became a fixture on that network's *Morning Joe* show.

However, the constant exposure ran the risk of the Charo effect. Charo was a Spanish singer and comedian who was a fixture on television talk shows in the 1970s and 1980s, who wore out her welcome after a decade or so. And unlike paid media—commercials—Trump had little control of the content.

But The Donald took the risk and reaped the reward. Trump was not buying air time with other people's money. Instead, he went on every news channel and answered every question. He gave cable news access like no other candidate.

Trump's mastery of the news led to a comical situation in which after airing a report on the highlights of Trump's latest free-wheeling speech, the news network would air a commercial showing Jeb Bush delivering the same boring speech to the same small crowd that aired in the same commercial the day before. In mid-July 2015, the two sat at 16 percent each on the *RealClear Politics* poll average. By year's end, Trump stood at 35 percent and Bush at 4.3 percent. Bush had spent $49 million on television ads. Trump had spent zero at that point.

Earned media was a controversy throughout the campaign. On March 1, as the results came in from the Super Tuesday primaries and caucuses, on Fox News Megyn Kelly and media critic Howard Kurtz discussed media coverage of the race.

> KELLY: If you look at the numbers even on the nightly newscasts, the time they devoted just last night to Donald Trump versus the other two, it was six minutes Trump, I think seven seconds, Rubio. I mean, the disparity was remarkable.
>
> KURTZ: There's a clear imbalance. And we've all had banners awaiting Trump news conference, which shows how he can hijack the news cycle. But a lot of that attention has been negative. But because Trump rode so vociferously

against the media, even negative attention helps him, because his fans say the media is just part of the establishment—the political establishment. We like the fact that he pushes back, talks about for example loosening the libel law to make it easier to sue news organizations. So Senator Cruz, I guess, has a point and now he has a talking point in at least one state outside of his home state, but it's still an uphill battle and the establishment is apoplectic now about Trump.

For years, television pundits complained about all the money rich donors spent on political campaigns, even while their networks milked elections for advertising revenue. Trump minimized ad purchases by maximizing news coverage. Now the talking heads complained that was unfair.

As the schlonging showed, Trump played the political experts with ease. They took his bait in an effort to discredit him. In so doing, they trapped themselves into giving him wall-to-wall television coverage over the Christmas weekend while he relaxed at Mar-a-Lago with his wife, children, and grandchildren.

Schlonged gave way to Auld Lang Syne, and Pulitzer Prize-winning humorist Dave Barry wrote his annual year-in-review column.

"On the political front, the big story is Donald Trump, who declares his candidacy for president and lays out a bold, far-reaching vision for America consisting of whatever thought is flitting through his mind at that particular moment. Trump is deemed to have no chance by veteran Washington-based political experts with vast knowledge of what all the other veteran Washington-based political experts think," Barry wrote.

On New Year's Eve, Krauthammer disclosed his winner of year, a choice that Ed Henry said surprised him.

"Well, you should be, but you should also remember that I'm a straight shooter. The obvious political winner in the United States this year is Donald Trump. The most astonishing, unexpected political rise in recent American political history. I would say with the exception of Jeremy Corbyn becoming the leader of the Labour Party, you know, a board-certified communist, the most unlikely. And, you know, I never let feelings get in the way of my ironclad judgment. Although I would say that the thing that probably tipped me over is when Trump, after a lot of hesitation, came out against the killing of journalists. That's what sealed the deal for me," Krauthammer said.

Henry then played a video clip of Trump, saying, "I mean, I got to tell you, Krauthammer is terrible. He is so unfair to me. He is the worst. He is the worst. And I'm not allowed to criticize him, so I am going to be very nice. Krauthammer, he is terrible, he's terrible. You have a guy named Steven Hayes. I never heard of this guy. When my name is mentioned, it's like he is a boil. He goes crazy."

To that, Krauthammer replied, "Let me just say, Mr. Trump, or Mr. Thrump, no diphthong in Krauthammer."

The good doctor knew candor and humor were good for the head. His fellow pundits in Washington could have used a few similar little mental-health therapies, even if they were the kind poured over ice and topped with a small ornamental umbrella.

And the Clintons should have stocked up on their favorite adult beverages because Trump launched the new year with his first paid television ad campaign. His target was not his Republican rivals but rather Bill Clinton's schlong.

The narrative from political experts was that Clinton would cream Trump in the general election because of the gender gap.

"Donald Trump's verbal attacks on women have done little to dent his meteoric rise, but a deeper look at his polling shows the threat of a gender gap ripping open if he becomes the GOP nominee. The billionaire businessman outdid himself during a rally in Michigan on Monday night, mocking Hillary Clinton for a disgusting bathroom trip she made during the most recent Democratic debate and commenting that Barack Obama schlonged her in the 2008 primaries," Steven Shepard of *Politico* wrote.

However, columnist Ruth Marcus of the *Washington Post* disagreed with this presumption of invulnerability for Clinton among women voters.

"Into this gender minefield lumbers Trump, characteristically unbound and deploying a weapon that none of Clinton's Democratic opponents, past or present, has dared to mention. He played the Bill Card," Marcus wrote on December 28.

After pointing out how President Clinton preyed on women in the workplace, Marcus said ordinarily the sins of the husband are not visited upon the spouse.

"But Hillary Clinton has made two moves that lead me, gulp, to agree with Trump on the fair game front. She is (smartly) using her husband as a campaign surrogate, and simultaneously (correctly) calling Trump sexist. These moves open a dangerous door. It should surprise no one that Trump has barged right through it," Marcus wrote.

She did not know the half of it. Trump was about to launch his first television ad campaign. Two days after the Marcus column appeared, police charged comedian Bill Cosby with sexual assault in Pennsylvania. Also, Mrs. Clinton's top aide was Huma Abedin, whose husband, Anthony Weiner, had resigned from Congress on June 21, 2011, after tweeting a picture of a bulge in his underpants.

The audio of Trump's ad was simply a clip of Hillary Clinton's speech on April 5, 2013, to the Women in the World Summit: "Women's rights are human rights and human rights are women's rights once and for all. Let's keep fighting for opportunity and dignity."

The images, though, were of her, her husband, one of his paramours, Anthony Weiner, and lastly, Bill Cosby and her.

The ad ended with the screen turning black as her audio clip ended. Flashed in white letters were "true defender of women's rights" first, followed by "Trump, Make America Great Again!"

Trump, who had openly admitted to cheating on his first wife, dared to go there. He pointed out Clinton helped punish women who complained about her husband's mistreatment of them.

"She's not a victim. She was an enabler. She worked with him. Some of these women have been destroyed, and Hillary worked with him," Trump told Fox News on January 11, 2016.

He pointed to President Clinton settling Paula Jones's sexual harassment lawsuit for every penny of the $850,000 she sought. That lawsuit led to his impeachment trial and a five-year suspension of his law license because he committed perjury in deposition by denying he had an affair with Monica Lewinsky, which the lawyers for Jones wanted to use to help establish a pattern of sexual harassment by Clinton, even though that affair was consensual.

Within a week of the ad's premiere, Mrs. Clinton's twenty-four-point lead in the *RealClear Politics* poll average dropped to 8.6 points.

Trump had shown in one ad that he could schlong Bill Clinton.

C H A P T E R   2 5

NOTES FROM THE FRONT.

———◆———

THE NEW YEAR BEGAN WITH Trump doing something on January 5 no Republican had done probably since Alf Landon. Trump campaigned for the Vermont primary. Radio talker Mark Steyn also did something few pundits did in the campaign. He attended.

Most other pundits based their opinions on surveys. The numbers in polls made them seem scientific when they were not. But a typical pontification appeared in the *Atlantic Monthly* on March 1, 2016: "Who Are Donald Trump's Supporters, Really?" The story included not one quote from a Trump supporter. The story was all about polls in which callers asked anonymous people what demographic group they belonged to, followed by a string of multiple choice questions. Do not get me wrong. If properly designed, such polls are useful.

The story was not useful. It merely displayed the magazine's grand prejudices. "Non-college men have been trampled by globalization, the dissolution of manufacturing employment, and other factors, for the last few decades. In places like West Virginia, the mortality rate for middle-aged white men has grown since 1980, despite the fact that US GDP per capita has quadrupled in that time. The causes are mysterious, but one outcome could be deep anger and political extremism manifested in Trump," the story said.

The language was inflammatory. The press loved to stereotype Trump's supporters as angry white men in West Virginia who were goose-stepping to Trump's tune. That tune went: Springtime for Donald and hillbillies./ Winter for nonwhites and France.

If ignorant rednecks were the base of his support, why was Trump drawing so much support in New England? On Super Tuesday, his best results were in Massachusetts, where he drew 49.3 percent of the vote in a five-man race in the most educated state in the nation. Something was going on that spreadsheets and stereotypes could not explain.

Rather than just read the polls and extrapolate from the numbers who the Trump voters are, CNN applied journalism. It dispatched reporters to thirty-one cities to talk to 150 Trump supporters face-to-face.

"The voters pledging their allegiance to the Republican front-runner hail from all corners of the country. They work on farms, in nursing homes and run small businesses; they've voted for Mitt Romney and Barack Obama and participated in the tea party movement; they are high school students who will vote for the first time this November and retirees and veterans who came of age during World War II," CNN reported on January 28.

Trump's plan to keep out illegal immigrants attracted some naturalized citizens. At a Trump rally in Burlington, Iowa, Terry Sweet spoke of his wife, a native of the Philippines.

"It's not fair to her to let the illegals stay here. She does everything right. She works, she pays taxes, she votes," he said.

Other Trump supporters also favored immigration.

"If we have them all come in, they've all been inspected, and they've all gone through the rules and regulations to become a citizen, I want more. The more the merrier," Sherry Schell said at a rally in Sarasota, Florida.

Some Trump supporters opposed immigration.

"The people that are coming in here from China, Indonesia, and all of them countries, they're getting pregnant and coming here and having babies. They get everything, and the people that were born here can't get everything," Paul Weber said at a rally in Waterloo, Iowa.

Trump held rallies everywhere. Steyn had a great time at the one in Burlington, Vermont. Far from being Hitler at his Nuremberg Rally in 1934, Trump rocked and rolled a packed house that had to turn away hundreds. On January 9, Steyn wrote this description:

Trump has no teleprompters. He walks out, pulls a couple of pieces of folded paper from his pocket, and then starts talking. Somewhere in there is the germ of a stump speech, but it would bore him to do the same poll-tested focus-grouped thing night after night, so he basically riffs on whatever's on his mind. This can lead to some odd juxtapositions: One minute he's talking about the Iran deal, the next he detours into how Macy's stock is in the toilet since they dumped Trump ties. But in a strange way it all hangs together: It's both a political speech, and a simultaneous running commentary on his own campaign.

It's also hilarious. I've seen no end of really mediocre shows at the Flynn in the last quarter-century, and I would have to account this the best night's entertainment I've had there with the exception of the great jazz singer Dianne Reeves a few years back. He's way funnier than half the stand-up acts I've seen at the Juste pour rires comedy festival a couple of hours north in Montreal. And I can guarantee that he was funnier than any of the guys trying their hand at Trump Improv night at the Vermont Comedy Club a couple of blocks away. He has a natural comic timing.

However, his timing was not natural but honed by four decades in the media spotlight. He had something rare in modern politics; he could speak without a teleprompter. Perhaps that was what most impressed Steyn, a radio veteran who had to quickly learn to ad lib.

Obviously, Trump's speeches impressed voters because he made his political points using humor instead of hectoring audiences. His critics called him a carnival barker. What's wrong with that? Carnivals are a business. Fail to deliver, and you're fired.

Trump delivered.

CHAPTER 26

NEW YORK VALUES.

———◆———

IN THE EARLY 1990S, PACE Foods of Paris, Texas, launched a national television campaign for its signature picante sauce. The ad showed cowboys eating over a campfire. When the cook brings out more picante sauce, it was not Pace but another brand. A cowboy looked at the label and said they made the sauce in New York City.

New York City?

"Get a rope," another cowboy said, as the commercial ended.

Cruz was the senator from Texas, although he had spent fifteen of the last twenty years in Washington. He chastised Trump for a 1999 interview on *Meet the Press* with Tim Russert. Trump told Russert he had New York values.

"I've lived in New York City in Manhattan all my life, OK? So, you know, my views are a little bit different than if I lived in Iowa," Trump said.

New York City?

Get a rope.

In mid-January, Cruz made a big deal about Trump's New York values. On the Howie Carr radio show on January 13, Cruz said, "Listen, The Donald seems to be a little bit rattled."

Two nights later, at the sixth debate, this time on Fox Business News, moderator Maria Bartiromo asked Cruz just what he meant when he said Trump embodied New York values.

CRUZ: You know, I think most people know exactly what New
    York values are.
(LAUGHTER)
BARTIROMO: I am from New York. I don't.
CRUZ: What—what—you're from New York? So you might not.

At that point Cruz, a champion debater, should have backed off. He did
not. They were in South Carolina. He thought he was playing to the
crowd. He ended his answer, "And I guess I can frame it another way.
Not a lot of conservatives come out of Manhattan. I'm just saying."

Cruz's father was a native of Cuba and an evangelist. Trump had
mocked that saying not many evangelists came out of Cuba, a largely
Catholic country.

When Cruz finished, Trump laid into him.

TRUMP: Conservatives actually do come out of Manhattan,
    including William F. Buckley and others, just so you
    understand.
(APPLAUSE)
TRUMP: And just so—if I could, because he insulted a lot of
    people. I've had more calls on that statement that Ted
    made—New York is a great place. It's got great people,
    it's got loving people, wonderful people. When the World
    Trade Center came down, I saw something that no place
    on Earth could have handled more beautifully, more
    humanely than New York. You had two one hundred—
(APPLAUSE)
TRUMP: You had two 110-story buildings come crashing down.
    I saw them come down. Thousands of people killed, and
    the cleanup started the next day, and it was the most hor-
    rific cleanup, probably in the history of doing this, and
    in construction. I was down there, and I've never seen
    anything like it. And the people in New York fought and

fought and fought, and we saw more death, and even the smell of death—nobody understood it. And it was with us for months, the smell, the air. And we rebuilt downtown Manhattan, and everybody in the world watched and everybody in the world loved New York and loved New Yorkers. And I have to tell you, that was a very insulting statement that Ted made.

The audience applauded Trump's response, as did Trump's critics.

"Trump is right about the smell. It was the thing you couldn't imagine unless you were nearby. And it lingered for nine months," Podhoretz tweeted middebate.

"Yes—acrid, covered our town, and due to the fires that wouldn't die down deep at the site. It was the computers," Peggy Noonan of the *Wall Street Journal* tweeted back.

The next day, Mia Farrow tweeted a photo of firefighters at Ground Zero. Her caption was simply, "#NewYorkValues."

Trump had framed New York values properly. Manhattan and the rest of New York City went through hell on 9/11. Response to that horror decimated their police and fire forces. Mayor Rudy Giuliani attended hundreds of funerals, but through his tears, he kept the city together. He became America's mayor on 9/11.

The *New York Times* reported that Cruz, too, had united the city.

"That comment did something that might have seemed unthinkable only a week ago. It aligned Mr. Trump, a leading Republican contender for president, with three Democrats: New York's governor, Andrew M. Cuomo; New York City's proudly liberal mayor, Bill de Blasio; and even presidential candidate Hillary Clinton," the *Times* reported on January 16.

Mike Lupica, an anti-Trump columnist at the *New York Daily News*, lit into Cruz on January 15.

"He should go talk to people in the Rockaways or Staten Island, the hardened survivors who bound together after Hurricane Sandy, about New York values. Or finally he should go all the way downtown, and back to September 2001. Here is what New York values are: New York values are a young guy, a paralegal, literally giving somebody he doesn't know the shirt off his back on a subway because winter has finally come to the city and brought freezing temperatures with it. New York values are the New York taxi driver who traveled three boroughs across four days to find the guy who had left $1,400 in his cab, so he could return the money to him. You know what that really was? It was the real life of a city that Ted Cruz knows nothing about. He is simply another tourist here, one constantly on the make," Lupica wrote.

(Note to self: do not mock New York values on national television.)

Quinnipiac University poll assistant director Maurice Carroll was among those who exacted revenge on Cruz. He polled New Yorkers on what their values were.

"Note to Sen. Ted Cruz: New York values, as measured by this poll, include a lot of sympathy for homeless adults, kids, and veterans, and a strong desire to do more," Carroll told CNN on January 20.

The numbers were clear: 93 percent were very or somewhat sympathetic to homeless adults; 92 percent were very sympathetic to homeless children; and 84 percent were very sympathetic to homeless veterans.

New Yorkers did not forget. In the New York primary three months later, Cruz collected nary a one of the ninety-five delegates available, while Trump took ninety.

However, radio talker Glenn Beck was among those who said Trump exploited 9/11. A native of Washington state and a resident of Texas, Beck said on his radio show on January 15, "For Donald Trump to play that card was a despicable slap in the face to 9/11."

By the way, David Pace began his picante sauce company in 1947 in Paris, Texas, population 26,000. His national campaign in the 1990s worked by raising the sauce's profile. This enabled Pace to sell his company to Campbell Soup of Camden, New Jersey, for more than $1 billion.

Camden, New Jersey?

Get a rope.

CHAPTER 27

HE-MAN TRUMP-HATERS CLUB.

———◆———

AFTER GOING OH-FOR-2015 AGAINST TRUMP, twenty-two members of the conservative commentariat decided to go all in against him. The *National Review* published a very special edition on January 21—dated February 15, 2016—called "Against Trump." This was a last-ditch effort to stop the Trump Train.

"Some conservatives have made it their business to make excuses for Trump and duly get pats on the head from him. Count us out. Donald Trump is a menace to American conservatism who would take the work of generations and trample it underfoot in behalf of a populism as heedless and crude as The Donald himself," the magazine said in an editorial.

The call for civility came from a magazine whose editor had said on national television, "Carly cut his balls off with the precision of a surgeon." Each of the twenty-two signers wrote their feelings about him.

"Sure, Trump's potential primary victory would provide Hillary Clinton with the easiest imaginable path to the White House. But it's far worse than that. If Donald Trump wins the Republican nomination, there will once again be no opposition to an ever-expanding government. This is a crisis for conservatism. And, once again, this crisis will not go to waste," radio talker Glenn Beck wrote.

"Without even getting into his past support for a massive wealth tax and single-payer health care, his know-nothing protectionism, or his passionate defense of eminent domain, I think we can say that this is a Republican campaign that would have appalled Buckley, Goldwater, and Reagan," David Boaz, executive vice president of the Cato Institute, wrote.

"The GOP base is clearly disgusted and looking for new leadership. Enter Donald Trump, not just with policy prescriptions that challenge the cynical GOP leadership but with an attitude of disdain for that leadership—precisely in line with the sentiment of the base. Many conservatives are relishing this, but ah, the rub. Trump might be the greatest charlatan of them all," L. Brent Bozell III, president of the Media Research Center, wrote.

"Trump has made a career out of egotism, while conservatism implies a certain modesty about government. The two cannot mix," wrote Mona Charen, a senior fellow at the Ethics and Public Policy Center.

Others blasting Trump were Ben Domenech, publisher of the *Federalist*; radio talker Eric Erickson; Steven Hayward, a professor at Pepperdine University; novelist Mark Helprin; Bill Kristol, editor of the *Weekly Standard*; radio talker Dana Loesch; David McIntosh, president of the Club for Growth; radio talker Michael Medved; Edwin Meese III, a longtime staffer for Ronald Reagan; Russell Moore, president of the Ethics and Religious Liberty Commission of the Southern Baptist Convention; former federal judge Michael Mukasey, who was Bush 43's attorney general from 2007 to 2009; Katie Pavlich, editor of *Townhall*; John Podhoretz, editor of *Commentary*; R. R. Reno, editor of *First Things*; Thomas Sowell, a professor at Stanford University; columnist Cal Thomas; and *National Review* staffers Yuval Levin and Andrew McCarthy.

Six of the twenty worked for think tanks, two were professors, and three wrote for subsidized magazines; the *National Review* never showed a profit and lost $25 million in its first fifty years. Thus half the members of the He-Man Trump-Haters Club (and Charen) lived outside the free market, but somehow they understood capitalism better than Trump did.

Tucker Carlson, publisher of the profitable *Daily Caller*, had a problem with that. He wrote about it in a column five days after Against Trump came out.

"Consider the conservative nonprofit establishment, which seems to employ most right-of-center adults in Washington. Over the past 40 years, how much donated money have all those think tanks and foundations consumed? Billions, certainly. (Someone better at math and less prone to melancholy should probably figure out the precise number.) Has America become more conservative over that same period? Come on," Carlson wrote on January 26.

"Most of that cash went to self-perpetuation: Salaries, bonuses, retirement funds, medical, dental, lunches, car services, leases on high-end office space, retreats in Mexico, more fundraising. Unless you were the direct beneficiary of any of that, you'd have to consider it wasted."

He was onto something. He knew the conservative commentariat personally. He saw them not as facilitating the cause but impeding it.

"Conservative voters are being scolded for supporting a candidate they consider conservative, because it would be bad for conservatism? And by the way, the people doing the scolding? They're the ones who've been advocating for open borders, and nation-building in countries whose populations hate us, and trade deals that eliminated jobs while enriching their donors, all while implicitly mocking the base for its worries about abortion and gay marriage, and the pace of demographic change. Now they're telling their voters to shut up and obey, and if they don't, they're liberal," Carlson wrote.

Billionaire Conrad Black already had stood up for Trump in a column in the *National Review* on December 15, 2015.

Donald Trump—who, I should disclose, is an old friend, a fine and generous and loyal man, and a delightful companion—is striking very close to the heart of the American problem: the corrupt, dysfunctional political system and the dishonest media. My view, as persevering readers know, is that it all started to go horribly wrong with Watergate, when one of the most successful administrations in the country's history was torn apart for no remotely adequate reason and the mendacious assassins in the liberal media have been awarding themselves prizes and commendations for 40 years since. Ten times as many people believe Rush Limbaugh as Bob Woodward (and they are correct in that assessment), and Donald speaks in fact (obviously not ex officio) for many more people than Obama. I suspect the Bush-Clinton era, which had its moments, is ending, and that whatever happens next year, Donald Trump will have played an important role in it. But the desperation prayer of the liberals—that he will split the Republicans—will not happen: He was never going to run as an independent, and the Republicans recognize how great a bloc of voters he can bring to them. To adapt George Wallace's old phrase, he has shaken the American political system "by the eyeteeth," and it will be better for it.

The *National Review* and the tax-exempt class were the eyeteeth. They did not like being shaken or even stirred. Just like liberals in Washington, conservatives in Washington had their theory of how the world should run and to hell with the consequences. Theirs was a caveman conservatism. Free trade good, ugh. Tariffs bad, ugh. Immigration good, ugh. Walls bad, ugh. Military intervention good, ugh. And so on. If you disagreed or even dared question their beliefs, they accused you of hating Reagan.

Their hissy fit, as they say in Calhoun County, was not without precedent. The *National Review* ran similar temper tantrums against Patrick Buchanan's 1992 presidential campaign and Newt Gingrich's in 2012. In both cases, the magazine stopped conservative populist candidates and helped the Democratic Party candidate win. The *National Review* did not care. It was the oldest conservative publication in Washington. It rebuffed any threat from the right to its prominence, even if that empowered the left.

The very special edition of the *National Review* was great marketing. If Trump became president, the twenty-two would be the loyal opposition. If Trump lost, the twenty-two would be in the driver's seat to pick the 2020 nominee. However, their opposition to him showed independents and Democrats that Trump was not a caveman conservative, making him more attractive as a general election candidate.

Indeed, three months after the very special edition, Jonah Goldberg used the stalwart opposition to Trump in a fund-raising plea to readers.

"It's much more painful to pick fights with your friends. Our ideas become more difficult to lift when so many walk away from the effort. It's harder to stand up for your principles when former allies are trying to tear you down. But, simply put, this is the life we have chosen," Goldberg wrote on April 27.

"And since I started working here almost 20 years ago, I have never been more proud of *National Review* than I have been in 2016. We've refused to go with the flow at precisely the moment so many are getting on the bandwagon. (I take clichés and beat them to death with mixed metaphors.) Yes, we've lost some treasured longtime friends, but we've gained some wonderful new ones. We can lament the losses and hope they are temporary, but none of us regret doing what we felt was right: Standing up for our principles, telling the truth as we see it, and reporting the facts as we find them."

After months of predicting the demise of Donald Trump, on February 1, professional conservatives in Washington and New York City finally got to hit send on the obituaries they had written for him months earlier. That was the night of the Iowa caucuses. Cruz won 27.6 percent of the votes, good for eight delegates; Trump had 24.3 percent, good for seven delegates; and Rubio had 23.1 percent, good for six delegates.

The media hailed this as a great loss for Trump, a good showing for Cruz, and a huge victory for Rubio. The *New York Daily News* put clown makeup on a picture of The Donald on page one and headlined it, "Dead Clown Walking."

"*National Review* takes a victory lap over Trump," *Politico* reported.

Cruz won by 3.3 points after camping in Iowa for months.

"This is an enormous win. Ted Cruz is a conservative. There's no doubt about his principles," Editor Rich Lowry told Fox News.

Meanwhile, Fox News heralded as the reason for Trump's second-place finish his decision to skip the seventh debate a few days before the vote on Fox News.

The basis for this self-congratulations was that polls showed Trump would win and understated Rubio's performance. Rather than question the veracity of the polls (the vaunted Iowa Poll averaged a 7.5-point error in the previous nine contested races going back to 1988), the conservative commentariat spiked the ball, starting with David Brooks of the *New York Times*.

"In Iowa on Monday night, we saw the limit of Trump's appeal. Like any other piece of showbiz theatrics, Trump was more spectacle than substance. Many supporters may have been interested in symbolically sticking their thumb in somebody's eye, but they are reality TV watchers, not actually interested in politics or governance. They didn't show up. We can expect similar Trump underperformance in state after state," Brooks wrote.

After seven months, Brooks still saw Trump as a mere celebrity. "What happened in Iowa was that some version of normalcy returned to the GOP race. The precedents of history have not been rendered irrelevant. Ted Cruz picked up the voters who propelled Rick Santorum and Mike Huckabee to victory in previous caucuses. His is a Tea Party wing in the GOP. But its size and geographic reach is limited," Brooks wrote. "The amazing surge for Marco Rubio shows that the Republican electorate has not gone collectively insane. At the last moment, and in a state that is not naturally friendly to him, a lot of Republicans showed up to support a conservative who could conceivably get elected and govern."

But Trump and Rubio had spent little time in Iowa until the last ten days. The *Washington Post* reported that The Donald spent $300 per vote received in Iowa, Cruz spent $600, and Rubio spent $700. The budget buster was Bush, who spent a whopping $5,200 per vote in Iowa. Of course, others were spending other people's money. Trump spent his own and was prudent.

Still, the conservatives in the La La Land of Washington held a wake for The Donald and the voters he attracted to the party. Krauthammer said this the night after the vote.

> The other story is what's called the anti-establishment lane, which I think it is a complete misunderstanding of what's going on—that somehow Trump and Cruz are identical because they're anti-establishment. There's a huge difference between them: Yes, they're anti-establishment, but Trump is a populist, Cruz is a conservative. So people say, "Well, the anti-establishment vote in Iowa is over 50 percent." But that's the wrong way to look at it. You add up Cruz and Rubio, both of them conservatives, one more conservative fundamentalist if you like than the other. And what you have is 51 percent of Iowa is conservative and one quarter is populist. That tells me that the Republicans are likely to stay with their roots as a conservative party and not accept the siren song of the kind of populism that Trump is championing,

Sean Medlock of the *Daily Caller*, writing under the pen name Jim Treacher, celebrated.

"GOP voters are starting to realize that this isn't an episode of *The Apprentice*. This guy might actually get the nomination if actual Republican voters don't do something about it. I have no idea what will happen in New Hampshire—and neither do you, and neither does anybody else—but I'm tired of elderly Caucasians running for president. The Democrats are already giving us White and Whiter. They're already making us watch as two old coots jostle over the last hush puppy at Golden Corral," he wrote on February 2.

Andrew Rosenthal, editorial page editor of the *New York Times*, piled on. "It's impossible to predict when Donald Trump's supporters will finally have enough of his bombast and bigotry, or when (if ever) he will decide to cancel the 2015–16 season of his reality-show campaign and go home. But if he does, we are getting a pretty good idea of how it will happen—with an epic outburst of petulance," Rosenthal wrote.

While the pundits celebrated Trump finishing only second, another fellow who had won thirty congressional races offered a different take. Democrat John Dingell, who retired in 2015 after sixty years in Congress, tweeted the next day, "The GOP's Iowa Caucus, the morning after: Third is the new first. Second is the new last. And first is the same old crazy."

Dingell also tweeted, "Congratulations to Ted Cruz on winning the critically important primary state that also gave us President Santorum and President Huckabee."

But The Donald was dead, the pundits in Washington assured America. On February 4, 2016, the vice president of the He-Man Trump-Haters Club, Bill Kristol, tweeted, "New Hampshire prediction, 5 days out: Rubio 25, Cruz 22, Trump 19, Kasich 17, others single digits."

As usual, Kristol was wrong.

CHAPTER 28

NOT TAKING IT FOR GRANITE.

———————

TRUMP'S SHOWING IN IOWA HUMBLED him. While supporters said finishing second out of a dozen candidates in his first election was good, Trump did not like losing. On Twitter, he howled that the election was fixed. Then he went to New Hampshire, the Granite State, determined not to lose his big lead in the polls and in fact to bolster that lead in the first-in-the-nation primary.

"Heading into this contest, he was a bit more humble, acknowledging that he needed more than an outsize personality to win elections. He spent more time with voters one on one and allowed reporters more access. He was a bit more composed and—compared with his normal tone—made somewhat fewer controversial comments," Jenna Johnson wrote in the *Washington Post* on February 10, the day after his 19.5-point victory in a nine-candidate field.

Having ducked the Fox News debate before the Iowa caucuses, Trump showed up for the ABC News debate three nights before the New Hampshire primary. Trump regained the spotlight from Cruz, who had won in Iowa. Despite the usual spin that Trump had lost, the only question after the debate, the question was how big Trump's victory would be in New Hampshire.

Yuge, to use his terminology. Not only did he win by double digits, but he more than doubled the 15.8 percent his nearest rival, Kasich, pulled down. Trump's supporters buried Cruz, Bush, and Rubio. Kristol's numbers were a joke.

The next day, readers of the *New York Daily News* woke up to another silly depiction of Trump, not as a clown this time but as the sinister Joker from the Batman comic books. "Dawn of the Brain Dead," read the caption as it depicted Trump's supporters as zombies: "Clown comes back to life with NH win as mindless zombies turn out in droves."

CNN anchor Jake Tapper took the newspapers and other news agencies to task for deriding Trump and Trump's supporters.

"I think those are business decisions that they are making, not journalistic decisions. They think that will appeal to readers and allow them to carve out a niche to get clicks or have newspapers purchased. But, I think journalistically, to not take Donald Trump seriously is a mistake. And I think journalistically to attack people who support a candidate is the very height of elitism," Tapper told *The Wrap*.

"These are Americans exercising their right to vote and it's important to go out and meet them and talk to them and find out why they're supporting the candidates they're supporting. It's not my approach to journalism. My approach to journalism is to cover what's going on and try to understand it and understand the voters and the candidates, not to mock them."

America needed more journalists like Tapper and fewer pundits.

However, Washington knew best. Charlie Cook, a political-race handicapper who was popular in the capital, blew off the New Hampshire win.

"I still see Trump as more of a protest candidate, a vehicle for the angry, anti-establishment mood among many Republicans, rather than someone who many Republicans will see as a realistic president. It should be remembered that Trump's 34 percent New Hampshire performance means that 66 percent of Republicans did not vote for him," Cook wrote.

But the conservative commentariat was in alarm. The very special edition of the *National Review* failed. One of its collaborators, John Podhoretz panicked. "The most important takeaway, though, is this: The politics of resentment won Tuesday night. It hasn't had a showing like this in the United States maybe since the 1890s," Podhoretz wrote in the *New York Post*, as if people were happy with the status quo in 1932, 1980, or 2008.

"Donald Trump and Sanders have a remarkably similar and remarkably simple message, and it's this: You're being screwed. They agree that international trade is screwing you, that health care companies are screwing you and that Wall Street is screwing you," he wrote.

Of course, all this was true. Government regulations protected big business from competition, while outright subsidies financed some of them.

"Don't look for uplift. Don't seek vision. This is probably going to be the payback election—America at its worst," he wrote.

Trump's campaign was largely self-financed, and Trump was stingy. He did not feed his millions to the consultancy class, which led to great underestimations by the Washington press corps, who took as gospel the word of unemployed political consultants who resented The Donald.

However, he had one overlooked advantage in New Hampshire. His campaign manager, Corey Lewandowski, learned his trade there. This helped Trump prevail.

"He remains the favorite to win Tuesday night's primary, though Republicans in the state expect he will fall short of the 20-plus point lead he has touted on the stump. And that's at least partly due to a refusal to invest in analytics and organizational capacity on the ground—a structural deficit he suffers beyond New Hampshire," *Politico* reported on the day of the primary.

Yes, he fell short of twenty, winning only by 19.5 points. As Joe Kennedy said in a telegram to his son in 1960, "Dear Jack. Don't buy a single vote more than is necessary. I'll be damned if I'm going to pay for a landslide."

Before the primary, Byron York of the *Washington Examiner* asked former governor John Sununu if he knew of any Republicans who were voting for Trump. Sununu said only one, a guy who lived down his street.

He was Lou Gargiulo, chairman of Trump's Rockingham County operation.

"I think like most establishment Republicans, they thought if they kept promoting the narrative that Trump was a passing fancy and he would collapse, it would happen," Gargiulo told York after the election. "But this phenomena is the result of 25+ years of failed promises and lackluster leadership over multiple administrations from both parties. People have had it, and those in power don't want to accept the reality they can no longer maintain the status quo."

After New Hampshire, the conservative commentariat openly opposed the prospect of the Republicans winning back the White House with an outsider.

"Donald Trump is back in the pole position. His commanding performance across almost all demographics and voting blocs in New Hampshire is staggering. Worse, Hillary Clinton's disastrous performance among both swing and core Democratic voters in the Granite State suggests that the flamboyant, vulgar, intemperate businessman may be electable in November," Noah Rothman wrote in *Commentary* magazine the day after the election.

Washington's elite conservatives would rather have the socialist Clinton as president than the socialite Trump.

Given up for dead in Iowa, Trump learned, adapted, and routed the competition in New Hampshire. The next stop was South Carolina, where Bush had all the money, Rubio had all the endorsements, Cruz had all the credentials, and Trump had all the leads in the polls. In South Carolina, Trump gave his critics plenty of ammunition—and then sat back as they blew their feet off.

CHAPTER 29

ROPE-A-POPE.

THUS FAR IN THIS NARRATIVE, I have ignored the other candidates because they were largely as boring as dried oatmeal. But that does not mean I was not fond of a few of them. Bush in particular had been a fine governor of Florida and was instrumental in expanding gun rights as well as stopping a monorail boondoggle.

But having spent more than $100 million of other people's money just to lose big in Iowa and New Hampshire, Bush decided to make South Carolina his last stand. Throughout the campaign, he occasionally rose to a lackluster appearance at a campaign stops, but usually he was more boring than a baseball doubleheader. After an applause line fell flat at a small rally in New Hampshire on February 4, Bush said, "Please clap."

Two weeks later, at a rally in Summerville, South Carolina, Bush responded to calls for him to quit. "It's all been decided, apparently. The pundits have already figured it out. We don't have to go vote. I should stop campaigning maybe."

But he stuck it out, using the last debate before the South Carolina debate to defend his family's honor. That night, Trump spoke out against the second Iraq War. "Who are we fighting with? Who are we fighting for? What are we doing? We have to rebuild our country. But we have to—I'm the only one on this stage that said, 'Do not go into Iraq. Do not attack Iraq.' Nobody else on this stage said that. And I said it loud and strong. And I was in the private sector. I wasn't a politician, fortunately. But I said it, and I said it loud and clear. 'You'll destabilize the Middle East.' That's exactly what happened," Trump said.

That was blasphemy to neoconservatives, but he continued.

> TRUMP: Obviously, the war in Iraq was a big, fat mistake. All right? Now, you can take it any way you want, and it took— it took Jeb Bush, if you remember at the beginning of his announcement, when he announced for president, it took him five days. He went back, it was a mistake, it wasn't a mistake. It took him five days before his people told him what to say, and he ultimately said, "It was a mistake." The war in Iraq, we spent $2 trillion, thousands of lives, we don't even have it. Iran has taken over Iraq with the second-largest oil reserves in the world. Obviously, it was a mistake. George Bush made a mistake. We can make mistakes. But that one was a beauty. We should have never been in Iraq. We have destabilized the Middle East.

Moderator John Dickerson let Bush respond. This was good television.

> BUSH: So here's the deal. I'm sick and tired of Barack Obama blaming my brother for all of the problems that he has had.
> (APPLAUSE)
> BUSH: And, frankly, I could care less about the insults that Donald Trump gives to me. It's blood sport for him. He enjoys it. And I'm glad he's happy about it. But I am sick and tired of him going after my family. My dad is the greatest man alive in my mind.
> (APPLAUSE)
> BUSH: And while Donald Trump was building a reality TV show, my brother was building a security apparatus to keep us safe. And I'm proud of what he did.

(APPLAUSE)

BUSH: And he has had the gall to go after my brother.

TRUMP: The World Trade Center came down during your brother's reign, remember that.

(BOOING)

BUSH: He has had the gall to go after my mother. Hold on. Let me finish. He has had the gall to go after my mother.

TRUMP: That's not keeping us safe.

BUSH: Look, I won the lottery when I was born sixty-three years ago, looked up, and I saw my mom. My mom is the strongest woman I know.

TRUMP: She should be running.

The exchange was brilliant. Having won New Hampshire and now leading in South Carolina, Trump used the national broadcast to advance his general election campaign. He was not going to carry Republican baggage into that race. Hillary Clinton had voted to go to war. His words drew praise from CodePink, a feminist group opposed to Republican wars but not Democratic ones.

"I watched the debate last night and LOVED IT. It felt surreal to hear Donald Trump, the leading Republican contender for President, saying what we at CODEPINK have been shouting to the winds for 14 years now: that Bush and his cronies lied about WMDs, that the Iraq war was catastrophic, and that Bush never 'kept us safe' because 9/11 happened on his watch," CodePink cofounder Medea Benjamin told *Huffington Post*.

Neoconservatives were livid.

"On Monday, Rush Limbaugh lumped Trump in the same league as Michael Moore and Daily Kos bloggers for standing by his Iraq war conspiracy theory. Then on Tuesday, CNN released a poll that found Trump dropped 9 points after the debate—from 40 percent to 31 percent. On Tuesday night, every voter I spoke to at Trump's campaign event in Beaufort, South Carolina disapproved of Trump's comments.

Their views ranged from genuine disgust to mere displeasure," John McCormack of the *Weekly Standard* wrote.

Ah, Michael Moore, the man conservatives loved to hate. Well, one of the many men we loved to hate.

"Trump sounded at times like Michael Moore, and he brought back into the fray a host of poisonous questions that have not been seriously re-litigated since the election of 2008. But of far more concern to me going forward is that Trump's whole line of attack is built upon a highly questionable premise: To wit, that he was a consistent and outspoken opponent of the Bush administration's post-9/11 foreign policy," Charles C. W. Cook wrote in the *National Review.*

Cook insisted that there was no evidence that Trump spoke against the war. However, he did in a cover story in *Esquire* in August 2004. "Look at the war in Iraq and the mess that we're in. I would never have handled it that way. Does anybody really believe that Iraq is going to be a wonderful democracy where people are going to run down to the voting box and gently put in their ballot and the winner is happily going to step up to lead the county? C'mon. Two minutes after we leave, there's going to be a revolution, and the meanest, toughest, smartest, most vicious guy will take over. And he'll have weapons of mass destruction, which Saddam didn't have," Trump said.

However, he expressed those sentiments after the fact. Opponents of Trump dug out a 2002 interview with Howard Stern as evidence that he supported the war. Stern asked him if he supported the war.

"Yeah, I guess so. I wish the first time it was done correctly. Yeah, I guess so," Trump said.

That showed about as much enthusiasm for the war as Jeb Bush had for his lackluster presidential campaign. But thirteen years after the war began, veterans of Iraq War II also lost enthusiasm for the war, especially as Iran and the Islamic State took large swathes of Hussein's kingdom. A Facebook friend, Major James Pollock (retired), MD, explained this. He served with the Air Force Theater Hospital in Balad as part of the 332nd Air Expeditionary Wing in 2005–2006 and again with Special Operations Command in 2008.

"I am a decorated Iraqi veteran, a Wounded Warrior, and very close friends of 200 to 300 Operation Iraqi Freedom veterans. About 90 percent of the Iraq veterans in my circles are very pro-Trump, very anti-McCain, and not too fond of any Bush, including George W. Bush, for several good reasons," he wrote.

McCain's failure to fix problems in the VA hospitals, particularly the one in Phoenix, Arizona, drew particular contempt. Pollock was oddly paralyzed for twenty-nine hours and left with a lifetime of spinal pain due to a rare incident under anesthesia at the VA hospital in Miami, followed by years of whitewashing, as Pollock outlined in a 2015 op-ed. Pollock's military friends respected McCain's Silver Star service and POW status in Vietnam but despised his political career.

"Veterans are winners and envy true and proven leaders like Trump, who may vary on occasional topics but is overall a winners especially in areas central to veterans like border security and dealing with abuser nations," he wrote.

"Concerning Iran, their ability to gain a nuclear weapons for use has not faded. From my Iraq wisdom, (speaking with literally hundreds of the Jihad's worst) it is clear to me that Iran will not use their nuclear weapons as 'leverage' like rational nations, but will deploy them to use when a sufficient quantity of, say 10–100 are ready. The hard right in Iran and the Middle East honestly believe that using them is a must for their pathway to Heaven via their 'Great Imam' returning," Pollock wrote.

He also blasted pundits. "It is obvious to a five-year-old that people like Megyn Kelly, Republican operatives, and the establishment hard heads would love to see a brokered convention, but that is basically stealing an election. I, most veterans, and a large percentage of American voters would be very disturbed to the point of praying that Trump run as an independent," he wrote.

Americans betrayed Iraqi veterans just as they had Vietnam veterans. As the saying goes, the military went to war while everyone else went to the mall.

However, Trump's dump on Bush did shake some neoconservatives out of their slumber.

"Even though Donald Trump raised the shade of Iraq in typically bullying fashion, accusing former President George W. Bush of lying about Saddam Hussein's weapons of mass destruction, he put a finger on a point of neuralgia for Republicans. Indeed, until conservatives can drive this Banquo's ghost from the table, they will remain haunted, divided and unable to offer a governing alternative," Thomas Donnelly of the *Weekly Standard* wrote on February 17.

James Hohmann of the *Washington Post* said Trump lost badly in the debate. Hohmann included Trump's support of Planned Parenthood's nonabortion services. This could doom The Donald.

"Keep in mind that he said this in the buckle of the Bible Belt, just down the road from Furman and Bob Jones universities," Hohmann wrote.

Someday, I will write a piece about all the buckles the Bible Belt has.

Having taken on the conservative sacred cow that is Bush 43, Trump eyed bigger game—Pope Francis. During the South Carolina campaign, Pope Francis visited the Mexican-US border. A week before the visit, Trump called the pope out.

"I think that the pope is a very political person. I think that he doesn't understand the problems our country has. I don't think he understands the danger of the open border that we have with Mexico. Mexico got him to do it because Mexico wants to keep the border just the way it is because they're making a fortune, and we're losing," Trump told Fox Business News on February 11.

The pope's stop was in Juarez, Mexico, across the river from El Paso, Texas.

"He will be calling on us to look with compassion on a group of people who have suffered terribly and perhaps that will lead people to seek out some different solutions than are now being proposed," Bishop Mark Seitz of El Paso, Texas, told CNN.

With ninety-eight million Catholics, Mexico is second only to Brazil in Catholic population. However, the United States is fourth with sixty-six million, falling between the Philippines and fifth-place Italy. Before reaching Mexico, Pope Francis met with Patriarch Kirilli, head of the Russian Orthodox church, which split from Rome a thousand years ago. Obviously, the Holy See was an extraordinary diplomat.

But like many an American pundit, politician, and Rosie O'Donnell, Pope Francis was about to learn you do not thump Trump and walk away unmolested.

"Can a good Catholic vote for this man?" a reporter asked the Holy Father at his border visit on February 18.

Pope Francis made the mistake of answering the question. "Thank God he said I was a politician, because Aristotle defined the human person as 'animal politicus.' So at least I am a human person. As to whether I am a pawn—well, maybe, I don't know. I'll leave that up to your judgment and that of the people. And then, a person who thinks only about building walls, wherever they may be, and not building bridges, is not Christian. This is not in the gospel. As far as what you said about whether I would advise to vote or not to vote, I am not going to get involved in that. I say only that this man is not Christian if he said things like that. We must see if he said things in that way and in this I give the benefit of the doubt," the pope said.

That night on Fox News, Krauthammer tried to defend Pope Francis:

Trump did sort of jump the shark on this, and he reached for it. And you have to wonder, after everybody he has taken on, now he takes on the pope. Who is left? It's the big guy upstairs. Look, the reason I take this lightly is I don't think it be amounts to anything. What the pope said was a general statement that any religious leader could say, "If you only talk about walls and not bridges," that's not good. He does this in a general way. Trump takes it as an attack on him. Cleverly, I think. This is a state, South Carolina, that is not that friendly to papists, and the pope is a papist, apparently. So this is a good play. But it is meaningless. It gives him a day in the news, which is what he does brilliantly day after day. And it's not going to hurt him at all. In fact, it might help him.

Whoever told the pope it was a good idea to call out an American politician like that deserved a spanking. Trump not only called the pope on this one, but he raised the stakes Trump Tower high.

"If and when the Vatican is attacked by ISIS, which as everyone knows is ISIS's ultimate trophy, I can promise you that the pope would have only wished and prayed that Donald Trump would have been president because this would not have happened. ISIS would have been eradicated unlike what is happening now with our all talk, no action politicians," Trump replied.

Trump had taken the wall controversy and connected it to the Muslim refugee crisis, which threatened the very identity of Europe. Rape and violence accompanied the sudden invasion by millions of people fleeing the civil war in the Middle East.

> The Mexican government and its leadership have made many disparaging remarks about me to the pope, because they want to continue to rip off the United States, both on trade and at the border, and they understand I am totally wise to them. The pope only heard one side of the story—he didn't see the crime, the drug trafficking and the negative economic impact the current policies have on the United States. He doesn't see how Mexican leadership is outsmarting President Obama and our leadership in every aspect of negotiation.
>
> For a religious leader to question a person's faith is disgraceful. I am proud to be a Christian and as president I will not allow Christianity to be consistently attacked and weakened, unlike

what is happening now, with our current president. No leader, especially a religious leader, should have the right to question another man's religion or faith. They are using the pope as a pawn and they should be ashamed of themselves for doing so, especially when so many lives are involved and when illegal immigration is so rampant.

Americans sided with Trump on this one. The idea of a foreign leader trying to influence our election was bad enough, but for a *religious* leader to do so was too much. Vatican spokesman Father Federico Lombardi raised the white flag the very next day.

> This wasn't in any way a personal attack, nor an indication of who to vote for. The pope has clearly said he didn't want to get involved in the electoral campaign in the US, and also said that he said what he said on the basis of what he was told [about Trump], hence giving him the benefit of the doubt.
>
> The pope said what we already know, if we followed his teaching and positions: We shouldn't build walls, but bridges. He has always said that, continuously. He also said that in relation to migration in Europe many times. So this is not a specific issue, limited to this particular case. It's his generic view, coherent with the nature of solidarity from the Gospel.

Trump succeeded where Henry VIII failed. Trump had made a pope back down.

Having taken on the Iraq War and the pope, Trump won South Carolina and all its fifty delegates quite handily, despite being outspent by Bush and others, and despite all the Republican establishment in that state backing Rubio. Bush finished fourth and threw in the towel. Cruz and Rubio scrambled to be the great anti-Trump hope of the big donors who ran the party.

CHAPTER 30

RUBIO'S MAGIC MOMENT.

ROARING OUT OF SOUTH CAROLINA, Trump racked up his third straight win in the Nevada caucus on February 23, in a twenty-two-point romp over Rubio. With an eighty-two to seventeen to sixteen lead in delegates over Cruz and Rubio, Trump was in command heading into the eleven-state Super Tuesday contest on March 1.

But Rubio was about to make his move. A slick politician with a working-class background, he was the son of a bartender and a hotel maid from Cuba. Rubio began college on a football scholarship. His was a classic American tale of pulling oneself up by one's bootstraps. He married a Miami Dolphins cheerleader, and after earning the prerequisite law degree, he entered Florida politics, rising quickly to speaker of the House at age thirty-five. His ethnic background, good looks, and charm impressed the right people in the Sunshine State, including Jeb Bush.

In 2010, Rubio risked his career by challenging Governor Charlie Crist for the Republican nomination. With Tea Party support, Rubio ran Crist out of the party and then won a three-man general election when Crist ran as an independent.

However, while Rubio played the part of a young and upcoming political leader, politically, Rubio was an empty suit who listened to donors, not voters. His willingness to join the Gang of Eight, which wanted to grant citizenship to people who broke immigration laws to enter the United States, was a deal breaker for conservatives. Rubio found himself battling fellow Cuban American Cruz for the position as the main challenger to Trump. Cruz had the backing of Christian conservatives, but the establishment found Cruz less than trustworthy.

Trump had the momentum, but Cruz and Rubio were about to break his stride at the debate hosted by CNN and Telemundo on February 26.

Things began well for The Donald.

"My whole theme is make America great again. We don't win anymore as a country. We don't win with trade, we don't win with the military. ISIS, we can't even knock out ISIS, and we will, believe me. We will. We don't win in any capacity with health care. We have terrible health care, Obamacare is going to be repealed and replaced," Trump said. "We just don't win. You look at our borders, they're like Swiss cheese, everybody pours in. We're going to make a great country again. We're going to start winning again. We're going to win a lot, it's going to be a big difference, believe me. It's going to be a big difference."

But Cruz and Rubio decided to gang up on him. Rubio mentioned Trump's 2011 criticism of self-deportation, which maintained that if you deported enough illegal immigrants, the rest would follow on their own. This had worked during the Eisenhower administration. It was a part of Trump's plan in 2016.

Trump's use of Polish workers in construction and his hiring of immigrants in Florida also drew Rubio's wrath. That led to an interesting exchange.

TRUMP: I've hired tens of thousands of people over my lifetime. Tens of thousands.
RUBIO: Many from other countries instead of hiring Americans.
TRUMP: Be quiet. Just be quiet.
(APPLAUSE)
TRUMP: Let me talk. I've hired tens of thousands of people. He brings up something from thirty years ago, it worked out very well. Everybody was happy.

Meanwhile, Cruz attacked Rubio for being part of the Gang of Eight senators who supported amnesty for illegal immigrants. But his main target was Trump, who had donated money to the campaigns of some members of that gang.

"I really find it amazing that Donald believes that he is the one who discovered the issue of illegal immigration. I can tell you, when I ran for Senate here in the state of Texas, I ran promising to lead the fight against amnesty, promising to fight to build a wall. And in 2013, when I was fight against the Gang of Eight amnesty bill, where was Donald? He was firing Dennis Rodman on *Celebrity Apprentice*," Cruz said.

In response, Trump said, "You get along with nobody. You don't have one Republican—you don't have one Republican senator [endorsement], and you work with them every day of your life, although you skipped a lot of time. These are minor details. But you don't have one Republican senator backing you; not one. You don't have the endorsement of one Republican senator and you work with these people. You should be ashamed of yourself."

But Cruz, a master debater, tried to flip his comment:

You know, I actually think Donald is right. He is promising if he's elected he will go and cut deals in Washington. And he's right. He has supported—he has given hundreds of thousands of dollars to Democrats. Anyone who really cared about illegal immigration wouldn't be hiring illegal immigrants. Anyone who really cared about illegal immigration wouldn't be funding Harry Reid and Nancy Pelosi; wouldn't be funding the Gang of Eight. And, you know, he is right. When you stand up to Washington, when you honor the promise you made to the men and women who elected you and say enough with the corruption, enough with the cronyism, let's actually stand for the working men and women of this country, Washington doesn't like it.

Trump did well on Super Tuesday, winning seven of the eleven contests. Cruz took three. And Rubio took Minnesota for his first victory.

"Even though he lost Texas, Donald Trump was the clear winner for the Republican Party on Tuesday, ending the day as the unrivaled favorite for the nomination. On the Democratic side, Hillary Clinton strengthened her momentum, helped in part by a sweep of Southern states with large black voting populations," the *Washington Post* reported.

Cruz had done well and had sole control of second place. However, the donor class looked to the winner-take-all primary coming up in Florida on March 15, and stuck by Rubio. Suddenly, pundits praised Rubio like the North Korean press praised Kim Jong-un, although they fell short of saying he made eighteen holes-in-one in a single round of golf.

"GOP unity must be part of prying the Democrats from the White House and preventing Obama's hard-Left failures from being replaced with, most likely, Hillary Clinton's hard-Left failures, plus grift and graft. Marco Rubio is the only candidate who is inviting the Republican party's raucous factions into the same boat to row, in unison, toward the White House," syndicated columnist Deroy Murdock wrote in the *National Review* on March 1.

However, there were holdouts. A week later, Matt Lewis of the *Daily Caller* was not sure if he should back Rubio or Cruz:

Rubio has the potential to defeat Hillary Clinton and to be a very good president, but I could be wrong. At this point, I'm like the mom who wants to set her little girl up with the perfect young man she just met. But such an "arranged" marriage might not work; mom might not really know best. Still, not to sound paternalistic, but it's hard to sit by and watch people you love make the mistake of their lives by marrying the wrong person. This is especially true when the perfect young gentleman is right under their nose.

Then again, maybe Rubio's inability to win a GOP primary exposes a fatal flaw. It's possible that enduring a primary campaign tests someone's character, toughness, and mettle.

Campaigns face scandals and crises and hardships, and the ability to overcome these things does tell us something about you. Maybe the voters know more than I do?

Blasphemy. No real pundit ever considers the public is smarter than he. Certainly, the editorial board of the *Orlando Sentinel* never doubted itself.

"Marco Rubio is GOP's last, best hope," the board declared in endorsing him on March 9. The editorial ended, "We don't see eye to eye with Rubio on plenty of issues; his hardline opposition to abortion rights is just one example. But for Florida Republicans who are leery of Trump yet impatient for change, Rubio is now the best hope in the party's 2016 field."

Translation: "We don't see eye to eye" meant "We will endorse Clinton in November anyway."

Also, Lewis made the point that Rubio failed to win fourteen of the first fifteen states. How foolish. Pundits always see victory in defeat and defeat in victory.

"The tossup in Virginia means Rubio gained double digits in that debate," Jay Carney, columnist for the *Washington Examiner*, tweeted on March 1.

By toss-up, he meant a three-point loss by Rubio.

Reviewing the CNN/Telemundo debate, Seth McLaughlin of the *Washington Times* said Rubio had momentum.

"It took six months before the first opponent was able to land a memorable blow against Donald Trump on the debate stage, but Republican strategists—and the other candidates in the race—are hoping they have finally solved their problem with the party's front-runner," McLaughlin wrote.

"The key moment came when Sen. Marco Rubio of Florida leveled a triple-barrel blast at Mr. Trump, accusing him of hiring illegal workers to build Trump Tower, scamming students at Trump University and having little meat on the bones of his health care plan."

Unfortunately, his column appeared the day after Rubio lost fourteen of fifteen states on Super Tuesday.

Trump supporter Ann Coulter could not resist getting a shot in, tweeting on March 1, "Yes, GOP is horribly split! 65 million Americans on one side and 500 pundits, consultants, and lobbyists on the other!"

But Rubio at last he had won a state on Super Tuesday, followed by a win in Puerto Rico on March 6, giving him two of the states and territories that had voted. Two days later came the four-state contest, which made 150 delegates available. Rubio got two delegates.

Next up was Super Saturday, a four-state contest. Trump and Cruz seemed headed to a two-man showdown. Rubio's campaign decided to feud with Donald Trump, which was like him trying to beat Serena Williams at tennis. But provoking Trump was not that difficult. The campaign dusted off the old "small-fingered vulgarian" insult that *Spy* magazine used thirty years earlier to get under his skin. Rubio tested his remarks in a speech the day before Super Tuesday.

"He doesn't sweat because his pores are clogged with the spray tan he uses. Donald is not going to make American great again; he's going to make America orange," Rubio said.

That did not cut it. His next attempt did.

"The other thing he says is he's always calling me little Marco. And I'll admit, he's taller than me. He's like six two, which is why I don't understand why his hands are the size of a guy that's five two. I just see his hands—they're like this—and you know what they say about men with small hands," Rubio said.

After pausing long enough for his audience to snicker, Rubio answered, "You can't trust them!"

Of all the garbage tossed at Trump in the campaign, he took this one personally. Sure, he usually fired back at salvos tossed his way, but for some reason, "small-fingered vulgarian" bothered him to the point that it almost cost him the nomination. At the Fox News debate in Detroit, moderated by Bret Baier, Megyn Kelly, and Chris Wallace, Trump defended his manhood, to the embarrassment of millions.

RUBIO: Let's talk about Donald Trump's strategy and my strategy and Ted's strategy and John Kasich's strategy when it comes to ISIS. And on health care and on the important issues facing this country. But let's be honest too about all this. The media has given these personal attacks that Donald Trump has made an incredible amount of coverage. Let's start talking again about the issues that matter to this country. I'm ready to do that starting right here right now tonight.

BAIER: Mr. Trump, your response?

TRUMP: Well, I also happened to call him a lightweight, OK? And I have said that. So I would like to take that back. He is really not that much of a lightweight. And as far as— and I have to say this, I have to say this. He hit my hands. Nobody has ever hit my hands. I have never heard of this. Look at those hands. Are they small hands?

(LAUGHTER)

TRUMP: And he referred to my hands, if they are small, something else must be small. I guarantee you there is no problem. I guarantee.

BAIER: OK. Moving on.

Trump's refusal to let the damned thing go only encouraged his detractors to repeat it. Instead of castigating Rubio for his below-the-belt attack, Trump's critics embraced it and then called him vulgar for bring it up in the debate.

Well, he was. The debate slowed his momentum. Super Saturday was a split decision, with Trump taking Kentucky and Louisiana and Cruz taking Kansas and Maine. States where Christian conservatives organized well became Cruz territory. But Trump had twelve states, Cruz had six. Trump led Cruz in delegates 390 to 303 heading into a four-state contest on March 8. Trump took three states and seventy-three delegates. Cruz took one state and fifty-nine delegates.

Rubio took one delegate. That's right—one delegate, not state.

This appalled the donor class. Having blown $100 million on Bush—after blowing $400 million on Mitt Romney in 2012—they were desperate to stop Trump, but they stuck by Rubio until the end—which happened a week later, when Rubio lost Florida and dropped out.

You might say, Rubio's campaign came up shorthanded.

CHAPTER 31

IT'S OUR PARTY. WE'LL DESTROY IF WE WANT TO.

———◆———

RUBIO'S FAILURE TO GROW INTO a formidable candidate surprised no one but the upper crust of the party, who were in a panic.

In the movie, *Blazing Saddles*, bandits over ran the town of Rock Ridge, and the people begged Governor William J. Le Petomane for help. He called his cabinet together.

"Holy underwear! Sheriff murdered! Innocent women and children blown to bits! We have to protect our phony baloney jobs here, gentlemen! We must do something about this immediately! Immediately! Immediately! Harrumph! Harrumph! Harrumph," Le Petomane said.

Washington showed the same indifference to the economic plight of Republican voters. From congressional staffers down to the lowly pundits in the press, all they cared about was protecting their phony baloney jobs. Trump threatened their jobs.

Against this background, Mitt Romney made a pilgrimage to Salt Lake City on March 3, 2016, not because he was a Mormon but because he was a politician. Beforehand, he told the press he would make a major announcement that would stop Trump. Pundits hoped Romney would run.

"Could it be a third-party run? Would he selflessly offer himself as the unity candidate? Would he bring some decorum to this pitiful display of anger, corruption, radicalism and unhinged populism we've been subjected to? As bad as he was, he was better than anything going today. I hope he brings a 32-point plan to win back the White House.

Because, truthfully, the only thing a Romney 2016 presidential candidate should be is 'severely' unexciting. It's what America needs," David Harsanyi of the *Federalist* wrote on March 3, 2016.

Selflessly offer himself? He did that in 2012 and pancaked in the general election. But instead of making a major announcement, Romney merely excoriated Trump with a fervor and animus he never displayed against any political opponent, most notably Barack Obama. Trump's ability to dodge the donor class—which he once belonged to—infuriated the big-money interests. They could cut deals with Democrats but feared they could not with The Donald. Romney rode in to rescue the oligarchy.

"He's playing the American public for suckers. He has neither the temperament nor the judgment to be president," Romney said.

Romney also called him a fraud and added, "Dishonesty is Trump's hallmark." Romney also poked fun at his name but not his hands. A person of Romney's stature must exude dignity.

"Think of Donald Trump's personal qualities, the bullying, the greed, the showing off, the misogyny, the absurd third-grade theatrics. We have long referred to him as The Donald. He is the only person in America to whom we have added an article before his name. It wasn't because he had attributes we admired," Romney said.

Trump responded during a rally in Portland, Maine.

"I don't know what happened to him. You can see how loyal he is. He was begging for my endorsement. I could have said, 'Mitt, drop to your knees.' He would have dropped to his knees," Trump said.

He also said Romney should have won in 2012.

"Mitt is indeed a choke artist. He choked like I've never seen anyone choke. Other than Rubio," Trump said.

The Republican Party establishment went all in against Trump, whose losses in Kansas and Maine on March 5, 2016, delighted George Will.

"If Mr. Trump is the nominee, he will be opposed by the most recent Republican nominee, no way Romney could support him, which sort of fits because the Republican nominee will have be—said that the most recent Republican president should have been impeached, which gives you a sense of the chaos," Will said on Fox News on March 6, 2016.

Like many pundits who originally said Trump would not be nominated but would instead destroy the party, Will now advocated destroying the party if Trump won the nomination. "What the Republican Party needs to avoid blowing up is to get a binary choice between Mr. Trump and someone else," Will said.

However, David Stockman, Reagan's first director of the Office of Management and Budget, sided with Trump. Stockman had seen the duplicity in DC firsthand.

"Mitt Romney's viscious public attack on Trump is only the beard. It is merely the censored for-family-TV-version of what the entire neocon establishment and War Party is saying every day in the corridors of Imperial Washington," Stockman wrote on March 19.

"Needless to say, The Donald is taking names and will not be reluctant to do far more than kick offending posteriors. He will make it his business to hound, denounce, denigrate and dispatch the entire passel of neocon power brokers who have declared war on his candidacy."

The neocons knew this, as did their rich patrons. Rather than let the candidates make the case for themselves, the donor class fired a barrage of attack ads. Romney cut robocall endorsements for Rubio. The punditocracy cheered. They organized a #NeverTrump campaign on Twitter.

"In an ideal world the Republican Party would have someone more effective than Romney—a successful, popular two-term president, let's say—available to make the honest broker's #NeverTrump pitch. But we don't live in that world; what the party has in its post-George W. Bush brokenness are various compromised figures, none of whom are ideal anti-Trumps. And I do think Romney's speech would have been better— much better, to my mind—if he had acknowledged as much, by admitting his own mistake in accepting Trump's endorsement four years ago, and casting his intervention now as, in part, an act of penance," Ross Douthat of the *New York Times* wrote on March 3.

And Lowry, editor of the *National Review,* said the same thing about Romney.

"Imperfect messenger? Of course. But what is he supposed to do, sit around wringing his hands in private like so many others? Trump supporters always say that attacking Trump only helps him, but the empirical evidence for that is dubious. (Did it help him to get attacked in Iowa? Or hurt him that he wasn't attacked in New Hampshire?) Of course, if everyone took the advice not to attack Trump, he would coast to the nomination basically untouched, which would suit Trump's supporters just fine. Romney has a megaphone, and has gone out and used it. Good for him," Lowry wrote.

But Jon Meacham, a contributing editor at *Time,* took a different tack.

"Trump has managed to hijack the whole political party, and the pilots are asking why no one is on their side—the passengers are cheering for the guy who took over the plane," Meacham said on MSNBC.

But that showed the passengers did not like where the pilots had the plane headed. The pilots did please the *New York Times.*

"It is an excellent thing that the Republican leaders have noticed the problem they have fostered, now embodied in the Trump candidacy. But until they see the need to alter the views and policies they have expressed for years, removing Mr Trump will not end the party's crisis," the *Times* said in an editorial on March 5.

But Democratic governor Dannel Malloy of Connecticut praised Trump. "He's formidable, he understands voter anxieties, and he will be ruthless against Hillary Clinton. I've gone from denial—'I can't believe anyone would be listening to this guy'—to admiration, in the sense that he's figured out how to capture everyone's angst," Malloy told the *Times* on March 4.

Maggie Gallagher was a voice of reason at the *National Review.* She wondered openly whether the Republican Party was worth saving. "Trump is the symptom, not the cause. What we do next is a hard question. But let's first face the truth of where we are: The old Reagan coalition is dead, destroyed not by social conservatives but by business interests and the Republican elites," Gallagher wrote on March 4.

She nailed the problem. The donor class was willing to destroy the party in order to save the party.

For themselves.

The race was over by mid-March. Paddy Power, the venerable British gambling company, paid off bets on Trump winning the Republican nomination.

But the Republican Party apparatchiks stood in front of the schoolhouse door. There was no way they would allow Trump's riffraff army to win and take over their party. The pundits on the cable news companies accommodated the Republican insiders. The pundits and the party hacks were friends. They framed it as if Trump needed to win in Michigan and Mississippi to regain momentum.

He did. And Hawaii too. The people had spoken. Three days later, Dr. Carson endorsed Trump.

"What I've seen recently is political operatives and parties trying to assert themselves and thwart the will of the people. I find that an extraordinarily dangerous place to be right now. I want the voice of the people to be heard, I want the political process to play out in the way that it should play out. And I don't think the Republican Party would be very wise to adopt a 'let's stop this guy' policy and 'let's promote this guy' policy," Carson said on March 11.

Carson respected the people's decision, but others did not. Power brokers and the media were about to throw the kitchen sink at Trump. Unable to win the battle with better ideas, the Democratic Party launched a campaign intended to paint Trump and his supporters as white supremacists—even his African American supporters such as Troy Morton, who had said Trump showed him how to win.

Washington Republicans went along because the last thing they wanted to do was confront a Democrat. They would rather lose in November than lose their control of the party apparatus.

CHAPTER 32

PARTY LIKE IT'S 1968.

CHICAGO HAD A LONG HISTORY as a violent city. The Haymarket Square labor rally of May 4, 1886, ended with a bombing that killed seven policemen and four civilians. In the St. Valentine's Day Massacre in 1929, Al Capone's gang gunned down seven rival gangsters. In 2015, the city suffered 506 homicides, the most of any city in the land. Its nickname was Chiraq, implying it was as violent as that war-torn nation.

Trump scheduled a rally for March 11, 2016, at the University of Illinois at Chicago, which had on its faculty Bill Ayers, the Weather Underground terrorist, who told the *New York Times* "I don't regret setting bombs," and "I feel we didn't do enough," in an interview published on September 11, 2001. Never imprisoned for his violent crimes, Ayers taught at the university. Ayers was also the man who launched Obama's political career in his kitchen.

Ayers, the black-supremacist group Black Lives Matter, and other well-funded groups such as MoveOn decided to stop the rally. They organized thousands of "protesters" who threatened violence if Trump went ahead with his rally. Trump canceled. However, the Ayers army menaced Trump supporters anyway. Chicago had not seen such political recklessness from the left since the town hosted the Democratic National Convention in 1968.

"We shut Trump down! Beautiful gathering of anti racist youth," Ayers taunted in a tweet that night.

Cruz seized the issue and implied that Trump deserved to have the terrorist Ayers and his violent friends intimidate Trump and his supporters.

"When you have a campaign that disrespects the voters, when you have a campaign that affirmatively encourages violence, when you have campaign that is facing allegations of physical violence against members of the press, you create an environment that only encourages this sort of nasty discourse," Cruz told a rally in Cincinnati the next day.

Indeed, the New York Daily News also implied that Trump deserved to have organized rioters shut him down.

"Donald Trump's divisive hate tour exploded in violence Friday with a bloody stop in St. Louis and chaos in Chicago—while the tone-deaf hate-monger denied his role in the madness," the newspaper said not in an editorial, but as the first sentence in its news report.

However, the Democratic Party had long targeted Trump rallies by sending people to interrupt his speeches, hoping to provoke violence. The hecklers coordinated their efforts, a point the press glossed over. Instead, the press reports called the infiltrators "protesters." Once again, Byron York offered insights few pundits could. He attended rallies. He noted similarities in enthusiasm at Trump's rallies and Obama's in 2008.

"But there was at least one big difference from those old Obama rallies: As a general rule, far right-wing protesters did not systematically disrupt Senator Obama's rallies and as a result, dominate press coverage of those events. Now, the far left-wing version of that disruption has become the story of many Trump gatherings," York wrote in the *Washington Examiner* on December 15, 2015.

The left wanted to hijack news coverage of as many Trump rallies as possible.

"The protesters who come to Trump's events, many of them affiliated with some arm of the Black Lives Matter movement, have refined their techniques. It goes like this: They come to a rally, settle into the crowd, and then one of them begins yelling loudly, causing the crowd to react—usually with a chant of 'Trump! Trump! Trump!'—and then the protester tries to make the inevitable security removal as long and as noisy as possible," York wrote.

"Only after all that is done does another protester repeat the process. Then yet another protester does it. With sequential removals, a small group of demonstrators can screw things up for quite a while."

But the aim was beyond hijacking news coverage. These infiltrators set up the narrative of "violent" Trump rallies, which the press largely and eagerly accepted.

The payoff came on March 11, when Trump canceled at Ayers's college.

Chris Matthews of MSNBC was among the many pundits who blamed Trump for lefty organizers mobilizing mobs to intimidate Trump and his supporters.

> TRUMP: You know we can't have a rally in a major city. Whatever happened to freedom of speech? Whatever happened to the right to get together and speak in a very peaceful manner? So, it's a little bit sad to see this. In fact, it's a lot sad to see this. But, you know, I just felt for the benefit of safety, I don't want to see people hurt. I cancelled it for tonight.
>
> MATTHEWS: So, when you set up rally in Chicago, which is a city which is majority Hispanic and African-American now, I believe the statistics are, that you went into a situation where you knew there would be a lot of people on a Saturday that would have the time and the passion to come out like this fellow we're watching here on tape to come back and protest your situation. So, there was really no surprise here, was there, in what happened? Given the venue of your event tonight?
>
> TRUMP: Chris, it shouldn't matter, it shouldn't matter. You know, you're the first one to say it. It shouldn't matter whether it was whoever lives in the city. I mean, it shouldn't make a difference. Whether it's white, black, Hispanic, it shouldn't matter. I mean, if you have a rally, you have a rally.

Many pundits said Trump deserved it.

"How much blame does Donald Trump deserve for the violence at his rallies? It's a fair question, and the obvious answer is: a lot," Jonah Goldberg wrote.

Goldberg's defense of fascist tactics surprised many of his readers. And this was fascism because the threat of violence suppressed Trump's right to free speech. From Goldberg's perch in Washington, he argued that the shutdown was not necessary.

However, Trump's decision to call off the rally was prudent for two reasons. Not only did he avoid a violent confrontation, but he finally showed America what he faced at rally after rally.

But Mike Lupica of the *New York Daily News* was another fellow who blamed Trump for the actions of Ayers and the rest of the thugs.

"This all didn't happen in a vacuum in Chicago, of course. This wasn't only about Trump supporters on Friday, because the opposition on this night was more organized than a marching band. Moveon.org says that violence at Trump rallies is what produced the violence we saw in Chicago, as if that gives them the high ground here. Fat chance," Lupica wrote.

"Before the fighting had even stopped Friday night, Trump was already saying he was the victim as he made the rounds on the various cable networks. He talked about his First Amendment rights being violated, in the same campaign that has seen him talk about how he wants to 'open up' libel laws so it would be easier to sue newspapers in this country after another 'hit job.'"

But others stood up for Trump. Paul Mulshine of the *Star-Ledger* in New Jersey defended Trump against criticism from Cruz.

"I don't know who advised the Ted to take the side of those Chicago protesters against The Donald, but whoever it was should be canned like a ham," Mulshine wrote.

Mulshine also wrote, "Cruz's blame-the-victim mentality is one more common to liberals. What the heck does 'the culture of a campaign' have to do with a concerted effort by left-wingers to shut down a speaker? When it comes to the culture of campaigns, I know plenty of liberals who would get their panties in a bunch about the culture of Cruz's campaign. But that doesn't give them the right to shout him down at his rallies."

However, Maureen Dowd of the *New York Times* blamed Trump at a barbecue in Austin on the day after the near riot.

"He took a perfectly good reputation as a huckster and turned it into a reputation as a Hitler," Dowd told *Politico*. She added a few minutes later, "As a journalist, it's an exciting thing all the apple carts have been overturned and we're dealing with a lot of chaos, but as a citizen, it's just upsetting and disturbing. It's like 'Night on Bald Mountain'—there's all these forces being unleashed. It's interesting, but it's also frightening."

Likewise, Karen Tumulty of the *Washington Post* blamed the victim. "An already ugly presidential campaign has descended to a new level— one where the question is no longer whether Donald Trump can be stopped on his march to the Republican presidential nomination, but whether it is possible to contain what he has unleashed across the country. Violence at Trump's rallies has escalated sharply, and the reality-show quality of his campaign has taken a more ominous turn in the past few days. On Saturday, a man charged the stage in Dayton, Ohio, and a swarm of Secret Service agents surrounded the GOP front-runner," Tumulty wrote.

But this violence came not from Trump nor his supporters but from a Sanders supporter. She illogically insisted that Trump was responsible for stifling his own free speech, not Ayers and his posse of protesters.

"Now, the outbreak of violence in Chicago had again drawn focus to Trump's temperament and character, as well as whether he has played a role in inciting his supporters," Tumulty wrote.

Andrew McCarthy at the *National Review* cheered the trolls on. "It is ludicrous to argue that, because the hard Left is primarily responsible for the outbreak of chaos and violence that caused Donald Trump's Chicago rally to be canceled last night, it is wrong to condemn the thuggery Trump often encourages at his appearances," McCarthy wrote.

Free speech meant nothing to the conservative commentariat. But the Trump critics were correct: the left was not primarily responsible. It was solely responsible. The actions of Ayers and company were indefensible, but the *National Review* had staked its reputation on stopping him. There was no going back once the magazine crossed the line and began its crusade.

At the *New Yorker*, a very confused Jelani Cobb tried to explain how the violent protesters shutting down Trump were nothing like the violent protesters at the 1968 Chicago convention. The explanation came from a man who had not yet celebrated his first birthday when the convention happened.

"On CNN, John King opined that many of the demonstrators had come 'just to cause trouble,' and Neil Bush, brother to George W. and Jeb, pointed out the similarities between the images coming out of Chicago that evening and those of the chaotic 1968 Democratic Convention. This was a miscasting of history, and yet another demonstration of why the Republican establishment has been so inept in its attempts to contain the Trump phenomenon. It wasn't the demonstrators who recalled the insurgent fury of Chicago in 1968, it was the masses of Trump supporters, fists clenched in a fervor to reroute the country's trajectory, to seize it from those who've taken us down the path of national shame—to make America great again, even if they have to break a few eggs," Cobb wrote on March 12.

Of course it was 1968 all over again. Cobb was in deep denial. The images on television of chanting, militant, and threatening demonstrators shouting down Trump supporters went against the grain of an American people who believe in free speech. If Holocaust survivors in Skokie, Illinois, had to tolerate a march by neo-Nazis in 1977, then surely liberals in Chicago had to allow the Republican front-runner to speak freely to his supporters at University of Illinois at Chicago.

Marc J. Randazza, a Las Vegas-based First Amendment attorney, wrote in a commentary for CNN on March 12, "If you don't stand up for Trump's liberty today, someone may come for yours tomorrow. If we believe in free speech, we need to believe in Trump's as well."

Exactly. Jay Nordlinger of the *National Review* tweeted on the night of the near riots in Chicago, "I'm no Trumpkin. But if protesters shut down his rallies, I'll become one out of defiance and spite. Call it democratic solidarity."

Krauthammer had all weekend to concoct his response to the threat of violence shutting down the rally in Chicago on Friday. His explanation on Fox News on Monday, March 14, was tedious.

There are two separate phenomenon, the one obviously what happened in Chicago, is organized, and this is the far left, also the far right we saw it, in the '20's and the '30's, the tactic of shutting the opposition down. And it isn't only something happening in presidential politics. This is happening on campus all the time. Speakers who aren't allowed to speak, outside of the Trumps and the others. And we're talking about the norm on campus, which is that the left acts in a totalitarian way to control who speaks. That's a phenomenon, it should be condemned, and Trump and the supporters who are the victims here, are not to be blamed.

There's a second phenomenon, which is other events which are happening in Trump events, and you get as Mara [Liasson] said, Trump winking and nodding saying, you know, in the old days we carried them out on a stretcher, meaning we used to beat people like that until they were unable to walk. We saw on tape a guy hitting, sucker punching a demonstrator in the face, and then saying on camera, if we see him again, we may have to kill him. That's lynch talk, and when asked about it, Trump said I don't condone it. That's great. But he refused to condemn it. And that I think is really unconscionable.

The Pulitzer-winning Krauthammer brushed aside as "a phenomenon" the actions of an organized mob and saved his toughest salvos for Trump.

Krauthammer was a Goliath. In the Bible, Goliath protected the Philistines. In Washington, the Goliaths protected the government.

On television, he fell in line with his newspaper employer, the Pulitzer-winning *Washington Post*, which also saw nothing wrong with such intimidation. In fact, the newspaper blamed Trump for it.

"If there were any doubt about Mr. Trump's culpability as an instigator, it was erased Friday during a press conference announcing his endorsement by Ben Carson. Mr. Trump doubled down on his complaints about protesters—'bad dudes,' he called them Thursday night—and defended his supporters' right to 'hit back.' Little wonder, then, that there were clashes later that day between Trump supporters and protesters at an event in Chicago, prompting Mr. Trump to cancel the event with too-little, too-late protestations about wanting to avoid violence," the newspaper said in an editorial on March 12.

Another of the newspaper's Pulitzer winners, Kathleen Parker, accused Trump of shoving the press.

"As Donald Trump continues to surge forward as the most-likely Republican nominee, perfectly sane people are beginning to wonder: 'Was there something we missed? Maybe he's not really so bad.' Shed that self-doubt and purge the thought. You're not wrong—and he's that bad," Parker wrote.

However, her colleague Richard Cohen sided with Trump.

"While the protesters are entitled to make their case, so is Trump. If they have free speech, so does he. A silent protest is one thing; a mass attempt to shout him down—in other words, to silence him—is something else entirely. The response is often violence—an attempt to shut up the shut-uppers. To Trump's constituency, there is something particularly galling about college students—seen as spoiled and the establishment-in-waiting—silencing the candidate whom they revere as their champion," Cohen wrote.

But Cohen was only a Pulitzer nominee. What did he know?

At the *New York Times*, they did not have to bother with Pulitzers. The *Times* had on board a Nobel laureate in economics, Paul Krugman. He was a professor at Princeton, who offered all the political insight of a twelve-year-old.

"But how does a party in thrall to a basically unpopular ideology—or at any rate an ideology voters would dislike if they knew more about it—win elections? Obfuscation helps. But demagogy and appeals to tribalism help more. Racial dog whistles and suggestions that Democrats are un-American if not active traitors aren't things that happen now and then, they're an integral part of Republican political strategy," Krugman said.

He had good ears because only dogs hear dog whistles, racial and otherwise. The Pulitzer-winning *New York Times* editorial board needed no dog whistles. It blew the factory whistle. Subtlety was for fools. "The Trump Campaign Gives License to Violence," the newspaper headlined its editorial on March 14.

Trump deserved to face an angry mob threatening violence, the newspaper said. In fact, he deserved violence. The editorial did not mention Chicago. At all. And the images of the Chicago near-riot disappeared from cable news as well, replaced by images of security guards removing hecklers—or as the media called them, "protesters."

However, another *Times* columnist, Ross Douthat, who was no fan of Trump or his supporters, nevertheless framed the event properly.

"The Chicago protest-cum-riot over the weekend almost certainly played into Trump's hands. It handed him yet another wave of free media (of course), and it changed the story around Trump's rallies (at least for many casually engaged voters) from 'Republican presidential candidate rants to his followers and encourages violence' to 'Republican presidential candidate shouted down by leftist mob'—which would be a winning narrative for almost any conservative politician, but especially for one whose appeal rests in part on the backlash against PC," Douthat wrote.

Such clear thinking and independent analysis were the reasons that Douthat never had won and never would win a Pulitzer, which no longer represented the best in journalism but the most pedestrian Goliath.

CHAPTER 33

LAWYERING THE ELECTION.

—————◆—————

THE PROTESTS BACKFIRED. TRUMP CARRIED Cook County—the home of Chicago—in the Illinois primary with 41 percent to 23 percent for Cruz on March 15. Trump took four states plus the Northern Marianas, losing only Ohio to Kasich, its governor. Rubio lost Florida and dropped out. Trump stretched his lead over Cruz to more than 250 delegates, after starting the day less than a hundred delegates ahead.

Trump was in command. But his opponents who had burned tens of millions of dollars trying to stop him—and who savaged him on cable news around the clock—were not about to gentlemanly concede.

"There is still time to defeat Trump's effort to win the Republican nomination—he has won about 35 percent of the overall vote so far and has about 44 percent of the delegates chosen. And even if Trump were to be the official nominee, there would be no reason not to mount an independent Republican candidacy in the general election. Either way, we can prevail—or go down fighting, with flags flying and guns blazing," Kristol wrote on March 11.

Just as Judge Elihu Smails went all in to stop Al Czervik and the caddies, the Republican establishment went all in against Trump and his hooligan supporters. Party officials vowed they would be sticklers for the rules. Haley Barbour, a former chair of the Republican National Committee, made this clear in the *Washington Post.*

"I expect a candidate to go to Cleveland with the necessary 1,237 delegates to be nominated on the first ballot. If not, we will have a contested convention, a rarity in modern US politics," Barbour wrote.

Barbour had explained the Republican National Committee's plan to stop the party from nominating the party's front-runner. They would lawyer the selection. Delegate selection was a two-step dance. In most states, voters stated their preference for the presidency, and later, party officials appointed the actual delegates. The plan was simple. Republican insiders would appoint Cruz delegates to the slots Trump won. If this meant they had to vote for Trump the first few ballots, they would. The integrity of the party did not matter. Keeping control of the party was the goal. If this meant electing Hillary Clinton, well, every war has its collateral damage.

There was some confusion among the pundits about a brokered convention—in which someone not in the running originally received the nomination—and a contested convention in which the second-place finisher challenged the leader.

Trey Mayfield of the *Federalist* was cheery about the proposal, in an article on March 10, 2016, headlined, "Brokered GOP Conventions Often Produce a Winning President." Yes, so successful that the last time Republicans brokered a convention (in 1940), they lost, and the last time Democrats did (in 1952), they lost as well. There was a reason parties stopped doing this.

After Trump's big win on March 15, David French of the *National Review* told readers to fight on. The #NeverTrump movement reminded me of those Japanese soldiers stranded on islands who continued fighting decades after World War II ended.

"Any normal race would be over. But this is not a normal election. We've gone from a race where the political wing of the conservative movement is at stake, to a contest where America finds itself teetering on the edge of political violence not seen since 1968. In such circumstances, patriots simply do not give up, and they especially don't give up while there are still glimmers of hope," French wrote.

Oddly, French was angry at Kasich for staying in the race after winning Ohio, as was Jennifer Rubin of the *Washington Post*, who pointed out that Kasich was mathematically eliminated from getting to 1,237 delegates.

"So what is the purpose, really? Kasich is infatuated with the attention and addicted to the limelight. If you had any doubt, his rambling and sanctimonious victory speech (vowing not to take the low road to the White House) should have removed any doubt. This is not someone ready to literally or figuratively give up the stage. For once, he is getting respect and TV coverage. Why give that up?" Rubin wrote on March 15.

Well, the same was true of Cruz, but David Brooks, the nominally conservative columnist for the *New York Times*, said Cruz was the party's one hope.

"Donald Trump is epically unprepared to be president. He has no realistic policies, no advisers, no capacity to learn. His vast narcissism makes him a closed fortress. He doesn't know what he doesn't know and he's uninterested in finding out. He insults the office Abraham Lincoln once occupied by running for it with less preparation than most of us would undertake to buy a sofa," Brooks wrote on March 18.

Brooks did not explain why Trump was "epically unprepared." I doubt he could. Trump had forty years' experience as the CEO of a Queens real-estate company that he grew into an international, multi-billion-dollar corporation. But the putdown of Trump by Brooks came from a man who in 2005 met a freshman senator named Barack Obama and immediately pronounced him fit for Mount Rushmore.

"I remember distinctly an image of—we were sitting on his couches, and I was looking at his pant leg and his perfectly creased pant, and I'm thinking, a) he's going to be president and b) he'll be a very good president," Brooks later wrote.

Not only was Brooks epically ill-suited to judge executive ability, but the electability factor also was a false concern. David French knew better.

"I'll never forget the moment I understood the true depth of support for Trump. My wife's uncle died weeks before the first primary. At his funeral, the pastor said that one of his greatest regrets is that he knew he would pass away before he had a chance to vote for Donald Trump. I've never heard that said of any candidate, much less a man so unworthy of such devotion. But he was following his leader. No one else had stepped up to earn his trust," French wrote.

CHAPTER 34

WHITE TRASHING.

————◆————

LIKE MANY READERS, I DID not understand why Trump's critics were so nasty and hateful. Then I realized, for most critics, Trump was not the threat. Trump's voters were. Glenn Reynolds, author of *An Army of Davids*, recognized Donald's army.

"Trump's rise is, like that of his Democratic counterpart Bernie Sanders, a sign that a large number of voters don't feel represented by more mainstream politicians. On many issues, ranging from immigration reform, which many critics view as tantamount to open borders, to bailouts for bankers, the Republican and Democratic establishments agree, while a large number (quite possibly a majority) of Americans across the political spectrum feel otherwise. But when no respectable figure will push these views, then less-respectable figures such as Trump or Sanders will arise to fill the need," Reynolds wrote on August 9, 2015.

The only threat Sanders supporters posed to power brokers in DC was giving them more power. The cry for more government was the sound of money in a town built on government.

But Trump's working-class support frightened the Republican elites just as it had the Democratic elites eight years earlier. Campaigning for president, Barack Obama told his deep-pocket donors in San Francisco on April 6, 2008, about his trip to the hills of Pennsylvania. His mother was an anthropologist, and Obama shared her analytic skills. Clinton supporter Mayfield Fowler covertly taped his comments. Hoping to undermine his candidacy, she shared them with the world a few days later.

"You go into some of these small towns in Pennsylvania, and like a lot of small towns in the Midwest, the jobs have been gone now for twenty-five years and nothing's replaced them. And they fell through the Clinton administration, and the Bush administration, and each successive administration has said that somehow these communities are gonna regenerate and they have not. And it's not surprising then they get bitter, they cling to guns or religion or antipathy to people who aren't like them or anti-immigrant sentiment or antitrade sentiment as a way to explain their frustrations," Obama said.

Many conservatives in Washington denounced Obama for saying that, not because they did not believe it wasn't true, but because Obama said it. I shall prove this by comparing two *National Review* articles, roughly eight years apart.

"Obama is also part of a long tradition on the Left of being for the working class in the abstract, or as people potentially useful for the purposes of the Left, but having disdain or contempt for them as human beings," Thomas Sowell, a columnist and Stanford economist, wrote on April 15, 2008.

But Obama's attitude was the same as staff at the *National Review.* They disdained the working class too. Trump's popularity brought this to the fore in an article, "The Father-Führer," by Kevin D. Williamson on March 28, 2016. The title implied that Trump supporters were Nazis.

"If you spend time in hardscrabble, white upstate New York, or eastern Kentucky, or my own native West Texas, and you take an honest look at the welfare dependency, the drug and alcohol addiction, the family anarchy—which is to say, the whelping of human children with all the respect and wisdom of a stray dog—you will come to an awful realization. It wasn't Beijing. It wasn't even Washington, as bad as Washington can be. It wasn't immigrants from Mexico, excessive and problematic as our current immigration levels are. It wasn't any of that," Williamson wrote.

The problem was laziness, he wrote. "The truth about these dysfunctional, downscale communities is that they deserve to die. Economically, they are negative assets. Morally, they are indefensible. The white American underclass is in thrall to a vicious, selfish culture whose main products are misery and used heroin needles. Donald Trump's speeches make them feel good. So does OxyContin. What they need isn't analgesics, literal or political. They need real opportunity, which means that they need real change, which means that they need U-Haul. If you want to live, get out of Garbutt, New York."

Williamson left Amarillo, Texas, as a young man for college and began his journalism career later in Mumbai, India. Change the location of his essay to Mumbai and "the whelping of human children with all the respect and wisdom of a stray dog" would have been less acceptable. Change the location to Ferguson, Missouri, and the *National Review* would have dumped Williamson just as it did John Derbyshire in 2013. The donors who kept the publication alive would not countenance certain racial prejudices.

To paraphrase Sowell in 2008, Williamson was part of a long tradition of being for the working class in the abstract, or as people potentially useful for his purposes, but having disdain or contempt for them as human beings. He mocked people who received disability checks for on-the-job injuries and the like.

"And that's where disability or other government programs kicked in. They were there, beckoning, giving men and women alternatives to gainful employment. You don't have to do any work (your disability lawyer does all the heavy lifting), you make money, and you get drugs," he wrote.

His complaint was valid. Many received monthly checks for on-the-job injuries that did not exist. Disability lawyers bought off the administrative law judges who approved the claims. But this fraud was rampant in the very cities Williamson said Trump supporters should migrate to.

Liberal blogger Ian Welsh objected. He said wages for white male factory workers in America had declined steadily since 1968, the year he was born. Automation, affirmative action, the tripling of immigration, the surge of women in the workplace, and free trade all contributed to this decline.

"The quality of life for the average white male peaked in 1968. Then, you call them trash, they have almost no good jobs, and you're surprised they're angry? You think they aren't human? You think they are Jesus, and can be treated like crap for longer than most of them have been alive and that there won't be consequences? You think that because other people are treated even worse, they will sublimate their own mistreatment? That's not just immoral, that's crazy stupid," Welsh wrote on March 17.

Rick Manning of Americans for Limited Government also lambasted the magazine and its writer for trashing people who earn a living.

"It is one thing in a political context to say, 'We don't like this candidate over another candidate.' That's perfectly legitimate, but in this article, Kevin Williamson, the author, attacks the people who support Trump, he attacks the people who work for a living," Manning told *Breitbart News* on March 18.

It isn't really about Trump when you get down to it. It's about people who feel they've been left behind by an economy where we see our jobs exported overseas, where we see environmentalists shutting down a factory, shutting down the mills, and we see government regulations working against [us]. We feel as if the government itself is working against us, and the system is all rigged to benefit the people who have lobbyists in DC and against the people who are just trying to make a living and raise their families and go to church and do all the things we do in our lives that don't have anything to do with what's happening in Washington, DC or state capitals or even our local town halls.

And it's those people that Kevin Williamson in the *National Review* article basically said, "It's your fault. Stop being a crybaby. Load up your trucks and move to the big city and see what you can do there." And it was fundamentally wrong. It was morally reprehensible, and so I felt I had to call him out.

But of course Williamson had to trash working people. The conservative commentariat raged with hate. Imagine how humiliating it would be to lose one's power to people who engage in "the whelping of human children with all the respect and wisdom of a stray dog."

However, the Washington conservatives merely mimicked their liberal friends, who thought they were better than everyone else in the United States. The brainiest people in America politics were acting like Mel Brooks as King Louis XVI in the comedy *History of the World, Part 1.*

COUNT DE MONET: It is said that the people are revolting.
KING LOUIS XVI: You said it. They stink on ice.

In real life, the king lived in the Palace of Versailles. He lost his head in the French Revolution. Fortunately for the denizens of Versailles, DC, the electorate in the United States shunned the guillotine.

We built Versailles, DC, on a mountain of debt. In the first seventeen years of the twenty-first century, the federal government tore up a balanced budget and went on a spending spree, adding $14 trillion to the national debt. At one point in 2009, the federal government borrowed forty cents for every dollar it spent. Both Democratic and Republican Congresses, and Presidents Bush 43 and Obama plundered the nation's future to keep the welfare state rolling. The near doubling of the federal budget and the government's power created an economic boom for the politicians, their staffers, the bureaucrats, and the lobbyists.

"In fact, if you have any doubt, if you looked last year, the numbers that we saw put out showed that six of the top 10 wealthiest counties in America—six of the top 10 wealthiest communities in America, by county, according to median income—are in and around the Washington, DC, area. That tell you anything about where we're growing the economy in this nation?" Governor Scott Walker of Wisconsin said on February 6, 2015, at a tribute to Reagan at Reagan's alma mater, Eureka College.

Topping the list was Loudon County, Virginia, with a median income of $117,680 in 2014—more than double the national average, and five times the poorest county in the land, Buffalo County, South Dakota, which is home to the Crow Creek Sioux Tribe reservation. Literally, the chiefs enjoyed five times what the Indians did.

On January 28, 2016, Carlson of the *Daily Caller* called the nation's capital the most corrupt city in the world.

Everyone beats up on Washington, but most of the people I know who live here love it. Of course they do. It's beautiful, the people are friendly, we've got good restaurants, not to mention full employment and construction cranes on virtually every corner. If you work on Capitol Hill or downtown, it's hard to walk back from lunch without seeing someone you know. It's a warm bath. Nobody wants to leave.

But let's pretend for a second this isn't Washington. Let's imagine it's the capital of an African country, say Burkina Faso, and we are doing a study on corruption. Probably the first question we'd ask: How many government officials have close relatives who make a living by influencing government spending? A huge percentage of them? OK. Case closed. Ouagadougou is obviously a very corrupt city.

That's how the rest of the country views DC. Washington is probably the richest city in America because the people who live there have the closest proximity to power. That seems obvious to most voters. It's less obvious to us, because everyone here is so cheerful and familiar, and we're too close to it. Chairman so-and-so's son-in-law lobbies the committee? That doesn't seem corrupt. He's such a good guy.

Trump and his supporters threatened that way of life, which is why Brooks earlier called him "epically unprepared to be president" more than a decade after pronouncing Obama as epically prepared because he had a crease in his pants. David Brooks was as clueless about the people as Mel Brooks was. The difference was Mel Brooks was playing a role for laughs in a movie. People took David Brooks seriously.

CHAPTER 35

THE TRUTH ABOUT BRUSSELS.

———————

"DONALD TRUMP FINDS NEW CITY to Insult: Brussels," read the head-line in the *New York Times* on January 27, 2016. Dan Bilefsky and Claire Barthelemy, ferreted out reaction to a statement Trump made on Fox Business network to host Maria Bartiromo. Trump had a month ear-lier said that some Muslim immigrant neighborhoods in England were no-go zones in England where police feared to tread. Officials denied this, but police officers told the London newspapers off the record that such zones existed. Trump continued to rail against the kid gloves politi-cians placed on police when dealing with Islamic crime and terrorism.

"There is something going on, Maria. Go to Brussels. Go to Paris. Go to different places. There is something going on and it's not good, where they want Shariah law, where they want this, where they want things that—you know, there has to be some assimilation. There is no assimilation. There is something bad going on," Trump said.

The *New York Times* wanted to report that Belgium was aflame in anger against The Donald. Instead, the reaction was tepid.

"Rudi Vervoort, the president of the Brussels region, said through his spokeswoman that he was surprised by Mr. Trump's words. 'We can reassure the Americans that Brussels is a multicultural city where it is good to live,' said the spokeswoman, Leonôr da Silva, listing the city's virtues: green spaces, a tolerant culture and its central place in Europe," the *Times* reported.

Two months later, Trump's warning came true. Muslim terrorists blew up a subway station in Brussels, killing thirty-four people and wounding hundreds more. The attack on March 22, drew little reaction from President Obama, who was in Havana giving a speech to Cuban communists. Matt Drudge reported Obama spent fifty-one seconds of an hourlong speech on the subject. He then went to a baseball game without further comment. Obama learned nothing from the San Bernardino attack on December 2, 2015.

The next day, while Brussels tried to recover from the bombing, Obama and his wife went to Argentina where they danced with professional tango dancers, as if they were auditioning for *Dancing with the Stars*. Obama was in full postpresidential mode.

However, Trump spent the morning of the blast on television shows reassuring the American people that, as president, he would better protect them from acts of terrorism. The free world needed a leader. Obama did not want the job, so Trump filled in.

Trump went on *Good Morning Britain*, having agreed to an interview weeks earlier. Host Piers Morgan shared in the *Daily Mail* his impression of The Donald's plan to deal with terrorism.

"Let's be honest with ourselves, right now ISIS is winning this war and will continuing committing utter carnage on our streets on an ever graver and more barbaric scale until they are stopped. I don't have the answers to how to do that," Morgan wrote.

"But I don't hear any good ideas coming from any world leaders at the moment either, and it's their highly paid jobs to work it out. Instead, I see a global paralysis driven by fear, confusion and woeful lack of leadership. And it will only get worse. Hate Donald Trump all you like, but at least he seems to recognise the magnitude of the threat and at least he has firm proposals for how to try to defeat it."

Something was up in London and Paris and Brussels. But just as the people were too afraid of being called stupid to say the emperor wore no clothes in the Hans Christian Andersen tale "The Emperor's

New Clothes," the American people were too afraid of being called racist, Islamophobic, and xenophobic to tell the truth about Islamic terrorism.

Trump was not afraid to tell the truth, which was why his supporters were willing to overlook flaws that would have brought down any other candidate.

CHAPTER 36

THE CHALKENING AND THE RIOTS.

———

LOCATED IN ATLANTA, EMORY UNIVERSITY is a prestigious private institution with $6.7 billion in its endowment fund, and an academic staff of 13,225 people serving 14,513 students. On March 22, James W. Wagner was in his thirteenth year as university president, earning more than $1.2 million a year. The day earlier, a group of students met with him to complain that someone was marking "Trump 2016" in chalk on the sidewalks and other places on campus—three weeks after the Georgia Republican primary ended. The students said they felt intimidated and unsafe.

Rather than laugh in their faces, Wagner held their hands and assured them that the mean Trump bogeyman would not sleep under their beds. He wrote a lengthy e-mail to the rest of the campus.

"After meeting with our students, I cannot dismiss their expression of feelings and concern as motivated only by political preference or oversensitivity. Instead, the students with whom I spoke heard a message, not about political process or candidate choice, but instead about values regarding diversity and respect that clash with Emory's own," Wagner wrote.

Conservatives mocked this. How can grown men and women fear a little sidewalk chalk? The incident was a reminder of what a racket higher education had become, turning young adults into overgrown children who could not handle a simple political message not to their liking. Elliptical talk about microaggressions and the like were tools used to coerce conformity from anyone who might question the socialistic indoctrination that has become common on so many campuses in so many fields.

Newt Gingrich took to Twitter to complain. "As an Emory alum I am worried about the fragility and timidity of some students. In the age of ISIS how can a name in chalk be frightening? Emory has me worried because I thought college was a place to grow up and explore ideas not a place to hide and be intimidated by trivia," he tweeted.

The nonsense embarrassed even the liberal newspapers. The headline in the *Washington Post* on March 24, read, "Someone wrote 'Trump 2016' on Emory's campus in chalk. Some students said they no longer feel safe."

The *New York Times* reported on April 1, "The students felt that there was an anti-diversity subtext to the so-called chalking written on campus about Mr. Trump, the Republican front-runner whose divisive comments about Muslims, women, Hispanics and disabled people have offended his critics but have tended to embolden his supporters."

The story should have been an April Fool's joke, but it was real. And supporters of Trump loved the clutching of the pearls by the little snowflakes on campus. The chalkening spread to other campuses.

Of course it spread. This is America. There is no quicker way to get an American to do something than by telling him he cannot do it.

Just seventy-two years earlier, a nation's young men scaled vertical cliffs after landing at Normandy in a hail of German fire. Now we had big galoofs cowering because someone scribbled a name in chalk on the campus sidewalk. The situation was so surreal that even Lowry, editor of the anti-Trump *National Review*, screamed at the insanity.

"What has become known on social media as 'the chalkening' demonstrates how some college kids can't be exposed to the simplest expression of support for a major presidential candidate without wanting to scurry to the nearest safe space. By this standard, a 'Make America Great Again' hat is a hate crime waiting to happen. It's not clear how any of these students can turn on cable TV or look at the polls for the Republican nomination these days without being triggered," Lowry wrote on April 7.

But Lowry blamed Trump. "The reaction to the chalkening is a testament to the electric charge surrounding Trump. He is like the Washington Redskins of political candidates—so politically incorrect that some people can't bear to see or hear his name. (The *New York Times* columnist Charles Blow actually refuses to use it.) This branding isn't prudent positioning for a general election, but it makes Trump a perfect vehicle for provoking the other side, and it's in that thumb-in-the-eye spirit that the Trump chalking is spreading," Lowry wrote.

As I reviewed hundreds of their columns and commentaries throughout the nomination process, I came to realize pundits overthink. A lot.

Eventually, Emory President Wagner did the right thing. "Emory stands for free expression!" he wrote on March 25.

In chalk.

But Amanda Obando Polio, a freshman from El Salvador, felt violated and threatened, and the *Washington Post* gave her safe space to express herself. "It was not for the chalking but for what it reminded me of; that America is changing and it could potentially transform into a nation with a leader who continually degrades people from various social groups," Polio wrote.

"When I came to the United States, when I applied and received a student visa, when I boarded that plane in August, I did not sign up for this. It might be naïve to expect that this country was going to be the land of opportunity. But America can't be proud of giving foreigners that impression anymore now that offenses that ignite social protests happen so often.

"The worst is that I see this without necessarily calling the USA my home. The people who protested, (who are not the entire Latinx community), do. How is life here when you, your family, and friends get discriminated against by a presidential front-runner?"

A month later, on the other side of the nation, Hispanics rioted at Trump appearances in Costa Mesa, California, and Burlingame, California. The press called the rioters "protesters." The *Los Angeles Times* cheerily headlined its news report, "Trump spurs a fresh wave of Latino activism." Trump had nothing to do with the lawlessness.

"Protest organizers in Southern California said the anti-Trump demonstration spread through word of mouth and involved mostly young people, including many high school and college students. They brought with them Mexican flags, which were once discouraged at immigrant rights rallies for fear they would be regarded as un-American," the newspaper reported on April 29.

"But in reaction to Trump, the Mexican flag has re-emerged, unfurled and unapologetic and a symbol for a new generation of Latino activists. Protesters said they have no hesitation about putting their heritage on display, especially when it comes to the rise and rhetoric of Donald Trump."

A few weeks earlier, the newspaper was not as fluffy when reporting about chalked messages on the sidewalks of the University of California–San Diego, headlining a report on April 12, "Pro-Trump graffiti to 'Build the Wall' at UC San Diego Latino center spark outrage."

The report quoted Kevin Antonio Aguilar, a doctoral student in Latin American history at the university, who had posted his thoughts on Facebook. "We in the Latin American community on campus demand that the individuals responsible for this racist attack face the proper repercussions for these actions."

While I have avoided castigating news reporters in this volume, neither story in the *Los Angeles Times* quoted a Trump campaign official or indicated that any of the five reporters tried to contact the other side in their reporting. Such reporting reflects the anticonservative bias in some newsrooms.

But paid and organized leftist hecklers had long stalked Trump's campaign rallies. In Chicago in March, Bill Ayers test-marketed the threat of riots. A month later, liberals used Latinos to inch the violence forward. *National Review* Washington editor Eliana Johnson was first among those who blamed Trump, making that case on Neil Cavuto's Fox News show on April 29.

"Well, one really important thing, Neil, is not to confuse where the bad behavior is coming from. Mr. Trump and his campaign have behaved badly in encouraging and fomenting violence inside their rallies. And, these protesters are behaving badly fomenting and encouraging bad behavior outside the rallies. The fact that there are protesters that are behaving badly does not [absolve] the Trump campaign or Mr. Trump for what he's done," Johnson said.

However, others at the *National Review* rejected such nonsense. On that same day, David French headlined his article, "Dear Mainstream Media, Don't You Dare Whitewash Anti-Trump Violence." French wrote, "Just imagine for a moment the shrieking outrage if Trump supporters had tried to flip a car outside a Hillary Clinton rally. Imagine the fury at the sight of a bloody man wearing a Hillary shirt."

Writing "Trump 2016" on a sidewalk in Georgia was wrong, but rioting in California was "Latino activism."

CHAPTER 37

UNDER HIS SKIN.

———————

BY THE TIME THE ARIZONA primary and Utah caucuses arrived, the race had winnowed to a two-man contest between Trump and Cruz, although Kasich stayed in to keep his sixty-six delegates from the Ohio primary from going to Trump. Arizona clearly supported Trump's call for a wall, while Mormons agreed with Romney and disliked Trump. He took all fifty-eight delegates in Arizona, while Cruz took all forty in Utah.

But as with Rubio's small-handed gesture a few weeks earlier, Trump was about to trip over another petty insult. The Republican establishment continued to hope they could keep Trump short of the 1,237 delegates needed to win a first ballot vote. Their plan was to then hijack the convention and the nomination.

Enter dirty trickster Liz Mair. Scott Walker fired Mair from his campaign after she used social media to mock Iowa. This time, she used the social media to mock Trump's wife. Mair found a photo of her posing naked for *GQ* when she was a model and posted the photo online. The caption read, "Meet Melania Trump. Your next first lady. Or you could support Ted Cruz on Tuesday."

The Donald took the bait. Trump tweeted, "Lyin' Ted Cruz just used a picture of Melania from a *GQ* shoot in his ad. Be careful, Lyin' Ted, or I will spill the beans on your wife!"

That was the reaction Mair wanted. She had nothing officially to do with the Cruz campaign, but she had made it her mission to stop Trump. All the cool kids in Washington and New York wanted to. Not only did he react, but he reacted in such a way that made it seem like Heidi Cruz had a sex scandal. But while Trump was equating his wife's work as a model with Cruz's wife's work at Goldman Sachs, the public was looking at Mrs. Trump's photo and thought he meant a sex scandal. This was a huge mistake by Trump.

Cruz held a press conference on March 24, to denounce Trump. "It's not easy to tick me off. I don't get angry often. But you mess with my wife, you mess with my kids, that will do it every time. Donald, you're a sniveling coward and leave Heidi alone," Cruz said.

Chivalry was not dead. He took the high road that Trump gave him. "We don't want a president who traffics in sleaze and slime. We don't want a president who seems to have a real issue with strong women," Cruz said.

He was the last hope of the party's insiders. Cruz matched Trump both in his ability to speak on his feet and in ruthlessness as well. Throughout the debating season, Trump was the polar bear who slayed the beluga whales. He felled Bush, Carson, Rubio, and the rest. Meanwhile, Cruz was the arctic fox, staying a safe distance from the polar bear while feeding on the scraps left by him. Now the two squared off.

The press pounced on this controversy like a cat on a bowl of cream. "Donald Trump's latest rude comments about Ted Cruz's wife are raising new alarms among Republicans about the party front-runner's ability to win over women, especially in a potential fall presidential match-up with Hillary Clinton," an unbylined story in the *Chicago Tribune* read.

Accompanying the story was a photo of Mrs. Cruz looking lovingly into her husband's eyes. The caption read, "Ted Cruz embraces his wife Heidi after announcing his candidacy for the Republican presidential nomination."

The *Chicago Tribune* report on March 25, was a sharp contrast to a report on the same day in the occasionally reliable *National Enquirer*, headlined, "Dirty Politics! Shocking Claims: Pervy Ted Cruz Caught Cheating—With 5 Secret Mistresses!"

However, the story named no names and said only that private detectives were investigating rumors. Nevertheless, some people took the weekly tabloid's story as gospel. Online radio talker Rob Zicari identified three of the women, who included Katrina Pierson, a spokeswoman for Trump. She denied having an affair with Cruz.

"Speaking for myself, the article is trash and 100 percent false," Pierson said in an email to the *Washington Post*.

The press passed on the story until Cruz blasted the story while campaigning in Oshkosh, Wisconsin, that afternoon. "Sen. Ted Cruz (R-Tex.) blamed Donald Trump and his henchmen for planting a *National Enquirer* story that accused him of extramarital affairs. Vehemently denying the story as garbage and complete and utter lies, the Republican presidential hopeful took his longest step yet toward refusing to back Trump if he wins the party's nomination," David Weigel of the *Washington Post* reported.

However, the *Daily Beast* and other news outlets pointed to Rubio's ill-fated campaign as the probable source of the report.

"A half-dozen GOP operatives and media figures tell The Daily Beast that Cruz's opponents have been pushing charges of adultery for at least six months now—and that allies of former GOP presidential hopeful Marco Rubio were involved in spreading the smears," the *Daily Beast* reported.

The *National Enquirer* had an interesting history in presidential politics, having broken the story of John Edwards having a mistress and love child even as the national press praised the 2008 presidential candidate for standing by his wife when she battled cancer. Indeed, Cruz was secondary to Blake Shelton on the cover that week, as the tabloid reported Shelton had cheated on singer Miranda Lambert with nine different women.

On the other hand, the *National Enquirer* also reported that during their presidencies, divorce was imminent for Clinton, Bush 43, and Obama.

The situation became comical, with Trump's spokeswoman denying reports that Cruz was cheating, while in forty-eight hours, the narrative on Cruz went from defender of his wife's honor to possible adulterer.

But Trump learned his lesson. He eased off tweeting his thoughts and his insults. To be a president, one must act presidential. Also, Trump needed to expand his staff from a small band of yes-men. He had not invested enough time and money in his political organization. The imperfect messenger needed to stop ignoring his Achilles heel and get help.

He did.

CHAPTER 38

BETTER CALL PAUL.

————◆————

HAVING CAMPAIGNED NEARLY DAILY FOR nine months, Donald Trump decided to take some time off the campaign trail after the primaries on March 22. His oldest child, Ivanka, gave birth to her third child, son Theodore James Kushner, on March 27. But The Donald kept working. He always did. Paul Solotaroff in his *Rolling Stone* profile on September 9, 2015, made that clear. Trump's father, Fred, instilled that in his sons.

"Though Fred lived and died a very rich man, he made his kids work like peasants. The three boys spent summers pulling weeds and pouring cement, learning the building trade from the subfloor up, while the two girls toiled in his real estate office in the bowels of Coney Island. Trump tells the story of being dragged by the nose to join Fred on his rounds collecting rents," Solotaroff reported.

Donald Trump told the writer how he used to collect rents.

"We'd go on jobs where you needed tough guys to knock on doors... You'd see 'em ring the bell and stand way over here. I'd say, 'Why're you over there?' and he'd say, ''Cause these [expletives] shoot! They shoot right through the door!'" Trump said.

This was a work ethic he passed along to his eldest sons, Eric and Donald Jr. "I was a dock attendant for a couple of summers, then went into landscaping...My brother and I are probably the only sons of billionaires who can operate a D-10 Caterpillar," Donald Trump Jr. said.

As for Ivanka, as a model, she made the cover of *Seventeen* at sixteen, but she also learned business from the ground up. "I did less-than-glamorous internships in sweltering New York—the South of France wasn't an option," she said.

All three worked for the company. Trump planned to turn the company over to them should he win the presidency. And winning the presidency was what Trump was all about in 2016. His plan to use earned media (nothing in life is free, kiddo) to rise to the top of the field and dominate the race worked. But as the April primaries neared, and the inevitability of his nomination grew, Trump needed to expand his operation beyond Corey Lewandowski—his campaign manager— and their small posse. Trump needed someone his age who could tell him to grow up.

Roger Stone, a longtime Trump political confidante, had urged him to run a more traditional campaign and even left the campaign after two months in the summer of 2015 over Trump's insistence on doing the campaign on the cheap. Trump proved right. It would be difficult to pair a rebel's message with a slick and well-oiled campaign organization. Trump extemporaneous speaking style suited that message, as did the rambunctious nature of his campaign.

However, enough was enough. Stone suggested Trump hire Paul Manafort to run the convention because Cruz and others were trying to pluck off the delegates Trump earned. Stone and Manafort had learned Republican presidential politics forty years earlier. Manafort did the teaching. Ahead of the 1976 convention, Manafort was President Ford's floor manager who kept delegates from straying to Reagan's side. Stone worked to shanghai Ford delegates.

Stone explained how he worked. In one case, he flew to Rhode Island to wine and dine Providence mayor Buddy Cianci.

"I was trying to peel him off Ford. I said, 'Think about it.' We finished dinner and he went right to a phone and called Manafort. Manafort had everything tied down so tight we couldn't move anything. He kicked our ass. He knows how to negotiate, just like Trump," Stone told David Catanese, senior political editor of *US News and World Report*, nearly forty years later.

Reagan hired Manafort for his 1980 campaign. Manafort worked for Vice President Bush's nomination in 1988 and Bob Dole's in 1996. It was at the 1988 Republican convention that Trump first met Manafort.

"Trump was in town and curious to see how a convention was really run; Manafort thought it'd be neat to get his picture with The Donald. The two convened in a trailer outside the Louisiana Superdome during a steamy weekday for a friendly chitchat," Catanese reported on April 21, 2016.

And twenty-eight years later, Trump needed Manafort. Cruz was picking off delegates in state conventions that should have gone to Trump.

"A lot of these losses Trump had that he is bellyaching about could have changed with good staff work," lobbyist Frank Donatelli, a White House political director for President Ronald Reagan, told Catanese.

Meanwhile, Lewandowski fell victim to the *j'accuse* justice the press occasionally indulges in. One of its own—Michelle Fields—filed a false charge of battery against Lewandowski following a Trump press conference at Mar-a-Lago after victories in Hawaii, Michigan, and Mississippi on March 8. As Trump left, Fields moved toward him. Lewandowski blocked her.

"I wasn't called upon to ask a question during the televised press conference, but afterwards Trump wandered around, stopping at every reporter to take their questions. When he approached me, I asked him about his view on an aspect of affirmative action," Fields reported at *Breitbart News*. "Trump acknowledged the question, but before he could answer I was jolted backwards. Someone had grabbed me tightly by the arm and yanked me down. I almost fell to the ground, but was able to maintain my balance. Nonetheless, I was shaken."

In Washington, ladies clutched their pearls in shock as if it were the 1880s.

"In a year of floors falling away under one's feet (such as the assumption that nearly all Americans demand a minimal level of civility in public life), the Corey Lewandowski story represents one more gob smack.

That Donald Trump stands by the belligerent Lewandowski tells us more of what we already knew about Trump, and also hints at the coward beneath the blowhard," Mona Charen wrote.

While the Juniper police in Florida charged him with battery, a security video clearly showed she was not yanked down. The prosecutor decided to drop the case. But Fields had damaged him, as politics is not always about the facts but about perception.

However, Manafort had baggage too. His list of clients included former Ukrainian president Viktor Yanukovych, who had ties to Vladimir Putin. The Orange Revolution overturned Yanukovych's victory in the 2004 presidential race, but six years later, Manafort helped get him elected again. He did good work and received nice fees.

But the days of doing the campaign on the cheap had ended. Trump hired the guy who had stopped Reagan in 1976. Now Manafort had to stop the Republican Party insiders, who ganged up on Trump in Wisconsin.

CHAPTER 39

TRUMP THUMPED.

AFTER MULTIPLE STATE PRIMARIES ON March 22, 2016, through the New York primary on April 19, 2016, there was only one primary: Wisconsin. The party was about to badger Trump in the Badger State, as Governor Scott Walker and his political machine backed Cruz. Milwaukee-based radio talker Charlie Sykes pitched in. And the money for the negative TV ads rolled in.

However, Wisconsin already was Cruz country. Months earlier, Nate Silver at *FiveThirtyEight* had figured out a path for each candidate to the 1,237 delegates needed to win the race. Silver said Cruz needed thirty-three of the forty-two delegates in Wisconsin, while Trump needed but eighteen.

But Cruz's shellacking of Trump—a thirteen-point win—exceeded his high expectations. Cruz won thirty-six delegates, while Trump settled for six.

"Now tonight, here in Wisconsin, a state that just three weeks ago the media said was a perfect state for Donald Trump, but the hard-working men and women of Wisconsin stood and campaigned tirelessly to make sure that tonight was a victory for every American," Cruz said in his victory speech on April 5.

Actually, no one said that. The press was beginning to admit that the race was over, and Trump had won.

"Tonight is a turning point. It is a rallying cry. It is a call from the hard-working men and women of Wisconsin to the people of America: we have a choice, a real choice," Cruz said.

Krauthammer thought otherwise. Having been burned all summer and winter long, like a Cleveland Indians fan in August, he was not about to get his hopes up over a sweep in Milwaukee.

"The most stunning result of Wisconsin is the solidity of Trump's core constituency. Fundamentalist Trumpism remains resistant to every cosmic disturbance," Krauthammer wrote on April 7, 2016. He continued:

"He managed to get a full 35 percent in a state in which:

+ He was opposed by a very popular GOP governor (80 percent approval among Republicans) with a powerful state organization honed by winning three campaigns within four years (two gubernatorial, one recall).
+ He was opposed by popular, local, well-informed radio talk show hosts whose tough interviews left him in shambles.
+ Tons of money was dumped into negative ads not just from the Cruz campaign and the pro-Cruz super PACs but from two anti-Trump super PACs as well.

"And if that doesn't leave a candidate flattened, consider that Trump was coming off two weeks of grievous self-inflicted wounds—and still got more than a third of the vote. Which definitively vindicated Trump's boast that if he ever went out in the middle of Fifth Avenue and shot someone (most likely because his Twitter went down—he'd be apprehended in his pajamas), he wouldn't lose any voters."

I must correct Krauthammer. He was the victim of lousy journalism. The actual Fifth Avenue quote mocked Trump's critics for making fun of his supporters. "They say I have the most loyal people—did you ever see that?—where I could stand in the middle of Fifth Avenue and shoot somebody, and I wouldn't lose any voters. OK. It's like incredible," Trump said in Sioux City, Iowa, on January 23, as reported by Jenna Johnson of the *Washington Post*.

Nevertheless, Cruz's big win delighted his supporters—both financial and political—as did a win in Colorado the following Saturday.

To the surprise of many voters in other states, while candidates "won" delegates, party officials appointed them. Cruz worked to have his delegates appointed—people who would vote for Trump on the first ballot, then Cruz afterward. Also, Cruz wanted to assure that neoconservatives would write the rules and platform the party would adopt at the national convention. He was, after all, a top-notch lawyer who had argued and won cases before the U.S. Supreme Court.

But his campaign went too far. Colorado, not Wisconsin, would be the turning point in the campaign, or rather the end of the road for the efforts of the conservative commentariat to derail Trump.

Cruz won Colorado in a convention closed to voters. The state party handed Cruz thirty-four of thirty-seven delegates. Leaders did this without the support of the rank-and-file. Party officials tweeted afterward, "We did it. #NeverTrump."

After Matt Drudge posted the tweet on his *Drudge Report*, the Colorado Republican did what Anthony Weiner did after Andrew Breitbart caught Weiner posting a naughty selfie on Twitter. The party deleted the tweet and told everyone someone had hacked its account.

Manafort went to work, using a previously scheduled appearance on *Meet the Press* to denounce Cruz and his campaign. "He's threatening. You go to these county conventions, and you see the tactics, Gestapo tactics, the scorched-earth tactics," Manafort said.

The Donald struck back, too, writing a column in the *Wall Street Journal* that blasted the Colorado Republican Party tactics. Party officials canceled the traditional caucus in favor of a closed convention in August 2015, after Trump took the lead in the national polls.

"I, for one, am not interested in defending a system that for decades has served the interest of political parties at the expense of the people. Members of the club—the consultants, the pollsters, the politicians, the pundits and the special interests—grow rich and powerful while the American people grow poorer and more isolated," Trump wrote.

"No one forced anyone to cancel the vote in Colorado. Political insiders made a choice to cancel it. And it was the wrong choice.

"Responsible leaders should be shocked by the idea that party officials can simply cancel elections in America if they don't like what the voters may decide."

Pundits saw Trump's point.

"I think Cruz could have won the majority of the voters anyway, in Colorado. But it's a smell test. The rules are the rules. Yes, of course, that's right, but it's a smell test for people. And I think you're seeing this in more and more places, so Trump's going to try to exploit that as he was outmaneuvered in Colorado undoubtedly," radio talker Laura Ingraham said on Fox News on April 11.

The Colorado convention was a three-card monte game, but on the same show, A. B. Stoddard of *The Hill* praised the manipulation by Cruz. "You can call him an evil genius, but Ted Cruz really got to work on this stuff obviously a long time ago and was completely prepared for a system that he could milk and exploit in a crafty way, and he's done that very successfully. It's just going to take more than tweeting and rallying and going on calling into TV shows," Stoddard said.

Of course, Cruz's plan was to stop Trump from reaching the majority threshold of 1,237 delegates, which would lead to a second ballot, which Cruz would capture, thanks to Cruz's people having been appointed to Trump's delegate slots.

"Look, I think the assumption that Trump is making, his supporters are making, is that the only really fair way to do this would be something like a national primary, to have a direct correlation between the number of votes you get and number of delegates. But you know, in Florida, Trump wins 47 percent of the vote, he gets 100 percent of the delegates, I didn't hear anybody complaining about the unfairness," Krauthammer said.

Everyone had a fair shot in Florida. Colorado was an insider's game run by people who called themselves "#NeverTrump."

"This is really going to help Trump. The Colorado situation is just too weird and it's going to help them in the contest going forward. People who are looking for an outsider and who have a grudge and a complaint with the establishment of the Republican Party, this is really—he's playing it perfectly, and it will definitely help him in the contest to come," Stoddard said.

New York loomed next. Cruz had no chance of winning that primary given his mocking of New York values in January. But the #NeverTrump crowd never gave up.

"It's important for the anti-Trump forces to hold Trump, if possible, below 50 percent in New York for both sort of delegate reasons, and it's like logical for momentum reasons," Bill Kristol said on the *Hugh Hewitt Show* on April 15.

Below 50 percent? They could not keep him under 60 percent, as he took ninety of the ninety-five delegates available. Kasich won five. Cruz got zero.

By any measure, the race was over after New York. The Associated Press declared Cruz mathematically eliminated from the race. Trump had won 845 delegates; Cruz had won 559. Trump had won twenty-two states and territories; Cruz had won eleven. Trump had won 8,722,467 votes; Cruz had won 6,389,500.

Meanwhile, Manafort was schmoozing with unpledged delegates, 250 of whom attended a three-day miniconvention in Hollywood, Florida, following the New York primary. Cruz and Kasich attended. Trump did not. Instead, Manafort met with them and introduced them to his new hire, Rick Wiley, a well-respected Republican who had been Walker's political director.

Manafort spared no expense wining and dining them. He threw a lavish dinner in their honor, serving RNC members seafood platters of crab legs, shrimp cocktails, and oysters, *Politico* reported on April 24. Trump had the money to hire the right people to get the job done.

Meanwhile, Cruz would ride the momentum of Wisconsin to finish last in five of the next six primaries. But he hung in there. After all, the NBA playoffs had begun, and Trump was on no one's roster. Besides, there were no plans for another *Home Alone* movie.

CHAPTER 40

NATE SILVER TARNISHED.

MUHAMMAD SAEED AL-SAHHAF BECAME THE most ridiculed man in Operation Iraqi Freedom in 2003. As Saddam Hussein's information minister, al-Sahhaf, gained international infamy by making outlandish pronouncements of the invincibility of the Iraqi army even as the allies routed them. Reporters took to calling him Baghdad Bob, which moniker people subsequently applied to others who insisted on an unrealistic facade in the face of the inevitable.

Most of the pundits in 2016 fit that definition, but the mother of all Baghdad Bobs easily was Nate Silver, a trained economist who set up *FiveThirtyEight* on March 7, 2008, to track the presidential election. He weighted various public opinion polls for bias and then used them to predict the election's outcome. He gained fame by getting forty-nine of the fifty states right in 2008, and all fifty correct four years later. But the 2016 election was a disaster for him.

"Basically Trump is the Nickelback of presidential candidates. Disliked by most, super popular with a few," Silver tweeted on July 15.

A month later on August 6, the Baghdad Bob of the army of the Goliaths, wrote, "If you want absurd specificity, I recently estimated Trump's chance of becoming the GOP nominee at 2 percent."

On September 15, Silver upped the chances for Trump and Carson to 5 percent each. "So there are couple things to think about. One is that if you look back at history, you've never seen candidates like Donald Trump certainly or Ben Carson win a party nomination. And secondly, if you look at the polling, a lot of times a candidate who is leading the polls now mid-September didn't win the nomination, didn't even come close. Four years ago, Rick Perry was in the midst of a surge. Twelve years ago, Howard Dean was surging. Hillary Clinton was still away ahead of Barack Obama in 2008. Rudy Giuliani was leading the polls in 2008. I think people, there's so much interest in this election, in this campaign, people forget that polls five months before Iowa historically have told you very, very little," Silver told Anderson Cooper of CNN.

As Trump's numbers in the polls continued to rise in the fall, Baghdad Bob Silver wrote, "Dear Media, Stop Freaking Out About Donald Trump's Polls," on November 23.

"Right now, he has 25 to 30 percent of the vote in polls among the roughly 25 percent of Americans who identify as Republican. That's something like 6 to 8 percent of the electorate overall, or about the same share of people who think the Apollo moon landings were faked. As the rest of the field consolidates around him, Trump will need to gain additional support to win the nomination. That might not be easy, since some Trump actions that appeal to a faction of the Republican electorate may alienate the rest of it. Trump's favorability ratings are middling among Republicans and awful among the broader electorate," Silver wrote.

Of course, five months earlier, Trump's favorability rating among Republicans was so low, Silver's site wrote him off. "So, could Trump win? We confront two stubborn facts: first, that nobody remotely like Trump has won a major-party nomination in the modern era. And second, as is always a problem in analysis of presidential campaigns, we don't have all that many data points, so unprecedented events can occur with some regularity. For my money, that adds up to Trump's chances being higher than zero but (considerably) less than 20 percent. Your mileage may vary. But you probably shouldn't rely solely on the polls to make your case; it's still too soon for that," Silver wrote.

Two weeks later, Silver tried to answer critics who pointed out to the poll guru that the polls showed Trump was winning and winning big.

"Betting markets—as good a quantification of the conventional wisdom as you'll find on short notice—have him at 22 percent. Higher than Cruz. About twice where they have Jeb Bush. Trump is four times more likely to be the nominee than Christie is, they're saying. I think 22 percent is too high. It's also significant that not only have Trump-like candidates not won, but they haven't come particularly close to winning," Silver wrote on December 5.

And Silver insisted Trump's lead would not hold up. "Dude, this isn't complicated. Go back and look at past polling frontrunners at this stage of the campaign. They have a poor track record. By contrast, go back and look at who was leading in general elections in late October. They have a very good track record. The point of being empirical isn't that you love polls. It's that you learn from experience, and our experience tells us that polls aren't reliable predictors at this stage of the race," Silver wrote.

Such hubris. His experience in forecasting presidential races went back exactly two presidential races. He had forgotten the lesson of Groundhog Day.

Sometimes there are six more weeks of winter after the groundhog sees his shadow on February 2. However, just because it happened twice in a row, that does not mean it will happen again a third time. But it also doesn't mean it won't happen, because a groundhog's shadow on February 2 has nothing to do with the weather, other than the fact that it was sunny when he exited his burrow.

In a tweet on April 9, Silver scoffed at Manafort's assertion in the *Washington Post* that Trump would be the presumptive nominee by mid-May.

"This is delusional on the part of Trump's campaign. Math doesn't work," Silver tweeted.

While March had disappointed him, the first primary in April—Wisconsin—perked Silver back up. "My revised deterministic projections have him at 1,155, and the probabilistic version has him at 1,159," Silver wrote on April 13.

Silver calculated that Trump would need to pick up 194 of the 213 delegates selected in the New York primary and the five primaries on April 26. That was 91 percent.

Trump got 200—or 94 percent. That meant Trump needed only 51 percent of the remaining delegates to win the nomination outright. The number fell below 50 percent after 54 unpledged delegates in Pennsylvania made their first ballot choices known.

Trump had not only taken every state but every county on April 26. While Silver finally admitted the race was in Trump's hands, the forecaster was not yet ready to admit he blew the election.

"But I still have a couple of points of caution," Silver wrote on April 27. "One is that it isn't uncommon for candidates to run up the score in primaries that appear to be noncompetitive. In fact, this happens all the time. Polls usually call the winners right in primaries, but they often lowball their margins of victory. It isn't very motivating to turn out for a guy who's going to lose a state by 30 percentage points, even if doing so might win him an extra delegate under some obscure provision of the delegate rules. In Indiana, a genuinely competitive, winner-take-all race where Cruz is (theoretically) the clear alternative to Trump, that won't be such a problem."

Silver was the poll wizard who lost his way. He got there by exposing the bias of others. But in this campaign, his own prejudices against Trump and against Trump's supporters blinded Silver. He ignored the information that stared him in the face. Instead of admitting in July that Trump's chances looked good, Silver had gone on about Nickelback.

However, there is nothing bad about being wrong. This is how we learn. What makes it bad is when you are too pigheaded to admit you were wrong.

Just ask Muhammad Saeed al-Sahhaf.

CHAPTER 41

PATRIOTISM TRUMPS IDEOLOGY.

———◆———

To CALL BROOKLYN-BORN IRISH CATHOLIC Peggy Noonan a speech-writer for Reagan is to call Michelangelo a sketch artist. She wrote "Boys of Pointe du Hoc," the president's moving tribute delivered on the fortieth anniversary of D-Day. The best passage mourned the heroes who died making the impossible possible that day.

We stand on a lonely, windswept point on the northern shore of France. The air is soft, but 40 years ago at this moment, the air was dense with smoke and the cries of men, and the air was filled with the crack of rifle fire and the roar of cannon. At dawn, on the morning of the 6th of June 1944, 225 Rangers jumped off the British landing craft and ran to the bottom of these cliffs. Their mission was one of the most difficult and daring of the invasion: to climb these sheer and desolate cliffs and take out the enemy guns. The Allies had been told that some of the mightiest of these guns were here and they would be trained on the beaches to stop the Allied advance.

The Rangers looked up and saw the enemy soldiers—the edge of the cliffs shooting down at them with machineguns and throwing grenades. And the American Rangers began to climb. They shot rope ladders over the face of these cliffs and began to pull themselves up. When one Ranger fell, another would take his place. When one rope was cut, a Ranger would grab another and begin his climb again. They climbed, shot back, and held their footing. Soon, one by one, the Rangers pulled themselves over the top, and in seizing the firm land at the top of these cliffs, they began to seize back the continent of Europe. Two hundred and twenty-five came here. After two days of fighting, only 90 could still bear arms.

Reagan had to rehearse the speech several times before he could deliver it without crying.

By the summer of 2015, Noonan was the sextuagenarian sage of the *Wall Street Journal.* She missed Trump. Totally. Which was odd considering his life was so well-chronicled in the New York media. Perhaps she did not read the tabloids.

"He has shot up like a rocket since his June announcement but likely has a low ceiling and short staying power. He is not as popular with Republicans as Bernie Sanders is with Democrats," she wrote on July 9.

She doubted Trump's commitment to Republicans. "He doesn't call his hotels Republican Plaza. He spends much of his time knocking Republicans, setting himself apart from the party and its contenders. If he says something stupid and cheap it will reflect on him. If he should say something brilliant and wise it will not redound to the benefit of the GOP," Noonan wrote.

However, she did something the people in DC did not do. She talked with his supporters. Not to. With.

"They think he's real, that he's under nobody's thumb, that maybe he's a big-mouth but he's a truth-teller. He's afraid of no one, he's not politically correct. He's rich and can't be bought by some billionaire, because he is the billionaire. He's talking about what people are thinking and don't feel free to say. He can turn the economy around because he made a lot of money, so he probably knows how to make jobs," Noonan wrote.

"He is a fighter. People want a fighter. Maybe he's impolitic but he's better than some guy who filters everything he says through a screen of political calculation."

Noonan listened but did not agree.

"Mr. Trump is not a serious man, which is part of his appeal in a country that has grown increasingly unserious," Noonan wrote.

What turned her off was his description of illegal aliens who cross the border from Mexico. "When Mexico sends its people, they're not sending their best. They're sending people that have lots of problems, and they're bringing those problems with us. They're bringing drugs. They're bringing crime. They're rapists. And some, I assume, are good people," Trump said.

Noonan lit into him.

> But as to Mr. Trump's words, throughout our history other nations *never* sent their 'best' to America. My people and my friends, the Irish, were not Ireland's elite when they came in the late 19th and early 20th centuries. They had nothing back home; that's why they left. The landed gentry, the high-born, the educated and established—they didn't come here. They didn't have to! The wretched refuse did. And the Irish transition to America was not so smooth. There was plenty of poverty, overcrowding, addiction, criminality. We should always remember—and Mr. Trump, as a native New Yorker, should remember—that our city's arrest vehicles weren't known as paddy wagons for nothing.

He had gotten her Irish up, as they say. However, six months after declaring, "Mr. Trump is not a serious man," Noonan castigated Republicans for not taking him seriously. "I do not understand the inability or refusal of Republican leaders to take Mr. Trump seriously," she wrote on January 6, 2016.

Maybe they read the *Wall Street Journal*.

"They take his numbers seriously—they can read a poll—but they think, as Mr. Bush said, that his support is all about anger, angst and theatrics. That's part of the story, but the other, more consequential part has to do with real policy issues. The establishment refuses to see that, because to admit it is to implicate themselves and their leadership.

Political consultants can't see it because they don't think issues matter—not to them and certainly not to the dumb voters," Noonan wrote.

However, she still did not like Trump and likely never will. "It reflects badly on the party that Donald Trump—whom one journalist this week characterized as a guy running around with his hair on fire—had to become the party's 2016 thought leader," she wrote.

Why would the coauthor of eighteen books—including one on golf—not be a good choice as thought leader? He was a graduate of the University of Pennsylvania's Wharton School. The idea that only journalists or politicians have thoughts was ludicrous. Nevertheless, Noonan wrote him off as a lightweight. I wished Noonan, of all the pundits, got it right. She seemed to understand the people who followed Trump. Like her, they were the progeny of the people who passed muster at Ellis Island so long ago. Trump's call to build a wall and restrict immigration was not bigoted but traditional—and necessary.

She delighted me on February 16, when she wrote a column that redeemed her. She still was not then nor ever would be a Trumpkin.

"There are the protected and the unprotected. The protected make public policy. The unprotected live in it. The unprotected are starting to push back, powerfully. The protected are the accomplished, the secure, the successful—those who have power or access to it. They are protected from much of the roughness of the world. More to the point, they are protected from the world they have created. Again, they make public policy and have for some time," she wrote.

Noonan continued to listen. The day after Trump swept the five states that held primaries on April 26, he gave a speech in Washington on foreign policy. This was only his second scripted speech, the other being a well-received speech on Israel. Noonan reviewed the second speech in her next column.

"What Trump supporters believe, what they perceive as they watch him, is that he is on America's side," Noonan wrote in April 29.

"And that comes as a great relief to them, because they believe that for 16 years Presidents Bush and Obama were largely about ideologies. They seemed not so much on America's side as on the side of abstract notions about justice and the needs of the world. Mr. Obama's ideological notions are leftist, and indeed he is a hero of the international left. He is about international climate-change agreements, and leftist views of gender, race and income equality. Mr. Bush's White House was driven by a different ideology—neoconservatism, democratizing, nation building, defeating evil in the world, privatizing Social Security. But it was all ideology."

But what about Trump's speech itself?

"You could see this aspect of Trumpism—I'm about America, end of story—in his much-discussed foreign-policy speech this week. I have found pretty much everything said about it to be true. It was long, occasionally awkward-sounding and sometimes contradictory. It was interesting nonetheless. He was trying to blend into a coherent whole what he's previously said when popping off on the hustings. He was trying to establish that there's a theme to the pudding. He was also trying to reassure potential supporters that he is actually serious, that he does have a foreign-policy framework as opposed to just a grab bag of emotional impulses," Noonan wrote.

She was being polite. His speechwriter did not have much to work with. Unlike Reagan, Trump had not spent the last quarter-century immersed in foreign policy. But he got the big picture right, which all the wonks running for president and the wonk president himself had missed.

The copydesk headlined her column, "Simple Patriotism Trumps Ideology," but patriotism is an ideology. Patriotism may have fallen out of vogue. Patriotism may have embarrassed conservatives in Washington. Patriotism may have been cornier than the Iowa State Fair, but patriotism had gotten the country through its worst times. Those boys of Pointe du Hoc did not die for universal health care or privatizing Social Security. They died so their nieces and nephews could someday argue over these matters of smaller consequence.

Michelangelo studied anatomy. Noonan studied Americans. She did not agree with all of them, but she listened. In the end, she did a good service to her readers because of that.

CHAPTER 42

INSIDERS OUT.

————◆————

To call *Politico*'s "insiders" accurate in this campaign would be to call a sketch artist Michelangelo. The Washington-based news organization tapped into the wisdom of political consultants across the country via online polls for its "Insiders" feature and came up with the same vapid answers.

"Nine out of 10 Republican POLITICO Caucus insiders and eight out of 10 Democrats believe there's at least a 50 percent chance or better that Donald Trump, the voluble real estate mogul who announced for president this week, will make it onto the first primary debate stage. And many members of the Caucus were eager to sound off on him," the site reported on June 19, 2015.

The site named all the insiders surveyed in each article but never associated their names with specific quotes.

"We are all part of the biggest reality show in history now with Trump regrettably on center stage. Even he is curious as to where this magical mystery tour ends," said a New Hampshire Republican insider.

"He's a nut," said an Iowa Democrat.

"He's an ass," said a New Hampshire Republican.

On July 17, they lit into Trump again. "The Trump Circus is no doubt having the biggest impact on Ted Cruz. Cruz, the incumbent proxy for the disaffected GOP Hell No Caucus, has been virtually starved of oxygen since Trump entered the race," said an Iowa Republican.

And most of them said we had reached peak Trump.

"About three-quarters of Republican early state insiders say they believe Donald Trump has peaked—but many acknowledge that may also be wishful thinking," the site reported on July 24.

Then on August 7, the site reported, "Donald Trump's first presidential debate was a disaster."

Sound familiar? It should. These were the people who fed the pundits the inside scoop.

"Finally they put Donald Trump into context and his ignorance became glaringly apparent. Frankly I had to run out of the room every time he opened his mouth," said a New Hampshire Democrat.

On August 28, the site reported, "When asked what would sink the campaign of Donald Trump, the bombastic billionaire who continues to rise in the GOP primary polls, the most popular response from insiders was that Trump would eventually sink himself. But there was plenty of hand-wringing—and there were many potshots—from insiders on both sides of the aisle who said they were flummoxed by his seeming ability to defy political gravity."

Writers always should use the word *flummoxed* when the opportunity arises.

"Jeb Bush is the candidate most likely to take on Trump—and damage him—in the GOP primary debate next week, according to the bulk of insiders on both sides of the aisle. Among Republicans, 44 percent of New Hampshire insiders said that was the case, while 20 percent of Iowans offered that assessment. Iowa Republicans were evenly divided between Bush, Chris Christie and Carly Fiorina in guessing who would most aggressively, and successfully, challenge Trump, while 40 percent of Democrats overall pointed to Bush," *Politico* reported on September 11.

Six days later, scratch Bush. It was Fiorina.

"The majority of Republican insiders call former Hewlett-Packard CEO Carly Fiorina as the winner of the second primary debate the night before at the Reagan Library—and say Walker and Florida Sen. Marco Rubio were both losers," the site reported on September 17.

A month later, the insiders began noticing Trump was not going away.

"Twenty-two percent of Caucus Republicans said Trump has a 50-50 shot at becoming the Republican nominee; the same percentage said he has a 30 percent chance. The rest of the respondents were divided, with the majority saying his odds are still less than 50 percent. But more than 8-in-10 GOP respondents said those are better odds than they gave Trump a month ago," *Politico* reported on October 23.

Mind you, at that point, Trump had led the *RealClear Politics* average of polls for ninety-six consecutive days. And 78 percent of insiders were saying he had less than an even chance of winning the nomination?

But, to use the cliché of the season, this was an unconventional campaign, even though Trump's outsider-coming-in campaign was reminiscent of Barack Obama's upset of Hillary Clinton just eight years earlier. Trump won despite the naysaying by the insiders, who grasped at any and all straws in hopes of stopping Trump because his nomination would unmask their incompetence. The results in Wisconsin gave them one last hope.

"Republican insiders overwhelmingly believe this summer's national convention will require multiple ballots to select the presidential nominee. That's according to The POLITICO Caucus—a panel of operatives, activists and strategists in 10 key battleground states—with roughly 90 percent of respondents saying neither Donald Trump nor Ted Cruz will win the nomination on the first ballot in Cleveland," the site reported on April 9, 2016.

The people who wrote him off in June 2015 continued to write him off in April 2016.

"Donald Trump has one chance to win the nomination, and that is on the first ballot. Right now, I put his chances at about 40 percent, and that will require him to get some number of delegates from the unpledged delegates in states like North Dakota, Colorado, Pennsylvania, and a few territories," said an Iowa Republican.

Many of these insiders advised elected officials on policy. If they could not get right the one thing they were expert in—elections—just imagine the damage they could do in giving advice on fields outside their expertise such as health care, border control, and war.

Well, you don't have to imagine very hard, do you?

CHAPTER 43

THE AQUAMAN–GREEN ARROW POWER HOUR.

———————•———————

IF THE NEW YORK PRIMARY had not convinced Cruz, Kasich, and the #NeverTrump crowd that their mission was futile, the primaries in five states a week later should have. Their poll numbers were awful. Two days before the five primaries, the campaign managers for Cruz and Kasich announced they would team up like Aquaman and Green Arrow to stop Trump.

"To ensure that we nominate a Republican who can unify the Republican Party and win in November, our campaign will focus its time and resources in Indiana and in turn clear the path for Gov. Kasich to compete in Oregon and New Mexico, and we would hope that allies of both campaigns would follow our lead," Cruz campaign manager Jeff Roe said in a statement issued April 24.

John Weaver, Kasich's strategist, disclosed how it would work. "We will shift our campaign's resources West and give the Cruz campaign a clear path in Indiana. In turn, we will focus our time and resources in New Mexico and Oregon, both areas that are structurally similar to the Northeast politically, where Governor Kasich is performing well," Weaver wrote in a message to Kasich's staff. "We would expect independent third-party groups to do the same and honor the commitments made by the Cruz and Kasich campaigns."

Trump mocked the move. "Lyin' Ted and Kasich are mathematically dead and totally desperate. Their donors and special interest groups are not happy with them. Sad!" Trump tweeted.

The Cruz-Kasich alliance was dead on arrival.

"I don't think it's really going to work. I think Donald Trump is on track to get the delegates he needs, not necessarily 1,237, but to get the delegates he needs to get the nomination on the first ballot," Mara Liasson of NPR said on Fox News on April 25.

In the same panel discussion, King Krauthammer politely called it dumb. "It's extremely late. Had they worked this out a month or two ago where they each go one-on-one, Trump has said, 'I want to go one-on-one with Cruz.' Well, he'll get his chance in Indiana. But we're really at a point where this is the endgame."

Both Aquaman and Green Arrow—Which was which? Did it matter?—subsequently disavowed any knowledge of their campaign managers' actions.

The five-state primary on April 26, was a nor'easter that blew away Trump's competition as he stretched his lead over Cruz to 996 to 561. That 435-delegate lead meant that for the first time in the campaign, Trump owned a majority of the delegates awarded.

After his sweep, Trump showed why he dominated news coverage by giving a victory speech that was light on the cheers and big on the news, announcing that Bobby Knight would endorse him in the next primary in Indiana. He spoke for less than three minutes but then turned the event into a press conference, which meant the cable news networks had to cover him live for the next forty minutes, because Trump kept everyone guessing about what he would say next. This delayed Clinton's victory speech past prime time.

The next day, to divert attention from finishing last in five of the last six primaries, Cruz dumped Kasich in favor of Wonder Woman, as Cruz announced Carly Fiorina would be his running mate. At least the *National Review* saw her as Wonder Woman.

"How does she help Cruz, who is currently sputtering in second place and running out of chances to beat Donald Trump? She's strong and polished on the stump, equally at home giving a big policy speech, answering questions at a town hall, or offering one-liners on a late-night talk show. She's an outsider, in a year when political neophytes are all the rage. And most important of all, she has the best chance of any potential running mate to negate presumptive Democratic nominee Hillary Clinton's political strengths," Jim Geraghty wrote on April 25.

But he did acknowledge one minor technicality. "Cruz will, of course, have to wrest the nomination from Trump if he wants the chance to unleash Fiorina on Clinton," Geraghty wrote.

What Washington elitists failed to acknowledge was Cruz ran a terrible campaign—according to Rich Danker, who founded and ran Cruz's official super PAC, the Lone Star Committee. He issued a blistering memo on April 24. Danker faulted Cruz for not expanding his base beyond the conservative PAC.

"Many conservatives are perplexed that Ted Cruz could lose to Donald Trump when Cruz is undoubtedly the closest ideological approximation to Ronald Reagan since he left the scene. He's the perfect conservative, many said, so how could he lose in a conservative primary?" Danker wrote.

I think this analysis misunderstands how Reagan framed himself as a candidate. He was not running to be winner of the CPAC straw poll or get the most conservative endorsements. He made it clear he was running to revive the US economy and defeat the Soviet Union. Those were objectives that made it easy for any voter to support him. A majority ended up getting behind him because his ideas achieved those objectives, not because they dazzled on an ideological scorecard. Like Cruz, Reagan in 1980 had to get by better-funded establishment Republicans. But he didn't try to shrink the nominating contest into a conservative beauty pageant.

Danker faulted Cruz for concentrating too much effort on Iowa and blowing off New Hampshire. Nominees must finish in the top three in Iowa and the top two in New Hampshire, or as Danker put it, "There are three tickets out of Iowa, but only two out of New Hampshire." Only Donald Trump met that criteria, which meant the race ended on February 9.

But Danker was not through with Cruz, writing:

> Like his state strategy, Cruz was very selective when it came to media availability. He allotted more time for conservative media, and limited his appearances on mainstream outlets. He took press questions infrequently. A frequent image became Cruz delivering his talking points into a podium of microphones, and then hustling away to avoid reporters' questions.
>
> Trump basically took every legitimate media interview request that landed in his inbox. He held numerous press conferences and took lots of reporters' questions. He became such a staple of the television talk shows that he was afforded the rare privilege of phoning in his appearances rather than appearing on camera. While these appearances, most notably on CNN with Jake Tapper where he declined to condemn hate groups, occasionally froze his campaign in its tracks for days, they totaled up to nearly $2 billion in free media coverage, six times what Cruz earned. I would argue that this disparity was completely legitimate given the candidates' inverse attitudes toward media availability.

One can understand Danker's frustration. He raised money to pay for media while Cruz turned down media opportunities.

"Cruz tended to give the same stump speech at every appearance. Although he spoke without notes (a skill developed from his experience as a trial lawyer), the material in his speeches tended not to differ no matter the setting. He also sounded in part like a Baptist preacher (his father's vocation). This produced an oratory style that led Ryan Lizza to observe in the *New Yorker*, 'Cruz delivers every sentence, no matter how generic, as if he imagines himself reciting the Gettysburg Address.'

Tough, but true," Danker wrote. "Trump gave exclusively extemporaneous remarks at each rally. This gave him the ability to comment at each
stop on what was happening that day in the news, which led to more
earned media."

The big blow came a few paragraphs later.

"I believe Trump ran a better campaign than Cruz for two reasons:
1) Republican voters not only wanted an outsider candidate for president, they wanted that candidate to campaign like an outsider. 2) The
conventional strategies and tactics on running in the presidential primary had become so stale that an outsider with disdain for professional
politics found a new way to win using common sense," Danker wrote.

The end of the message said what most of his opponents learned.

"Donald Trump loses to Ted Cruz on a conservative scorecard, but
he did a better job on selling his conservative positions as the cures to
today's public evils," Danker wrote. "Part of that involves finding new
ways to sell old ideas. As Rush Limbaugh said once during this election,
people are never permanently converted. You have to keep engaging
voters by meeting them where they are looking for political leadership.
Again, Cruz seemed so wedded to a playbook that he couldn't get to
such a place. Trump drove away many conservatives by flunking on some
conservative precepts, but he more than made up for it by matching the
conservative ideas he did exalt to voters' top needs."

Voters? Ugh.

CHAPTER 44

JOURNALISTS AGAINST NEWS.

————•————

WHAT IS NEWS IS NOT too difficult to understand. Any news story must include at least one of these elements: proximity (local), prominence, timeliness, oddity, consequence, conflict, human interest, controversy, and impact. Consider therefore the following imaginary headline in a New York newspaper: "Local celebrity today makes surprise announcement to run for president and backs a popular idea his sixteen rivals oppose."

Trump was news. He was interesting. He created controversy and conflicts. His exploits attracted readers, viewers, and listeners. He dominated the news from the moment he joined the presidential race.

Nearly a year later, when Trump's nomination became obvious to even the lowliest cable news anchor, the political press did what it does best—stare at its navel. The cover of the May/June 2016 issue of *Politico* magazine showed Trump facing a media mob with the headline: "What Have We Done?"

Such conceit was irresistible to Fox News media critic Howard Kurtz, who panned the magazine's main story. "It's a study in self-flagellation, this argument that Trump would not be where he is today without being propped up by the press. Many of his detractors refuse to acknowledge that a non-politician is winning this thing by getting a record number of GOP primary votes, so the thing must be rigged by reporters," Kurtz wrote on May 3.

Kurtz had covered a fire or two when he was a reporter. He delighted in bursting media bubbles.

"Reporter Ben Schreckinger became the full-time Trump correspondent despite the fact that working for *Politico* is his first job out of college. Perhaps that's why he is so angry at criticism from Trump and his deputies and a lack of access, both of which are standard fare in the political big leagues," Kurtz wrote.

We lived in a time when senior editor applied to anyone nine months out of college. Six if he had a master's degree.

Former CNN anchor Campbell Brown contributed a piece—"Why I Blame TV for Trump"—to the *Politico* pity party.

I really would like to blame Trump. But everything he is doing is with TV news' full acquiescence. Trump doesn't force the networks to show his rallies live rather than do real reporting. Nor does he force anyone to accept his phone calls rather than demand that he do a face-to-face interview that would be a greater risk for him. TV news has largely given Trump editorial control. It is driven by a hunger for ratings—and the people who run the networks and the news channels are only too happy to make that Faustian bargain. Which is why you'll see endless variations of this banner, one I saw all three cable networks put up in a single day: "Breaking news: Trump speaks for first time since Wisconsin loss." In all these scenes, the TV reporter just stands there, off camera, essentially useless. The order doesn't need to be stated. It's understood in the newsroom: Air the Trump rallies live and uninterrupted. He may say something crazy; he often does, and it's always great television.

Her blast showed her confusion over what is news. Why would it not be news when the front-runner speaks for the first time after a humiliating loss? The story had all of the nine elements of news I listed.

Low news ratings reflected a disconnect between the audience and the networks over news. Often, people in the news media saw themselves as smarter than their audience. One thing I have learned in blogging is the medical doctors, military veterans, engineers, clergymen, executives, lawyers, factory workers, plumbers, car mechanics, beekeepers, and others who read my blog know much more than I do about life in general and their fields in particular.

In her piece, Brown trotted out the fallacy that the media exposure Trump earned was the same as paid advertising. "Trump's exposure has been three times greater than that of Cruz and Kasich combined. He received 50 percent of the exposure when there were more than a dozen candidates—a percentage that has only grown. Of course, by now, you've all also read the figure of close to $2 billion worth of free media the *New York Times* cited for Trump's TV bonanza. And that story was back in March. No campaign's advertising budget can compete," Brown wrote.

In rebuttal, Kurtz wrote, "Trump has seized much of the free air time by doing many, many more interviews than his rivals, and by driving the campaign dialogue—which all candidates try to do but are usually too cautious or dull to pull off."

Brown's unhappiness with Trump's nomination stemmed from believing television had more power than it did.

So yes, I believe Trump's candidacy is largely a creation of a TV media that wants him, or needs him, to be the central character in this year's political drama. And it's not just the network and cable executives driving it. The TV anchors and senior executives who don't deliver are mercilessly ousted. The ones who do deliver are lavishly rewarded. I know from personal experience that it is common practice for TV anchors to have substantial bonuses written into their contracts if they hit ratings marks. With this 2016 presidential soap opera, they are almost surely hitting those marks. So, we get all Trump, all the time.

Hers was a castor oil approach to the news. If it tasted good, it was not news. Kurtz schooled her.

"A huge portion of the media attention lavished on Trump is harshly negative, often from conservative and liberal commentators who oppose him on ideological grounds. Trump punches back hard, especially on Twitter, though he's toned it down of late. The billionaire actually benefits from denunciations by those his supporters view as members of a failed media/political establishment," Kurtz wrote.

Of course, the feeling was mutual from the failed media/political establishment. Many Trump critics detested his supporters. Out of retirement came Joe Epstein, seventy-nine, a conservative academic who was the editor of the Phi Beta Kappa Society's *American Scholar* magazine for a quarter century. He wrote an essay, "These Five Are the Best We Can Do?" in the *Wall Street Journal* on April 6.

"Is there something in our system of electing candidates that makes inevitable the rise of the mediocre and even the exaltation of the vulgar?" Epstein wrote.

He meant vulgar in the classical way—that is, "of the common people." When *Spy* magazine called Trump a "small-fingered vulgarian," it had nothing to do with profanity; it was rather a putdown of the outer-borough mentality Trump represented.

"So low have things fallen owing to Donald Trump that lifelong Republicans have told me that, in a Trump-versus-Clinton election, they are likely to hold their nose and vote for Mrs. Clinton," Epstein wrote.

But Epstein agreed with several of Trump's observations. "One saw Marco Rubio and thought, in another time a successful siding salesman. One saw Carly Fiorina and thought, in the old days a scolding grammar-school principal. One saw Martin O'Malley and thought, who let this guy off the used-car lot? One sees Hillary Clinton and thinks how exhausting it must be for her, day after day, to argue on behalf of all those things—justice, equality, fairness to women—that in their personal life she and her husband flouted," Epstein wrote.

But in dismissing two candidates for being salesmen showed his misunderstanding of politicians. In a representative democracy, they needed to become Ron Popeil—except instead of pitching Veg-O-Matics, they had to sell themselves. Trump was the best of this lot, and he knew the news game better than the pros.

To be sure, some of the answers Trump gave and some of the statements he made embarrassed his supporters as much as Jack Nicholson's Melvin Udall character embarrassed Helen Hunt's Carol Connelly character in the movie *As Good As It Gets*.

> CAROL: Why can't I have a normal boyfriend? Just a regular boyfriend, one that doesn't go nuts on me!
> HER MOTHER: Everybody wants that, dear. It doesn't exist.

So it went with presidential candidates in 2016.

As much as *Politico* tried to push its false narrative of a media hoodwinked and bullied into favoring Trump, the reality was Trump was the most news-friendly candidate in presidential history. He eschewed the big money ads in favor of press conferences, media availabilities, and rallies. This was a high-risk strategy that worked because it separated him from the politicians. Unlike Hillary Clinton or Ted Cruz, Donald Trump did not hide from the media. He granted interviews to outlets that were hostile to him. He even gave Megyn Kelly an interview, which she used for a prime-time special on the regular Fox network during the May sweeps.

This was how the system should work. Instead of hiding behind ads and canned speeches, candidates should stand before the reporters and the voters without a teleprompter. *Politico* asked, "What Have We Done?"

They had done their job.

CHAPTER 45

THEY GOT TRUMP RIGHT.

———————

THE END CAME QUICKLY. ON May 3, Donald Trump won Indiana, his seventh consecutive primary. That night, Ted Cruz took the stage in Indianapolis and conceded the race. This stunned his supporters and the Trump family.

"Downstairs in the pink-marbled lobby, a handful of Trump's longest-serving campaign staffers—those who believed in Trump back when few believed that the candidate would make it this far—gathered near a big-screen television to watch. They stood stoically, some with arms crossed or hands politely folded, and quietly listened to Cruz's closing words as a bank of cameras recorded their every reaction. Corey Lewandowski, Trump's embattled but faithful campaign manager, only occasionally looked up from his phone," Jenna Johnson of the *Washington Post* reported.

"When Cruz said the words that made the news formal, the lobby burst into cheers. As Cruz said that the voters had chosen a path, one woman yelled: 'Yes!' But the campaign staff remained quiet, so as not to be caught celebrating a rival's ultimate downfall. Two aides clapped. Lewandowski looked up from his phone and stared intently at the television, his eyes glistening. As the speech ended, he and a few other top aides embraced one another in a group hug that quickly began tighter and tighter, as if their grip communicated the screams of excitement that they couldn't yet yell."

After Cruz quit, Trump spoke to his supporters in the atrium of Trump Tower, which alternated with Mar-a-Lago as the venue for his victory speeches. He was somber and gracious. He called Cruz a tough competitor.

"I know how tough it is—it's tough, it's tough. I've had some moments where it was not looking so good, and it's not a great feeling. And so I understand how Ted feels and Heidi and their whole beautiful family," Trump said.

Rocky Balboa had won the title, but Apollo Creed had won his respect.

I did not want the nomination campaign to end. It was fun. The people had risen in anger and kicked the Republican Party right in the apparatchiks. Hard. What a fine moment in American history we had just lived through.

The conservative commentariat had declared Trump's supporters apostates. In Poca, West Virginia, we knew better. The ballot for the West Virginia primary included Donna Boley and John Raese as Trump delegates. Boley was in her thirty-second year as a state senator. At one time, she was the only Republican in that body. Outnumbered thirty-three to one, Boley had soldiered on. Raese was a hardcore conservative who challenged Jay Rockefeller and Robert C. Byrd. He lost of course, but he kept the lamp lit. Boley too. They were conservative when conservative wasn't cool.

Many old-line conservatives understood just that Trump was retaking the Republican Party from zealous ideologues. Patrick Buchanan, a senior advisor to Presidents Nixon, Ford, and Reagan, grew up when communism, not sharia law, threatened the land. He was an outsider looking in who did not like what he saw.

"The American political class has failed the country, and should be fired. That is the clearest message from the summer surge of Bernie Sanders and the remarkable rise of Donald Trump. When Trump ridicules his rivals as Lilliputians and mocks the celebrity media, the Republican base cheers and laughs with him," Patrick Buchanan wrote on July 27, 2015, proving that at age seventy-six, he had not forgotten how to write a compelling lead.

Like many old school journalists, Buchanan ripped the press. "Trump also benefits from the perception that his rivals and the press want him out of the race and are desperately seizing upon any gaffe to drive him out. The piling on, the abandonment of Trump by the corporate elite, may have cost him a lot of money. But it also brought him support he would not otherwise have had," Buchanan wrote.

He liked Trump's odds—a year before the convention.

"If his poll numbers hold, Trump will be there six months from now when the Sweet 16 is cut to the Final Four, and he will likely be in the finals. For if Trump is running at 18 or 20 percent nationally then, among Republicans, it is hard to see how two rivals beat him," Buchanan wrote.

He followed up his "Could Trump Win?" column in July with "Can Trump Be Stopped?" on October 19.

"One cannot lose Iowa and New Hampshire. Thus, today's task for the Republican establishment. Between now and March, they must settle on a candidate, hope his rivals get out of the race, defeat Trump in one of the first two contests, or effect his defeat by someone like Carson, then pray Trump will collapse like a house of cards," Buchanan wrote.

"The improbabilities of accomplishing this grow by the week and will soon start looking, increasingly, like an impossibility—absent the kind of celestial intervention that marked the career of the late Calvin Coolidge."

Buchanan's assessment came not from a desire to fit in with his peers, but rather a simple reading of history. Phyllis Schlafly at ninety-one also backed The Donald.

"Trump is the only hope to defeat the Kingmakers. Because everybody else will fall in line. The Kingmakers have so much money behind them," Schlafly told Jo Hahn of *Breitbart News* on January 10, 2016.

For more than a half century, Schlafly had railed against the donor class, writing in 1964, "They dictated the choice of the Republican presidential nominee just as completely as the Paris dressmakers control the length of women's skirts."

But just as women eventually rose and ignored the Parisian designers, so the Republican electorate rose and ignored the edict of the Republican establishment to nominate Jeb Bush.

Trump's nomination repudiated the post-Reagan party. All the money Bush had, all the endorsements Rubio had, and all the support Cruz had from politicized Christians were not enough to quell the rebellion.

The race was over even before 2016 began, but few admitted it. Pundits oversold Trump's second-place finishes in Iowa and Wisconsin, but his support was overwhelming. His crowds were large and noisy. His ratings were high. After Super Tuesday, King Krauthammer folded.

"You look at the math, you look at the odds, you'd say absolutely, they are too late. It isn't as if it's impossible but the math is completely in Trump's favor. This evening looks like it's going to continue the trend. It's going to take a major event," Krauthhamer said on Fox News.

The king was not happy, but his acceptance of the facts was why he was king. Liberals eagerly embraced a Trump nomination, anticipating a loss to Clinton.

"Watching him morph into a pol in real time and wriggle away from the junior-varsity G.O.P chuckleheads trying to tackle him is hypnotic. He's like the blond alien in the 1995 movie 'Species,' who mutates from ova to adult in months, regenerating and reconfiguring at warp speed to escape the establishment, kill everyone in sight and eliminate the human race," Maureen Dowd of the *New York Times* wrote on March 5.

But others realized it was no movie. On March 10, *Salon* columnist Camille Paglia admitted she was wrong about him.

Nevertheless, Trump's fearless candor and brash energy feel like a great gust of fresh air, sweeping the tedious clichés and constant guilt-tripping of political correctness out to sea. Unlike Hillary Clinton, whose every word and policy statement on the campaign trail are spoon-fed to her by a giant paid staff and army of shadowy advisors, Trump is his own man, with a steely "damn the torpedoes" attitude. He has a swaggering retro machismo that will give hives to the Steinem cabal. He lives large, with the urban flash and bling of a Frank Sinatra. But Trump is a workaholic who doesn't drink and who has an interesting penchant for sophisticated, strong-willed European women. As for a debasement of the presidency by Trump's slanging matches about penis size, that sorry process was initiated by a Democrat, Bill Clinton, who chatted about his underwear on TV, let Hollywood pals jump up and down on the bed in the Lincoln Bedroom, and played lewd cigar games with an intern in the White House offices.

Chris Wallace of Fox News was contrite.

"I think one of the things you learn is that you don't know as much as you think you know, that for anyone foolish enough to think they're an opinion maker or opinion shaper, this has been a lesson that the American people will make their own decision for themselves," Wallace told *Politico* on March 1.

Wesley Pruden, editor in chief emeritus of the *Washington Times*, delighted in calling his younger colleagues out.

"The lions of the legacy media have never understood the barely controlled rage of the Bible-believing unwashed at being scorned, disdained and despised, and along comes a man with a club and an eye for someone to hit with it. Grandma Grundy would forgive him a little cussin'. Some of the lions pretend to have learned a lesson, but it's not that they were wrong, it was the people who were wrong and stubbornly unwilling to be educated. Some of the pundits are clinging to the hope that The Donald will be stopped and punditry will be redeemed," Pruden wrote on March 4.

CHAPTER 46

WHY GOLIATH FAILED.

———————

TRUMP CLINCHED THE NOMINATION THE day after Leicester City clinched the British Premier soccer title for the first time in its 132 years of existence. Bookies had given the team five-thousand-to-one odds of winning when the season began.

"A guy just won the Republican nomination for president by spending no money, hiring no pollsters, running virtually no TV ads, and just saying what he truly believed no matter how many times people told him he couldn't say that," Ann Coulter wrote on May 4, eleven months after she predicted his victory.

However, just about everyone else in the punditry was wrong. Each pundit had his own reasons for missing the story of the year. I offer thirteen reasons.

Arrogance. Pundits believed they were smarter than the American people, especially white males without college degrees in West Virginia, or as I call them, neighbors.

Bubble. I realize this was the cliché explanation, but that only meant the explanation has its limits. If someone is outside your ken—as Nixon supporters were to Pauline Kael in 1972—perhaps you should not judge them so harshly. That applies to my judgment of Washington pundits as well.

Celebrity. Krauthammer and other cable news celebrities dismissed Trump as being a mere celebrity on TV.

Dinero. A cottage industry grew of being a Republican strategist—a common cable-news identification—who dumped on Trump. Also, the tax-exempt periodicals and think tanks relied on donors to stay alive, and he who pays the piper calls the tune.

Elitism. Gossip queen Liz Smith saw his dislike of the hoity-toity from the get-go forty years earlier, and his social betters did not like him either. Manhattanites carried on the tradition both in New York and Washington, where many of them had moved.

Free trade. Washington took as gospel that free trade was good for America. Outside the capital, it was not. But in Washington, if you were too dumb to believe in free trade, then you could not be president.

George Wallace. I doubt many pundits lived among Muslims or illegal aliens. Prejudices work both ways. The beliefs that Muslims shared the ecumenical values of other religious people in America and that illegal immigrants were the same as legal immigrants led to dismissing Trump as a racist, which meant he could not possibly win.

Herd mentality. Everybody who was anybody in Washington said Trump had no chance, so how could he have a chance?

Investment. Just as Trump's supporters became invested in his success, his detractors became personally invested in his defeat. This explained Bill Kristol's continuous, calamitous cries of peak Trump.

Joke. Not taking Trump seriously proved fatal.

Knowledge. Pundits made personal attacks on the man without knowing who he was. But if they bothered to look at him as human, it would be harder to attack his person.

Lazy. Rare was the Byron York who dared talk to a Trumpkin.

Make America Great Again. To intellectuals—and just about every pundit aspired to be one—patriotism was the last refuge of the scoundrel. Therefore, all patriots were scoundrels.

I doubt any of the people who missed the Big Story hit all thirteen of those reasons, and I leave room for people who hit zero of them. But they missed it and then insisted the bough would break, and The Donald would fall.

He did not fall because the rules applied to politicians. He was not one. People cut him slack because he sought the office not for fortune or fame, which he already had. Mike Lupica of the *New York Daily News* was dismissive but insightful when he wrote on June 8, 2015, "Donald Trump already has what he honestly believes is the best job in the whole world, which is being Donald Trump."

However, the biggest reason so many failed to see Trump coming was the belief that one of the other contestants would rise and slay him. They based this on the assumption that the Republicans had the best field of candidates since Reagan dined alone, which was dangerous because, as Jerry Belson wrote in a script for *The Odd Couple* TV show, you must "never ASSUME, because when you ASSUME, you make an ASS of U and ME."

Bush was great at fund-raising but lousy at vote-getting. Of all Trump's opponents, he was the best of the lot. We know this because he was the one Trump targeted first and hit the hardest until Bush dropped out. The rest were tiresome and boring.

One other assumption that drove the doomsayers to their demise was that this was an unusual election year full of surprises.

Well, Trump was unusual, but the path to his victory was pretty routine. Like Reagan, he won the debates and piled up primary wins early and often. Trump succeeded because, like Reagan, he could speak through the media filters to get his message across. In Reagan's 1980 presidential campaign, his critics, too, called Reagan racist and stupid and dismissed him as a celebrity and a joke.

On the night Cruz conceded and the race ended, Chris Stirewalt of Fox News spoke. "I remember sitting in this very building on the day that Donald Trump announced, and I said, well, you know, it's a fringe situation, and you know, these people, and it's not going to happen. What happened is he annealed a group of supporters particularly around the issue of immigration."

He is the only man in America outside a glassblower who would use *annealed* correctly in a conversation.

Those who wrote off Trump when he entered the race now will write tomes to explain what happened. It boiled down to four words: Make America Great Again.

CHAPTER 47

TRUMP CANNOT WIN (REPRISE).

———————

WHEN TRUMP ENTERED THE PRESIDENTIAL race, Chris Cillizza of the *Washington Post* pronounced Trump's candidacy dead on arrival. Nine months later, Cillizza made the same argument in the general—that Trump was too unpopular to win.

"The less the general election focuses on Clinton, the better for Clinton and Democrats. It's as simple as that. There are very few people in the political arena who could possibly knock Clinton down to second billing. Trump is one of them. And not in a good way, if you are a Republican with an eye on reclaiming the White House," Cillizza wrote.

Had Karl Rove learned anything? In a column in the *Wall Street Journal* on January 6, he wrote, "If Mr. Trump is its standard-bearer, the GOP will lose the White House and the Senate, and its majority in the House will fall dramatically."

Had Jonah Goldberg learned anything?

"I honestly believe that Trump would crash in the general election like so much blue ice from an Aeroflot jetliner. I don't think he can flip any of the states in the Democratic blue wall, and I think there's a strong likelihood he'd fail to hold onto some of the states in the Republican red wall. Talk to political handicappers in Arizona and Utah, for instance, and they will tell you he's very likely to lose there and take other Republican candidates down with him," Goldberg wrote on April 30.

Why am I bothering with these losers, you may ask.

You know something? You're right. Let us look at the winners. *Dilbert* creator Scott Adams made his prediction on April 27: "Landslide."

Patrick Buchanan wrote on February 26, "America is crossing into a new era. Trump seems to have caught the wave, while Clinton seems to belong to yesterday. A note of caution: This establishment is not going quietly."

Rush Limbaugh said on May 4, "Hillary Clinton doesn't have a prayer. I don't care about the Electoral College. I don't care about anything else. Just like in terms of the people that are fed up with Washington and the establishment, as we sit here today, she is the lone candidate representing what obviously so many Americans, Republicans and Democrats for their own reasons right now happen to despise. She's losing the vote in every state, and yet the Democrats expect her to triumph. Where is her momentum?"

We shall see how he does in November when it is November.

But on May 3, 2016, Donald's army laughed at last at that army of Goliaths who had dismissed him as a clown.

About Don Surber.

—————•—————

Don Surber is a true American. An Army veteran, he graduated from Cleveland State University and spent thirty years writing for the Charleston Daily Mail. He spent twenty-seven of those years serving as an editorial writer and columnist, never losing his bold viewpoint and confident edge.

Surber became concerned about responsible media coverage during the 2016 election cycle and has written this book as a vindication for Trump supporters everywhere.

Surber has written two other books, *Exceptional Americans: 50 People You Need To Know* and *Exceptional Americans 2: The Capitalists*. Both are available at Amazon and on Kindle.

Surber lives in West Virginia coal country with his wife of thirty-eight years, Lou Ann. They have three adult children.

40940415R00142

Made in the USA
Middletown, DE
27 February 2017